The Northern Rhodesia Copperbelt 1899-1962

The Northern Rhodesia Copperbelt 1899-1962

Technological development up to the end of the Central African Federation

Francis L. Coleman
MA Dip Ed PhD

Senior Lecturer in Economics and Economic History
Rhodes University Grahamstown South Africa

Manchester University Press

Augustus M. Kelley Publishers

©1971 FRANCIS L. COLEMAN

Published by the University of Manchester at
THE UNIVERSITY PRESS
316–324 Oxford Road, Manchester M13 9NR

UK ISBN 0 7190 0419 5

USA
AUGUSTUS M. KELLEY PUBLISHERS
305 Allwood Road, Clifton, N.J. 07012

Library of Congress catalog card No. 72 149805
US ISBN 0 678 06784 8

PRINTED AND BOUND IN THE REPUBLIC OF IRELAND BY THE BOOK PRINTING
DIVISION OF SMURFIT PRINT AND PACKAGING LIMITED, DUBLIN.

Contents

Illustrations

Figures

Plates

Preface

In the course of a single life-span an inhospitable, disease-ridden wilderness in the heart of tropical Africa has been transformed into one of the major copper producing areas in the world. This study is an attempt to explain and describe the rise of the modern industry from a technological point of view, the main theme being the work of the early, lone prospectors, leading to the rise of the various mining companies, with the enormous technical and economic issues involved creating in turn the need for huge combines in the form of the Anglo-American Corporation and Rhodesian Selection Trust. Linked with this is the story of Nchanga, the largest copper producer in the Commonwealth. From its small beginning, with the discovery of a rock outcrop in a stream, the history of the venture is traced to its present dominance, with a capital of £28 million and an annual output of well over 175,000 tons of copper.

I was fortunate in having access not only to the records of the mining companies but also to a large quantity of unpublished material which was specially sent out to Rhodesia from the London office of Rhodesian Selection Trust for my use and which is now at the head office of Roan Selection Trust at Ndola in Zambia. My debt of gratitude to this group, as also to their colleagues in the Anglo-American Corporation, is very great.

In addition to written material, both published and unpublished, several Copperbelt 'old-timers' placed their vast personal knowledge and experience at my disposal. Neil Wilkie and Neville Airey in particular spent many hours discussing various technicalities and reminiscing with me. Professor George Shepperson of Edinburgh University and Dr Richard Gray of London gave me invaluable advice throughout. Nevertheless, all the opinions expressed and conclusions reached, unless explicitly stated otherwise, are my own.

The management of the Nchanga mine provided me with the material from which the maps and diagrams were drawn, and the early photographs were taken by the late J. C. Ferguson and W. Scrymgeour.

Appendix I originally appeared as a note in the *South African Journal of Economics*, vol. 37, No. 2.

To my wife, who typed the proofs and kept the children quiet, this book is affectionately dedicated.

F. L. C.

To Veronica

Glossary of technical terms

see also Introduction

Geology

Anticline A folded rock structure with the flanks downwards. Opposite of *syncline*.

Assaying Testing ores for mineral content, particularly for valuable minerals.

Footwall Rocks lying immediately below an ore-body.

Gangue Earth in which ore is found.

Hanging wall Rocks lying immediately above an ore-body.

Leaching The removal, usually by solution in water (e.g. rain) or weak acids, of some mineral or minerals in the rock. It is a chemical process, not to be confused with physical washing out.

Lode A formation containing valuable minerals in which one dimension is very much greater than the other two. Normally a lode is steeply inclined.

Ore-body Rock containing a mineral or minerals of commercial importance that may either now or in the future be mineable at a profit.

Oxide, copper oxide ores Those containing oxidised copper minerals. The main types found on the Copperbelt are the carbonates, malachite and azurite, with some copper oxide (cuprite) and copper silicate (chrysocolla). Generally these oxide ores are referred to on the Copperbelt as 'oxide' or 'acid soluble'. Malachite and azurite can usually be concentrated, similarly to the sulphides, by flotation. Cuprite floats only with difficulty, whilst chrysocolla does not respond to flotation at all and requires separate treatment.

Outcrop Rock exposed at the surface.

Sub-outcrop Rock coming close to, but not reaching, the surface.

Sulphide copper ores   Those containing copper in the form of sulphides. The main forms found on the Copperbelt are chalcocite, bornite and chalcopyrite. Carrollite is a copper/cobalt sulphide mineral.

Syncline   A folded rock structure with the flanks upwards. Opposite of anticline.

Mining

Ancient workings   Pre-European mine workings generally abandoned by the time of discovery.

Casing   Lining for drill holes to keep out water or to prevent collapse in soft ground.

Crosscuts, drives, drifts   Passages tunnelled more or less horizontally underground. They serve various purposes, for example, haulage, prospecting and dewatering. They are generally referred to in terms of their depth and general direction.

Drills   There are various types—diamond, shot, churn—which are used according to circumstances. *Diamond* drills provide a core sample, can be used in any direction (e.g. underground), are good in hard rock, but otherwise are slow. *Shot* drills provide a core but not such a satisfactory one as a diamond drill. They are also slower but have the advantages of being good in soft ground and providing large diameter holes suitable for drainage or ventilation. *Churn* drills have the advantages of shot drills, but do not provide a core. However, the sludge can be sampled. Shot and churn drills are only used vertically downwards.

Inclines   Passages which are not horizonal, but are generally excavated downwards. An exception is a *raise* which is a passage into the ore-body inclined upwards from underground. A *winze* is a similar passage inclined downwards from underground.

Shafts   (*a*) Incline(d): diagonally downwards from the surface. (*b*) Vertical: vertically downwards from the surface. Sub-incline or sub-vertical shafts are similar but begin at a level below ground.

Introduction

The mining and treatment of copper ore

Commercial copper is generally found not as pure metal but as either sulphides or oxides of the metal, deposited, often in very small and irregular quantities, in otherwise worthless rock. The actual values of the minerals which are economically workable naturally depend on various other factors such as the size of the deposits, their geographical location and the specific, technical problems involved in the actual mining and treatment. Thus, although the world average of copper mineralisation in ore is 1·5 per cent, deposits of as low as 0·7 per cent are profitably exploited where their large size, amenity to treatment and convenient location justify development. The Copperbelt is actually most inconveniently situated in the heart of Africa, some 1,500 miles by rail from the coast, with a further 6,000 miles by sea from Beira to the markets of Europe. When it is considered also that the pioneering days were fraught with disease and considerable hardship, it becomes clear that only substantially better than average yields of metal would justify the enormous expenses involved. In fact, many millions of tons of ore averaging around 3·5 per cent copper were shown to exist, this percentage of metal being more than double the world average, so that from very early on in the history of the Copperbelt the physical difficulties involved have been regarded as obstacles which had to be overcome rather than deterrents which could justify abandoning the enterprise.

Mining The first step in the recovery of the metal is mining, which may be done either by underground methods or by the 'open pit' technique. Both are widely used throughout the world. Several open pits are being operated on the Copperbelt at present, mainly at Nchanga, but with one at Mindola, one at

Chambishi and a new one being developed at Bwana Mkubwa. Although the technique, which involves the removal of the ore by digging down from the surface, is relatively economical, it requires the presence of ore-bodies comparatively close to the surface. As the bulk of the Copperbelt ore-bodies lie deep, the more complicated and costly underground methods must be employed. Shafts have to be sunk and from them tunnels are driven towards the ore-body, to develop which and extract the ore a whole network of smaller tunnels and shafts have to be excavated. Electric power has to be led underground, compressed air is required for ventilation, and drainage facilities must also be provided. In addition, basic materials, waste rock, ore and a labour force all require transportation.

Three basic mining techniques are in use on the Copperbelt, all with modifications to meet specific local conditions. Some mines employ several different methods to cope with varying problems on the same property.

Open stoping (or more correctly, sub-level stoping) is largely used at Nkana and the Roan Antelope. The ore is removed in a series of workings, or 'stopes', at regular intervals along the ore-body. Supporting the stopes are pillars of ore which are left behind by the miners until the adjacent stopes have been emptied of ore, when they are drilled and blasted from workings, usually in the footwall, the ore being then drawn off. The system has the advantage of permitting large-scale operations, but does lead to dilution of the ore with waste rock, which lowers the grade predicted from drilling and also adds to the problem of concentrating the ore later. It can also involve wastage in that caving may occur before extraction is complete. Only where the remaining ore values are sufficiently low for this not to matter is this technique justifiable. The unsupported hanging wall (overlying rock) eventually breaks, or 'caves' into the abandoned workings and this caving may continue right to the surface, where a crumbling and highly dangerous pit, up to fifty feet or more deep, may appear in the 'bush'. Clearly, no surface development can take place above such underground workings.

Where the ore is sufficiently rich to warrant total extraction, as at Chibuluma, a 'cut and fill' technique is employed: the stopes are filled with waste material to prevent caving before the pillars are removed. Although more expensive, this method ensures a more complete and cleaner extraction of the ore.

The larger and thicker ore-bodies are generally mined by a caving method, either on a continuous front, as at Nchanga, or in blocks. This latter technique is widely used at Mufulira. A thin, narrow stope is mined under a block of ore, completely undermining it and causing the roof to collapse by its own weight. It is similar so far to the 'open stoping' method, with the essential difference that the hanging wall consists of ore, not of waste rock. Thus, instead of drilling and blasting the ore as in the other methods, the weight of the overlying rocks is used to break it up. The broken ore is drawn off from below. This method is relatively cheap to operate and ensures a substantial recovery of the ore, but at the cost of some dilution with waste rock.

Concentrating After mining, the ore consists of lumps of rock throughout which are disseminated tiny particles of copper-bearing minerals which must be separated from the rock before the copper can be obtained from them. As a preliminary to this the ore is crushed, usually in two or more stages, until it has been reduced to pieces of no more than three-eighths of an inch in size. The crushed ore is then fed into ball mills—large horizontal revolving cylinders, each about a quarter full of steel balls. As the mills revolve the ore is ground by the action of the steel balls as they climb up the side of the mill and fall back on the pulp. The outflow is sized in a classifier, the fine material passing to the flotation plant and the coarser fraction returning for regrinding.

If the ore consists of sulphide minerals the flotation process is straightforward. After suitable chemicals have been added and the pulp of ore and water violently agitated, air is introduced. The fine mineral particles cling to the bubbles at the top and may be skimmed off. The waste material, known as 'tailing',

2

sinks and is pumped to the unsightly tailings dams which are a feature of the Copperbelt towns. After filtering, and sometimes drying, the concentrated minerals are ready for the smelter.

More complex problems arise when the ore contains both copper and cobalt, when two flotation circuits are required to separate the two minerals. In the case of ore containing a mixture of sulphide and oxide copper, as at Nchanga, a differential flotation procedure must be adopted to separate the two for their subsequent very different treatment. The sulphide concentrate is railed to Nkana for smelting, but the oxides are sent to the leach plant, where they are converted to a copper sulphate solution by treatment with dilute sulphuric acid. The copper is then recovered by electrolysis.

Smelting   After mixing with a flux—usually of a silicous nature for the Roan Selection Trust concentrate, and a lime flux for the Anglo-American product, which already contains an excess of silica—the concentrate is loaded into a reverberatory furnace, a box-like structure built of refractory bricks and 110 ft long. At one end there is provision for feeding in pulverised coal with pre-heated air.

As the charge melts, it collects in the bottom of the furnace in two layers, the lower, heavier layer—the 'matte'—being a mixture of copper and iron sulphides, while the upper layer (slag) consists of a mixture of silicates. The slag is skimmed off periodically and taken away to be dumped: the matte is tapped off when required from a tap-hole near the bottom of the furnace, then carried off in ladles holding some twenty tons to the converters.

The converters are steel, brick-lined cylindrical furnaces, lying horizontally on rollers so that they can be rotated. In them, air under pressure is blown into the molten matte, resulting in the iron and sulphur present being oxidised. Molten copper alone remains at the end of the process.

The oxidisation of the iron and copper sulphides takes place in two separate stages. First of all the iron sulphide is oxidised to iron oxide, which combines with silica flux added to the mixture to form slag, which is skimmed off and returned to the reverberatory furnace. The remaining copper sulphide is further oxidised to form metallic copper. Both these reactions generate considerable heat, sufficient to keep the contents of the converter in a molten state. At Mufulira the sulphur dioxide gas is lost, but at Nkana it is recovered to form the base for the sulphuric acid required in the electrolytic process and for the leach plant at Nchanga. The Roan Selection Trust group will undoubtedly process its own sulphur dioxide in due course.

Copper from the converters is about 99·4 per cent pure. After it has been cast it is known as 'blister' copper because when cooling the residual gases form small blisters on the surface. Much copper was sold in this form in the past, but there is now substantial demand for even purer forms of the metal. To achieve this increased purity the molten copper is transferred to anode furnaces, similar in size and shape to the converters, in which pulverised coal is used to maintain a high temperature. In these furnaces, compressed air is blown through the copper to oxidise the remaining sulphur, and the old-fashioned technique of 'poling' is used to remove the oxygen in the copper. This involves the insertion of large, green, hard-wood tree trunks into the molten mass. Despite its apparent crudity, this still remains the best way of carrying out this final process in the furnace. The resulting copper, 99·8 per cent pure, is cast into anodes and sent to the refinery.

Refining The refining process involves the passing of an electric current between the plates of impure copper (anodes) and sheets of pure copper (cathodes) immersed in an acid copper-bearing solution. During the process, copper is dissolved from the impure plates and deposited on the pure sheets. In the 'tank-house refinery' are hundreds of lead-lined tanks in which electrolysis takes place until the anodes are too small for further use, after twenty-eight days, when they are returned to the smelter to be melted and cast into fresh anodes.

Meanwhile, the impurities in the anodes have either passed into the electrolyte solution or are in sediment at the bottom of the tanks. This sediment—'slimes'—is removed and treated to obtain the gold, silver and other valuable metals which may be present. Similarly, part of the electrolyte is continuously being removed and treated.

The cathodes, now 99·98 per cent pure, are either sold as such or cast into specific shapes—wire bars (for rods and wire), cakes and slabs (for copper sheeting), billets (round bars for pipes), or ingots (for preparing copper-based alloys such as bronze or brass).

1 The background

The activities of Rhodes and his colleagues in the 1880's and 1890's can be adequately judged only when considered against the background of prospective mineral wealth in Central Africa, mingled in rumour and fact, which had developed as a result of the missionary and exploratory activities of previous decades.[1] Although Rhodes thought that a 'second Rand' might be found in Southern Rhodesia, it seems likely that he also hoped to find further quantities of minerals to the north of the Zambesi. Any such discoveries would have been of great value to him in increasing traffic and thus furthering the cause of the Cape to Cairo railway on which he had set his heart. And, most important, it can be taken for granted that Rhodes, the imperialist, envisaged any mineral discoveries as being in British territory. Yet in the mid-1880's, Rhodes' dream of British territory stretching the length of Africa seemed as far away as it had ever been. He had only narrowly prevented the Transvaal Boers from occupying Bechuanaland, and it seemed highly probable that the Belgians, Germans and Portuguese between them would seal off the British possessions from expansion to the north. They could do this legitimately, for the Berlin Conference of 1884 had not banned further European expansion in Africa, but simply laid down the rules under which it was to be carried out. The notification of acquisition of territory was required to permit of objections being lodged, and effective occupation—government officials, missions, traders, settlers— was needed. Fortunately for Rhodes, the conference agreed that 'spheres of influence' would be recognised; it was on these that he pinned his hopes.

Yet haste was essential, and it was in the realisation of this

[1]For further information on this topic, see Appendix I.

that Rhodes acted. Rumours of gold in Lobengula's country led to John Moffat being sent to make a treaty with him, in spite of protests from the Transvaal and Portugal, the treaty being followed by a mineral concession negotiated by C. D. Rudd, F. R. Thompson and Rochfort Maguire. Rhodes carried matters further on a visit to London in 1889, when he allied with Harry Johnston and Lord Gifford, the chairman of both the Exploring Company and the Bechuanaland Exploration Company, in an offer to Lord Salisbury to take over for Britain all the interior of Africa north of the Zambesi and attend to its finance and administration until such time as the British public should appreciate its value and significance to themselves. Thus when Lord Gifford formally applied to the British government for a charter authorising the above to be put into effect, he was supported by Rhodes, Alfred Beit and Rudd, who represented the Matabeleland concession. The objects of the proposed company were quite straightforward:

1 To extend the railway and telegraph systems northwards in the direction of the Zambesi.
2 To encourage emigration and colonisation.
3 To promote trade and commerce.
4 To develop and work mineral and other concessions under the management of one powerful organisation, 'thereby obviating conflicts and complications between the various interests that have been acquired within those regions, and securing to the native chiefs and their subjects the rights reserved to them under several concessions'.

When the government agreed to grant the charter which formally established the new British South Africa Company, apart from granting extensive powers of legislation and administration (along with instructions to prevent any liquor trade with the African peoples and to put down the slave trade), it deliberately failed to define the company's sphere of operations precisely; this was to be 'the region of South Africa lying immediately to the north of British Bechuanaland and to the north and west of the Transvaal and to the west of the Portuguese dominions'. In this way the British 'sphere of influence', as

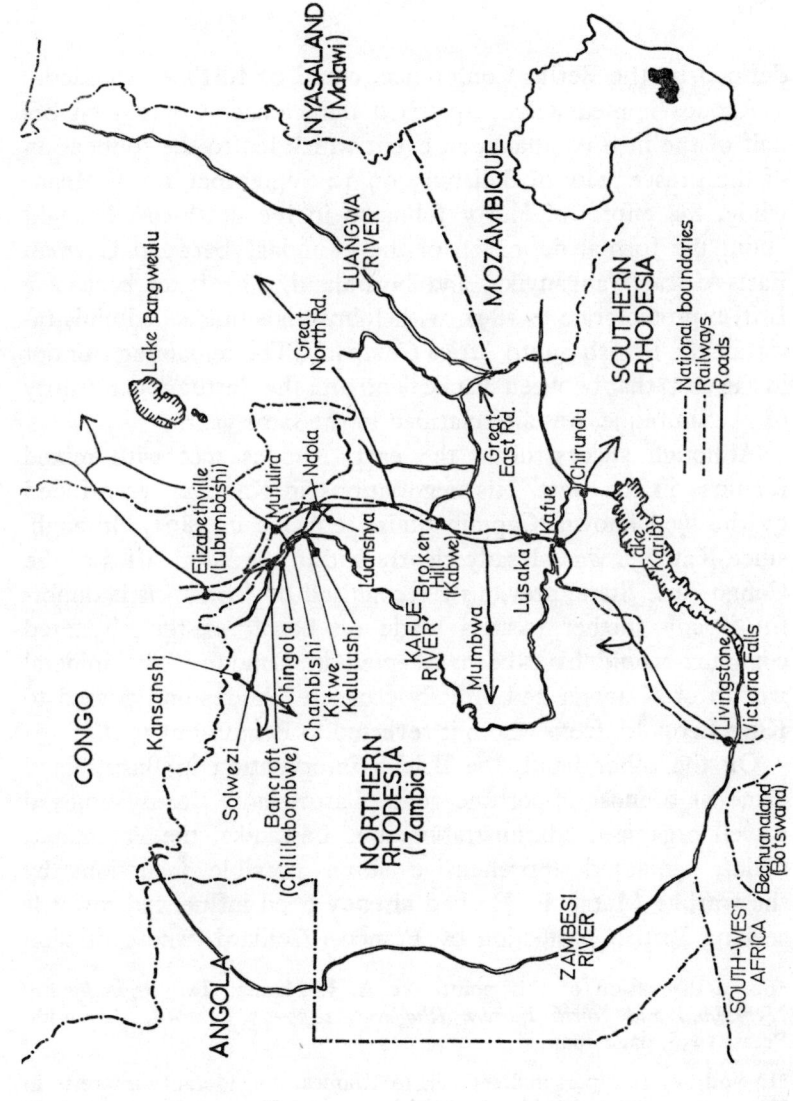

Fig. 1
Northern Rhodesia

defined by the Berlin Conference, could be further extended.

Rhodes immediately despatched the Pioneer Column on behalf of the new company, an event which led to the foundation
of the present city of Salisbury on 12 September 1890. Meanwhile, the efforts of Harry Johnston in the north-east brought
about the formal definition of the boundary between German
East Africa (Tanganyika) and Nyasaland. The latter became a
British protectorate in 1891, with Johnston acting as Administrator for the British South Africa Company. The remaining frontier
in the east, that between Manicaland and the Portuguese territory
of Mozambique, was also clarified in the same year.

Although successful in the east, Rhodes met with mixed
fortunes in the west. His negotiations in Katanga were foiled
by the well known 'Captain Stairs' episode in 1891, although,
since Katanga was already clearly within the boundaries of the
Congo Free State, previously recognised by Britain, it is doubtful if any further treaties made on behalf of the chartered
company would have been accepted in London.[2] The mineral
wealth of Katanga had already escaped Rhodes and passed to
King Leopold, from whom it reverted to Belgium in 1908.[3]

On the other hand, the British intervention in Barotseland
came at a most opportune time. Barotseland already enjoyed
a well organised administration, but Lewanika, the Paramount
Chief, remained apprehensive about possible incursions by
the warlike Matabele. He had already been influenced towards
seeking British protection by François Coillard, whose mission

[2]For a discussion of this point, see A. J. Hanna, *The Beginnings of
Nyasaland and North Eastern Rhodesia, 1859–95*, Oxford, Clarendon
Press, 1956, page 160.

[3]In spite of this personal setback to Rhodes, considerable interests in
Katanga copper are held by the British company Tanganyika Concessions
Ltd, in which the British South Africa Company was represented (see
chapter 2). Rhodesian Anglo-American Ltd also acquired large holdings
in Tanganyika Concessions in 1952–53. The British South Africa
Company now forms part of Charter Consolidated. Rhodesian Anglo-
American and Rhodesian Selection Trust have become Zambian Anglo-
American and Roan Selection Trust respectively subsequent to the
break-up of the Central African Federation and the independence of
Northern Rhodesia as the new State of Zambia.

station for the Paris Evangelical Society had been established in Barotseland since 1884. Further favourable reports from Bechuanaland turned the scale in favour of Frank Lochner, who arrived at Lewanika's court at exactly the right moment. The treaty, which was signed on 27 June 1890, constituted an important step in the modern mining history of Northern Rhodesia. By it, and the further agreements signed in October 1900 and August 1909, Lewanika ceded to the British South Africa Company a monopoly of the mining and commercial rights within the territory under his jurisdiction, whilst his own constitutional position was safeguarded. That portion of his territory actually occupied by the Barotse people was prohibited to prospectors, the boundary of Barotseland and North Western Rhodesia being subsequently extended in such a way as to embrace the ore-bearing regions beyond the Kafue.[4]

[4]It has sometimes been suggested, notably by the late J. E. 'Chirupula' Stephenson, that the present Copperbelt did not fall within Lewanika's jurisdiction, although Lewanika himself claimed this was the case. If we accept Stephenson's contention, its significance, in terms of the British South Africa Company's right to royalties and of economic and political development in general, was momentous. For his exposition of his theory, see J. E. Stephenson, *Chirupula's Tale*, Geoffrey Bles, London, 1937. The author was not fortunate enough to meet 'Chirupula' personally before his death on 15 August 1957, but had access to some of his books containing original marginal notes For a description of his funeral, etc., see the *Central African Post*, 19 August 1957. A more academic discussion of the point is contained in L. H. Gann, *The Birth of a Plural Society*, Manchester University Press for the Rhodes–Livingstone Institute (now the Institute for African Studies, University of Zambia), 1958, pages 135–6. After the assumption of all mining rights by the Zambian government in 1964, the issue naturally ceased to have any economic significance.

2 The early discoveries

The recognition of the Lewanika–Lochner concession by the British government led to the formation of several prospecting companies, the first of which was the Bechuanaland Exploration Company, registered on 25 April 1888 with Lord Gifford as chairman and Edmund (later Sir Edmund) Davis as one of the directors. This was the pioneer of the Edmund Davis group of companies active in Rhodesia. More important, though, within the context of Northern Rhodesia, were its later offshoots, the Northern Territories (BSA) Exploring Company, which in June 1899, was reorganised as the Northern Copper (BSA) Company, the Rhodesia Copper Company, the Rhodesia Broken Hill Development Company and the Rhodesia Copper and General Exploration and Finance Company—for all of which the Bechuanaland Exploration Company acted as 'managers in South Africa'— and the Kafue Copper Development Company and the Bwana Mkubwa Copper Mining Company, for which the parent company acted as 'agents'. All six were formed by Edmund Davis and allied interests.[1] T. G. Davey was the consulting engineer for the group, the prospecting activities of which were co-ordinated by the manager of the Bechuanaland Exploration Company, H. U. Moffat, who was later to become prime minister of Southern Rhodesia.

The first of the Davis 'offshoots', the Northern Territories (BSA) Exploring Company, which was registered in February 1895 in association with Rhodes, commenced operations almost immediately, when F. G. Burnham and Pearl Ingram, followed later by F. R. Lewis, were sent to prospect north of the Zambesi. From this year onwards prospecting licences were

[1]For the interrelationship of the companies relevant to the Copperbelt, see Fig. 9 (chapter 6).

granted to small companies or individuals, and a number of small finds were made, notably in the area north-west of Mumbwa, known geographically as the 'Hook of the Kafue' and, from 1902, when the various claims were amalgamated and acquired by the Northern Copper (BSA) Company, to geologists as the 'Big Concession'. The most important of these were the Silver King and Sable Antelope. Others included the North Star, True Blue, Wonder Rocks, Crystal Jacket, Blue Jacket, Bob, Loulou, Sugarloaf, Lishambika, Inyarka, Kwemba and Beehive.[2]

The other company to undertake pioneering work in Northern Rhodesia was Tanganyika Concessions Ltd, founded by Robert (later Sir Robert) Williams in January 1899, with a capital of only £100,000. Robert Williams, an Aberdonian, was, like Davis, an early associate of Rhodes. He had been interested in Rhodesia since 1891, when he founded the Zambesi Exploring Company to investigate the mineral possibilities on Rhodes' behalf. Originally his prospectors had sought, and failed to find, gold. But Williams was convinced that, notwithstanding previous failures, minerals would be found in Northern Rhodesia and further north, and in particular on the Congo–Zambesi watershed, which struck him as being geographically similar to the Rand. Thus motivated, and with the added hope of being able to further Rhodes' Cape to Cairo railway by creating traffic, he obtained from the chartered company a concession to prospect for a mineral area of up to 2,000 square miles and to stake up to 1,000 claims anywhere in Northern Rhodesia. In return, the British South Africa Company was to have a 35 per cent interest in these claims, and in addition, as part of Rhodes' railway scheme, Williams was to provide a steamer on Lake Tanganyika.[3] The township of Abercorn and

[2]For details of these mines, see J. A. Bancroft, *Mining in Northern Rhodesia*, British South Africa Company, 1961, pages 57–59 and 68–69; for an article on their subsequent fate, see 'The ghost mines of Mumbwa', *Horizon* (a magazine for Rhodesian Selection Trust employees), March 1961, pages 18–19.

[3]Rhodes himself possessed 2,000 £1 shares which subsequently rose in value to £25 a share.

the jetty at Mpulungu were subsequently built as the proposed terminus of the Rhodesian section of the railway, which has still not materialised. Williams also obtained from King Leopold of the Belgians, before the discovery of Kansanshi (see page 12) was known to either, a concession lasting five years over 60,000 square miles in Katanga, plus an annual subsidy of £10,000 in return for a guarantee of 60 per cent of the profits of any minerals discovered.

Having achieved his concession, Williams now 'played his hunch'. This was all it could be, in spite of his own convictions, for the evidence, as detailed in Appendix I, was meagre. True, ancient workings existed, but there was nothing to suggest that they were not almost completely worked out,[4] and in any case they were oxide deposits, notoriously expensive to treat and possibly small in extent, as the Hook of the Kafue finds subsequently proved to be. And if this was the case, with the railhead many hundreds of miles away at Bulawayo, with the intervening country ridden with malaria and sleeping sickness, with transport dependent, at least initially, largely on human porterage, the operations involved in extraction, refining and marketing would be financially suicidal. Only the discovery of more large deposits — either of very rich oxides such as those at Kambove,[5] discovered by the Emile Françqui expedition in 1891, or, better, of substantial, easily worked sulphides—would justify future development work. At the time of Williams' decision to go ahead only one major deposit of any nature and no trace of sulphides had been found. Yet

I instructed George Grey to proceed to the great divide between the Zambesi and Congo Rivers, and marked out on the map the most likely place to find minerals on that divide, and quoted in confirma-

[4]All the ancient workings had been abandoned when discovered by Europeans. This could be caused only by a removal of the motivation (perhaps pressure from slavers) or by exhaustion of the oxide ores (malachite and azurite) accessible to the native and amenable to his smelting techniques.
[5]Leopold and his advisers completely failed to realise the implications of this find. If they had done so it is unlikely that any concession would have been granted to other than Belgian interests.

tion the writings of Livingstone, Cameron and other explorers who had either heard of minerals or visited one or two of the old workings at or near that divide during the past seventy or eighty years, and with this idea I secured a concession . . . George Grey and his party . . . first discovered the Kansanshi mine and later opened up at an expense of about £100,000 the Katanga copper mines, proving the existence . . . [of] . . . probably the greatest copper fields in the world, extending over 250 miles in length, all within the area I had indicated.[6]

In fact the first major discovery made by Grey in Katanga was the extremely rich carbonate deposit of the 'Star of the Congo'. Not unnaturally, attention was now diverted from Northern Rhodesia to such effect that over a hundred other deposits had been found in Katanga by 1906, when the Union Minière du Haut-Katanga was formed to develop the new copper fields.

I had meantime at Rhodes' request [continued Williams] negotiated his Cape to Cairo Railway through to the Nile with King Leopold, but after a great struggle to secure its extension to the Congo border, and although I offered Rhodes, shortly before he died, a half interest in our mineral interests to assist his railway, we failed to get that extension, as his financiers demanded further mineral concessions from the Belgians.

It will be recalled that the chartered company held a 35 per cent interest in the claims of Tanganyika Concessions in Northern Rhodesia, that Rhodes personally possessed 2,000 £1 shares and that, by virtue of Williams' agreement with King Leopold, Tanganyika Concessions was to enjoy 40 per cent of the profits of the Katanga operations.[7] Rhodes' trustees, how-

[6]Sir Robert Williams, speech to annual general meeting of Tanganyika Concessions Ltd, London, 30 July 1925.

[7]Subsequently, in 1905, as a result of the amazing results of Williams' work, his concession was extended for a further period of four years, during the last three of which the Belgian Comité Spécial du Katanga agreed to meet half the expenses, but Tanganyika Concessions would receive only 20 per cent of the profits of any new mines discovered. After eight years' work, Williams was to place his organisation at the disposal of the Comité Spécial for two more years, during which period the

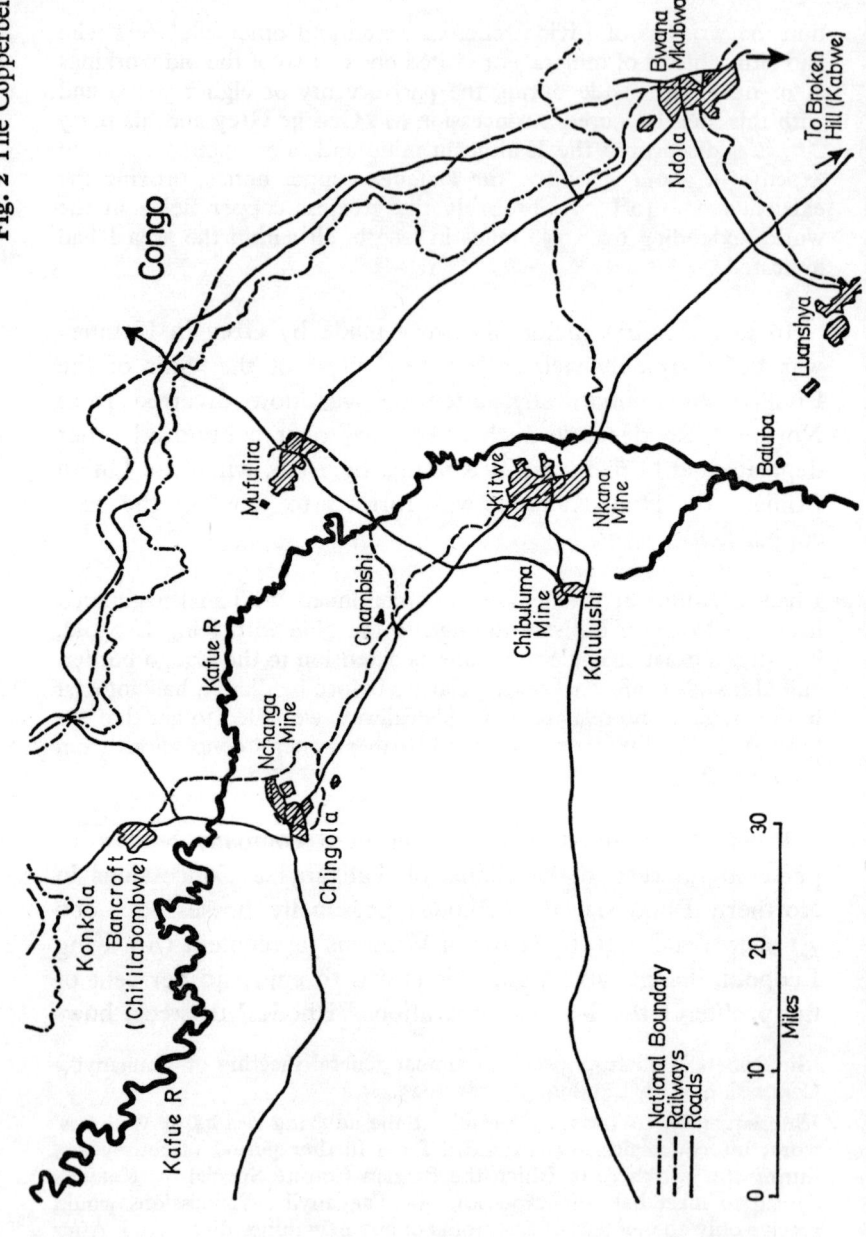

Fig. 2 The Copperbelt

Congo

Bwana Mkubwa

To Broken
Hill (Kabwe)

Ndola

Luanshya

Baluba

Mufulira

Kafue R

Kitwe

Chambishi

Nkana
Mine

Chibuluma
Mine

Kalulushi

Nchanga
Mine

Chingola

Konkola

Bancroft
(Chililabombwe)

Kafue R

National Boundary
Railways
Roads

0   10   20   30
              Miles

ever, felt that this percentage was inadequate and pressed Williams to negotiate for a greater share. The failure to achieve this and the consequent hold-up in the advance of the railway occasioned bitter criticism in Northern Rhodesia, especially from Leopold Moore in Livingstone, who enlarged at some length on the benefits which might be expected for the town once it stood on a rail link between the south and the future mining centres.

> ... there is promise of great activity in North West Rhodesia. That the principal field of operations will be the huge mineral belt, a portion only of which lies within our borders, is certainly a point to the bad for Livingstone; but we feel justified in assuming that any enterprise such as we have indicated could hardly fail to have highly beneficial commercial effects on its prospects.[8]

But

> The Beit and the Rhodes Trustees appear to have declined to afford any financial assistance, and this seems to point to their disbelief in the likelihood of the section now to be constructed ever forming part of the main trunk line.[9]

This setback, however, was only temporary. Williams immediately negotiated with the Portuguese for the building of the Lobito (Benguela) Railway to the Angola coast at Lobito Bay. In practice, geographical problems, the outbreak of the first world war and economic difficulties prevented the completion of this railway until 1931, by which time communications with the south were fully established. In any event it was not necessary

---

Comité Spécial would finance all the operations. Any new discoveries made during these two years would be placed in reserve. Thus the financial interrelationship between Tanganyika Concessions and Union Minière, although substantially beneficial to the former, was very complex. Again, though, the nationalisation of Union Minière by the Congolese government after independence has created a new situation which awaits further analysis.

[8] *Livingstone Mail*, 3 October 1908.
[9] *Livingstone Mail*, 5 December 1908. The proposed line to Tanganyika would have by-passed the present Copperbelt.

because immediately after Williams had secured the concession to build the Benguela railway he was approached by Dr Jameson, then Prime Minister of the Cape as well as a director of the chartered company, with a particular request to negotiate the extension of the Rhodesia Railway to the Congo border and thence to the Katanga mines. It was as a result of the ensuing negotiations between Williams and Jadot that Tanganyika Concessions formed a new company—the Rhodesia–Katanga Junction Railway and Mineral Company, with a capital of £1½ million—to connect the Rhodesia Railway to the Congo frontier, from which point it was extended to the mines by the Belgians in 1910.

With the formation of this company, which also took over control of the Kansanshi mine, Tanganyika Concessions had no major interests in Northern Rhodesia and concentrated thenceforth on its share of the Katanga prospects. The British South Africa Company was given 50,000 fully paid £1 shares for its interest in the mine, as a result of which transaction Kansanshi became exempt from royalty payments to the British South Africa Company. On the other hand, although the railway company enabled Tanganyika Concessions to shed most of its interests in Northern Rhodesia, it was the means by which the British South Africa Company was able to survive at all. Writing to Owen Letcher in August 1931, Sir Robert Williams remarked:

Dr Jameson, when he asked me after Rhodes' death to try to get a connection for the Rhodesia Railways to the Katanga mines, told me that unless I got this, the Chartered Company would go into liquidation as that Company, of which Dr Jameson was then the President, was losing £300,000 per annum under its guarantee of interest to the Rhodesian Debenture Holders.[10]

Kansanshi
The George Grey appointed by Robert Williams to investigate his theories about the mineral wealth of the Zambesi–Congo divide was a brother of Earl Grey of Falloden and a personal

[10]Quoted in O. Letcher, *South Central Africa*, African Publications, Johannesburg, 1932, pages 133–34.

friend of Rhodes. The expedition, which left Bulawayo at the end of the rainy season in 1899, consisted of five Europeans,[11] thirty-eight Africans, sixty-seven donkeys, eight oxen, seven horses and two pack mules.[12] A liberal quantity of trading goods and basic supplies, sufficient for one season, was carried. The party reached the Kafue on 30 May, but made no mineral discoveries worthy of mention until they reached the area previously designated by Williams.[13] In this area, on 6 September 1899, Grey was led by an old native chief, Kapiji M'Panga, to the ancient workings at Kansanshi. These workings covered a very large area. Pits over a hundred feet deep were to be seen, extended down to the water-table, and, in some cases, with trees growing out of them.[14] Obviously the workings were very old. Thousands of tons of oxide ore had already been removed, but whether or not this was by the initiative of the local natives is not clear. Normally the primitive smelting took place fairly close to the extraction site—that is, within a few miles, wherever suitable wood for charcoal and a water supply were available—but the fact that no smelting sites have been discovered within many miles of Kansanshi, and that the nearest ones are easily accessible from other sources of ore, suggests that either some form of overlordship was enforced, by which the ore was transported elsewhere for treatment, or that it was removed as an adjunct to the slave trade.[15]

The Kansanshi deposit is more closely related to the Katanga mines than to those on the present Copperbelt. Unlike the Copperbelt deposits, there are plentiful signs at Kansanshi of

[11]For an interview with W. R. White, the sole survivor in 1960, see *Horizon*, March 1961, pages 10–14.
[12]There is a photograph of the expedition in the *Northern Rhodesia Journal*, vol. 2, No. 3.
[13]For a full report on the activities of the expedition, see *Report on the Discoveries made by Mr George Grey's Expedition*, Tanganyika Concessions Ltd, London, 1903.
[14]Personal information: J. E. G. Williams.
[15]It is interesting to note in this connection that Grey complained in 1901 that the slave trade interfered with his own operations at Kansanshi. See L. H. Gann, 'The end of the slave trade in British Central Africa, 1889–1912', *Rhodes-Livingstone Journal*, vol. XVI, 1954.

the presence of copper. Most striking is an elliptical hill, practically free of vegetation, which rises to about a hundred feet above the surrounding tree-covered plain (see plate 1). Traversing this hill from north to south, and continuing to the south for a few hundred yards, are a series of veins of minerals, including copper oxides, which vary in width from about fifteen feet to a matter of only inches, the majority being in the region of five feet or less. A variety of colours are to be seen, depending on the type of mineral exposed. Grey was deeply impressed by what he saw, especially the scope and extent of the ancient workings. Nevertheless, nothing immediate was done. Not only was there no railway at all in Northern Rhodesia, but in any case, oxide ores were very expensive to treat. Thus Kansanshi remained merely as a base for subsequent explorations into the Congo, during which the famous Star of the Congo mine near the modern city of Lubumbashi was discovered.

It is not surprising that Tanganyika Concessions should decide to concentrate on Katanga rather than Northern Rhodesia, for Katanga was not only easier to prospect in—the copper outcrops, in the form of hills bare of vegetation, being comparatively easy to find—but at the same time the values of ore there were (and still are) much greater than anything found in Northern Rhodesia. Expectant optimism was evident as early as 1908:

The whole problem in Katanga is the question of producing and marketing the copper . . . The engineer's estimate is that he can turn out copper from the Star and Kambove at £10 a ton. [The estimate for Kansanshi was £18.] It will cost less than £10 a ton to send it to Europe. Add the profit of the Union Minière and this will make it less than £30 a ton. There is not a mine in the world, with the possible exception of the Rio Tinto, that can afford to sell copper below £38 a ton . . . Given the railway and efficient management, Katanga should control the world's copper supply and be the brightest spot in Africa.[16]

Thus, whereas good Rhodesian ores assay at 5 per cent copper or less, as early as June 1911 the Star of the Congo mine was

[16]*Livingstone Mail*, 26 December 1908.

producing ore which yielded 15 per cent copper.[17] Some assays of samples sent to London contained copper values as high as 33 per cent.[18] Ore which would have been considered a reasonable prospect elsewhere was sometimes used in Katanga as ballast on roads. It also proved possible in Katanga to send some ore, from Kipushi for example, direct to Belgium for treatment, which again helped to reduce capital expenditure.

The Rhodesia Copper Company: Roan Antelope and Bwana Mkubwa

Another important company which developed as a result of the Lochner concession was the Rhodesia Copper Company, in which the leading figure was Edmund Davis. The Northern Territories (BSA) Exploring Company formed by Davis and Rhodes in 1895 had become the Northern Copper (BSA) Company, and it was the latter which eventually amalgamated with other small groups to form the Rhodesia Copper Company, which is noted for the two very great discoveries of the Roan Antelope and Bwana Mkubwa.

Undoubtedly 1902 was a vital year in the economic history of Northern Rhodesia. Early in January, before the formation of the Rhodesia Copper Company at the end of the month, T. G. Davey, operating for the Davis group, stumbled across outcrops of lead, zinc and vanadium on a *kopje* or rocky hillock which he named 'Broken Hill' on account of its resemblance to a similar formation of that name in Australia. This fortunate occurrence was the result of Davey becoming lost in the 'bush'.[19]

On the formation of the Rhodesia Copper Company, Davey became its consulting engineer. About thirty Europeans were employed by Davey as prospectors, and it was one pair of these,

[17]See *Livingstone Mail*, 22 June 1911 and 12 August 1911.
[18]Bancroft, op. cit., page 51.
[19]For details, see his 'Report to the Directors of the Rhodesia Copper Company', 31 December 1902. A separate company to develop the mine—the Rhodesia Broken Hill Development Company—was founded in 1910.

W. C. Collier and J. J. Donohoe, who made the momentous discoveries referred to above.[20]

There were actually three Europeans—Collier, Donohoe and W. Sellers—in the party sent from Bulawayo early in 1902 to Davey, who was then at the Silver King mine in the Hook of the Kafue, but only the first two were sent on by Davey in the north-easterly direction which would bring them to the region of the present Ndola and Luanshya. They proceeded on their way together as far as Kapopo, where the first clue to the presence of copper was found. Here, as Livingstone and others had already recorded elsewhere, the local natives were using malachite as a treatment for tropical ulcers. Both Collier and Donohoe were experienced prospectors, each perfectly competent to proceed on his own. Thus, in order to cover the maximum possible amount of ground, the two agreed to separate and rejoin forces later at the village of Chiwala, a retired Arab slaver who enjoyed some measure of domination over the local inhabitants. Although Chiwala had apparently ordered the Africans in the area not to divulge the sources of the malachite used and claimed to the last that it came from Katanga (it may have done, for no recent native workings have been found in the area), an old man, whom Collier befriended by shooting meat for him, informed him where the ore might be found. On the following day Collier visited the indicated area, stalked and shot a Roan antelope, and to his amazement found that it had fallen on an outcrop of pure malachite—hence the name of the future mine. Although in fact it was thus discovered fortuitously, it

[20]There are many accounts in existence of Collier's discovery of the Roan Antelope, all of which show discrepancies in detail. In compiling this one I have used:

(a) Collier's account to Chester Beatty (address to the New York section of the American Institute of Mining and Metallurgy, October 1931).
(b) An interview with Collier in the Bulawayo *Chronicle*, 28 March 1934.
(c) Lucy Cullen, *Beyond the Smoke that Thunders*, Oxford University Press, 1941.
(d) O. Letcher, *South Central Africa*, op. cit.
(e) Personal accounts given to me by two of Collier's friends, N. M. Airey and W. Pickering.

would be most unjust to dismiss the find as depending on pure chance. Collier was an expert and already in a known copper-bearing region. It could, therefore, have been only a matter of time before the secrets were revealed, regardless of luck.

Near this outcrop Collier found some minor ancient workings, on which he pegged claims. The next day he investigated further, discovering a large open clearing, 100–300 ft wide and a mile long, which doubled back in the form of a hairpin, the arms of which were about two thousand feet apart. Collier pegged claims on each, one being named the Roan Antelope and the other Rietbok (another type of buck).[21] Trenching along the line of the clearing later disclosed copper oxides, such as malachite and azurite, very similar to the deposits found in the Congo. Nevertheless, the find was neglected until the revival of interest from 1923 (see chapter 4), partly because of the difficulties applying also to Kansanshi, but also largely because of the extraordinary find which Collier and Donohoe were almost immediately to make.

Having pegged the Roan and Rietbok claims, Collier proceeded at once to join Donohoe, with whom he was secretly led on 4 December 1902 to the most intriguing ancient workings ever to be found in Northern Rhodesia. There are two principal workings, parallel to each other and about thirty feet apart, on the north-eastern slope of a *kopje* which rises for some seventy-five feet above the surrounding plain. The first of these, which is about 750 yards long, varies in width from five to twenty-three feet. The second runs intermittently for almost 300 yards, with a width of four feet. Both vary in depth from two to thirty feet.

[21]There has been considerable controversy regarding the date of these discoveries. Irwin—the general manager of Roan Antelope in 1928—believed that the date was 1904 (letter to D'Eath of Rhodesian Selection Trust, dated 2 August 1948, in Rhodesian Selection Trust archives), and in fact further claims were pegged in the area for the Rhodesia Copper Company in that year. But the original date was almost certainly June 1902, the claims being all finally pegged in November. See letter from T. W. Baxter (Federal Archives) to Roan Antelope Mine dated 25 November 1948, in Rhodesian Selection Trust archives. The claims were finally beaconed and registered in 1913 in terms of the Mining Proclamation of 1912.

Obviously, a large quantity of high-grade malachite had been removed at some time in the past; equally, the deposit was not being worked when discovered and no smelters were found in the vicinity. (Subsequently, a smelting site which may have served the mine was discovered some miles away alongside a *dambo*, or grassy drainage area in the bush, which would have provided a water supply.)

J. E. G. Williams, who was employed there as an assayer from 1921, informed the writer that the remains found gave the impression that the early workers had either left in a great hurry, abandoning their equipment and extracted ore, or had been forcibly removed. There is an unresolved mystery here, but, as at Kansanshi, it seems probable that the mine was an accessory to the slave trade. Arab slavers were undoubtedly active in the area before the coming of European administration, the presence of Chiwala himself being living evidence. Apparently the focal point of the slave trade was a large tree, standing in Ndola and now preserved as a national monument, below which the caravans are reputed to have gathered before their arduous march to the coast. It is reasonable to suppose that the slaves might have been burdened with either smelted copper or malachite on their journey. Further west, of course, Portuguese slavers dominated, the actual areas of the respective spheres of influence not being perfectly clear. Thus, clashes between Arab and Portuguese agents in the Kansanshi and Bwana Mkubwa areas may well have occurred.[22]

Donohoe named the mine 'Bwana Mkubwa'—the Big Chief, or Great Master—a name which has aroused mild controversy ever since. C. M. Doke believed that it was named after the Administrator, Codrington.[23] A. E. Beech, writing in *Horizon* in

[22]For information on the slave trade see, *inter alia*, O. Letcher, *South Central Africa*, op. cit., page 125; M. Gelfand, *Northern Rhodesia in the Days of the Charter*, Blackwell, Oxford, 1961; J. M. Mowbray, *In South Central Africa*, Constable, London, 1912, page 118; H. and W. E. Masters, *In Wild Rhodesia*, F. Griffiths, London, 1920; L. H. Gann, 'The end of the slave trade in British Central Africa, 1889–1912', op. cit.; C. M. Doke, *The Lambas of Northern Rhodesia*, Harrap, London, 1931.
[23]C. M. Doke, op. cit., page 47.

March 1959, thinks it was in honour of Collier himself. However, it is fairly clear that when Donohoe had stayed with the
Native Commissioner at Kapopo, Francis Enilius Fletcher
Jones,[24] known to the local Africans as the 'Bwana Mkubwa', he
had promised to name a mine after him if one should be discovered. There is little doubt that Jones was the Bwana Mkubwa
in question.[25]

Exploratory work began in 1903, when four vertical shafts,
sunk to the 250 ft level in dry ground, disclosed considerable
reserves of rich oxide ore below the old workings. Nevertheless,
as in the case of the other discoveries, it was impracticable to
attempt to operate the mine without adequate transport facilities, and nothing further was done until the arrival of the railway. The line was opened late in 1909.

[24]This same F. E. F. Jones, along with J. E. Stephenson, founded the
bomas (district administrative headquarters) at Mkushi and Ndola.
[25]K. Bradley, *Copper Venture*, Mufulira and Roan Antelope Mines, 1952,
page 67, agrees, but more conclusive evidence is to be found in a pencilled
footnote by J. E. Stephenson in his own copy of *Chirupula's Tale*, op. cit.,
page 97 (copy in Rhodes-Livingstone Institute Library, now the Institute
for African Studies, University of Zambia, Lusaka). Collier also supported
this theory: see Bulawayo *Chronicle*, 28 March 1934.

3 The second stage of exploration and development

Bwana Mkubwa

During the interim period of waiting for the completion of the railway to Bwana Mkubwa the Rhodesia Copper Company was succeeded by the Rhodesia Copper and General Exploration and Finance Company, from which latter company the property was acquired by the newly formed Bwana Mkubwa Copper Mining Company in March 1910. This company, which was registered in London, had an initial capital of £600,000 in £1 shares. Development work now began in earnest from a number of vertical shafts with drives extending from them at the 100 ft and 250 ft levels. These showed the existence of a rich central lode, with poorer areas surrounding it.[1] Only the main central lode was developed at this stage, the ore reserves being estimated in 1913 at 55,000 tons of 12 per cent copper, with possibly double that quantity at 5 per cent. The assayer about this time was Mr Blackie, the grandson of the founder of the publishing firm of that name. All the estimated ore reserves lay in dry ground, water not being encountered until a depth of 270 ft was attained. This water proved excessive at greater depths, with the result that little attempt was made to deepen the workings.

A concentrator capable of handling ninety tons a day commenced operations in January 1913 and continued until September 1914, when the mine was temporarily closed on account of the shortage of labour and materials occasioned by the 1914–18 war and the low copper prices then prevailing. In fact this was premature, for the price of copper rose from £61 to £170 a ton by the end of 1916. From this rapid price rise Katanga reaped

[1] For full geological details, see J. A. Bancroft, 'Notes on the geology of the Bwana Mkubwa mine', *International Geological Congress Yearbook*, 1929.

the benefit and greatly increased its production, as may be seen from table 1.[2] It is clear from this table that the increasing demand and rise in prices during the 1914–18 war greatly

Table 1. Copper production (long tons)

Year	Katanga	N. Rhodesia	Average price per ton (£)
1908	–	589	–
1909	–	601	–
1910	–	782	–
1911	997	905	–
1912	2,492	1,972	–
1913	7,408	240	–
1914	10,722	218	62.6
1915	14,054	176	79.6
1916	22,149	167*	125·2
1917	27,462	132*	125·0
1918	20,237	96	113·5
1919	22,366	195	86·0
1920	18,961	130	80·4
1921	30,464	184	57·6
1922	43,362	180	61·6
1923	57,886	130	66·5
1924	85,379	89	60·0
1925	90,110	74	64·7
1926	80,639	708	63.6

*According to Dr Bancroft (op. cit., page 123) Bwana Mkubwa produced 2,845 tons of copper between June 1916 and March 1918. If this production was exported as concentrate it would not be reflected in the records as metal production. This would account for the apparent discrepancy.

[2]These figures, like those in tables 2 and 3, are extracted from *The Story of the Cape to Cairo Railway and River Route*, ed. L. Wienthal, Pioneer Publishing Co., 1923, vol. IV, page 64, for Katanga, and from T. D. Guernsey, *A Prospector's Guide to Mineral Occurrences in Northern Rhodesia*, British South Africa Company, Salisbury, 1952, Chamber of Mines *Year Books* and the Government Mines Department for Northern Rhodesia. A price list which does not always coincide with official figures is published in L. H. Gann, *A History of Northern Rhodesia*, Chatto & Windus, London, 1964, page 329.

stimulated production in Katanga, the dramatic drop in 1918 being largely accounted for by the epidemic of 'Spanish 'flu' which struck Central Africa in that year. The post-war depression is also clearly mirrored in these production figures. The Bwana Mkubwa company endeavoured to exploit the favourable situation brought about by the war by resuming production in June 1916, with the concentrator treating a further 69,374 tons which yielded 2,845 tons of copper.[3] Again, though, this was only a temporary measure, for the mine closed down once more in March 1918.

Provided the railway had at least reached as far as Broken Hill, it mattered little, as far as Kansanshi was concerned, how much further it progressed in Rhodesia (although a future branch line from Katanga might solve many difficulties in transport and supply to the mine). Even now, the nearest point on the Rhodesia Railway, at Kirila Bomwe (formerly Bancroft) is some hundred miles away. The transport problem to Kansanshi therefore still remains. Nevertheless, when the railway reached Broken Hill in 1906 Grey felt tempted, despite the difficulties involved, to endeavour to smelt some of the high-grade ore at the mine. He assembled a blast furnace at Broken Hill, and, profiting from the experience of the Northern Copper Company in the use of traction engines to provide transport to and from the Silver King, Sable Antelope and other mines in the Hook of the Kafue,[4] engaged a Captain Hamilton to construct a road suitable for these machines over the three hundred miles from Broken Hill to Kansanshi. The blast furnaces arrived at Kansanshi in 1907 and smelting began on a small scale in February 1908, the furnaces using local charcoal and fluxes, and producing over two tons of copper daily when in operation.[5] This was increased to over four tons a day by 1910, using a larger furnace, but the necessary supply of high-grade ore could not be maintained, with the result

[3]Figures quoted in Bancroft: 'Mining in Northern Rhodesia', op. cit., page 123.
[4]See report by Lord Gifford to a meeting of the Northern Copper Company, London, 1903, quoted by O. Letcher, op. cit., pages 75-7.
[5]E.g. 72 tons in twenty-seven days in May. *Livingstone Mail*, 22 August 1908.

that production fell to 1·25 tons a day.[6] This was completely un-economic, and led to the closure of the mine on the outbreak of war in August 1914, by which time some 2,800 tons of copper valued at £170,000 had been produced. By this date the property had been transferred to the Rhodesia–Katanga Junction Railway and Mineral Company. The mine then lay dormant until 1927.

The Nkana area
Many years ago, so the traditional accounts tell us, a girl named Nachimbala, a relative of Mushiri, the Paramount Chief of the Walamba, gave birth to a daughter. This child, who was born during a period of severe famine, was named Nkana in honour of the Nkana palm, the leaves of which were eaten by the tribe to prevent starvation. When Nkana reached womanhood she mar-ried a certain Yalobe. Their son, Nkana Yalobe, was the grand-father of the first Chief Nkana, whose grandson, the late chief, died in December 1961, aged 58.[7]

About three miles north of the present road bridge across the Kafue river, near the modern town of Kitwe and close to where the Wusikili stream flows into this river, a small outcrop of copper-mineralised rock has been exposed in the bed of the stream. It is still not absolutely certain who was the first European to see this outcrop. Two prospectors, F. Lewis and O. Baragwan-ath, who were based on the Silver King, may have reached it and pegged a claim there in 1901, after travelling up the Kafue by canoe.[8] This would, of course, have been some months before the

[6]At first a great future had been forecast for the mine, since the costing estimates for the mine were £18 a ton plus £1 a ton transport charges to Europe, i.e. a total cost of some £10 a ton less than any other producing mine. See the *Livingstone Mail*, 26 December 1908. The Katanga estimates were even lower. Only a fortnight earlier the same paper was berating the Rhodes and Beit trustees for alleged disbelief in the future, as evidenced in their attitude to the extension of the railway (see chapter 2, note 9).
[7]For his obituary, see the *Northern News*, 28 December 1961. In his youth, before being crowned in 1932, he had himself worked on the mine which was named after his father.
[8]Reported in *Horizon*, April 1963 The account had already formed the subject of a most interesting historical novel, *Trail of the Copper King*, by T. V. Bulpin, published by Timmins, Cape Town, 1959.

well-known expedition of Collier and Donohoe to the Roan
Antelope and Bwana Mkubwa. Certainly the reef was known by
1906, for a map produced in London in September of that year
by Edward Stanford and now in the geology files of the Anglo-
American Corporation clearly indicates it. Nevertheless, the first
time that attention was seriously drawn to the outcrop was in
1910, when J. Moffat Thompson, then assistant magistrate at
Ndola, was shown the outcrop by an African whom Bancroft suggests was Nkana.[9] He may have been the father of the late chief,
who was then only seven years old. Thompson pegged the outcrop, later selling the claims to Zeederberg of Bulawayo, who
eventually sold them to the Johannesburg financiers, Colonel J.
Donaldson D.S.O. and E. Sievewright.

Further conflicting information came to light in 1956 when
J. F. Kapnek, of Johannesburg, who had been connected with
mining in Southern Rhodesia since 1904, supplied a memorandum detailing his own activities to the late J. C. Ferguson, then
Director of Geological Surveys for the territory, by whom it was
shown to the author. Ferguson, who was an old friend of Kapnek,
was satisfied that the memorandum, as also a letter subsequently
written by Kapnek to the Secretary of Mines, Lands and Surveys
in Salisbury on 21 August 1957, are valid evidence.

In 1910 Kapnek and Theodore Berwitz sent out from Salisbury a Scotsman, Dark Fraser, to trade cattle on their behalf in
Barotseland. While on this venture, Fraser formed the opinion
that there were good prospects for coal, copper, gold and other
minerals in Northern Rhodesia and suggested to his employers
that he should undertake some prospecting on their behalf. As a result, relates Kapnek, he formed a syndicate which included Berwitz,
Eli and Harry Susman, who were then living at Livingstone,
Henry Ellenbogen, a former mayor of Bulawayo, Abe Fingleson
and himself. The syndicate contributed £75 a month between
them to the scheme, of which £60 was for monthly expenses—
native wages, food, picks, shovels, and other equipment—and the

[9]Bancroft, op. cit., page 66.

balance of £15 made up the wages of Fraser, who was also to receive a sixth share in anything he discovered.

In the course of his expedition Fraser located some small copper outcrops, one of them being the present Nkana deposit. Samples taken by him assayed around 4 per cent copper. Kapnek then claims that he submitted the assay results, along with samples, to the Bulawayo mining interests, without gaining any response. The claims, which had been registered in the name of Dark Fraser, were therefore abandoned. In view of the apparently great potential of Katanga, Kansanshi and Bwana Mkubwa, a minor outcrop of only 4 per cent copper was unlikely to have much speculative value at the time. It is known, however, that in 1916 H. C. Winnicott pegged two blocks of claims in the area for the Susman brothers, and these may have been the same claims. This action was very probably stimulated by the considerable rise in copper prices already noted above. The claims were registered as 'Nkana Copper' in 1916. The Susmans offered the claims to the Bwana Mkubwa company for nothing more than their expenses, amounting to £100. On this offer being rejected (perhaps not unexpectedly in the light of the frustrating results from the richer deposit at Bwana Mkubwa), the claims were sold to a William Lee for the same sum in December 1918. Lee now went to work trenching and sinking prospect shafts, and soon proved valuable deposits, ranging up to 4·6 per cent copper, in reefs several feet wide and totalling up to 1,800 ft in length. By June 1919 Lee was demanding £10,000 for his two blocks of claims. In the same month Lee and F. A. Unger, a representative of the Consolidated Mines Selection Company,[10] who had been inspecting Lee's property, were taken by Chief Nkana some fifteen miles to the north-west, where they were shown the ancient workings at Chambishi, which had previously been pegged by Collier and Donohoe in July 1903[11] and before that by George Grey in 1899.

The earliest known registration of these latter claims was on

[10]In 1928 this company was one of the participants in the formation of Rhodesian Anglo-American.
[11]There is no record of this except for a note found amongst Collier's papers after his death. Personal information: L. Tucker.

3 March 1913,[12] when they were registered in the name of the Rhodesia Copper and General Exploration and Finance Company, which company abandoned them in June 1917. They were re-registered on 2 January 1920 in the name of William Lee, transferred to the Messina Coal and Metal Mines in June of the same year and re-sold to Donaldson and Sievewright in 1924.

[12]It should be noted that all claims pegged before the Mining Proclamation of 1912 were recorded in the Mines Department, Ndola, from which department no further information could be obtained. See letter ref. RD 331/49 dated 23 December 1949 from the Registrar, Mining Titles, Livingstone, to Mufulira Copper Mines Ltd, in the Rhodesian Selection Trust files. Unfortunately, too, all the records dated prior to 1912 held by Copper Ventures, Rhodesian Selection Trust and the British South Africa Company were destroyed by enemy action during the 1939-45 war

4 Development and exploitation to 1939

After the impetus of the initial spurt of prospecting had lost momentum in the early years of the twentieth century, it seems clear that as far as Northern Rhodesia was concerned the results were relatively disappointing. Gold finds were negligible, the numerous small copper mines in the Hook of the Kafue were all either already failures or shortly to become so, and Kansanshi was too far away from transport facilities. Bwana Mkubwa, although apparently promising, was also a long way from the railhead, and in any case, its potential was soon to be shown to be greatly exaggerated: it has never, to date, been a paying proposition. What else remained? Old workings on oxide deposits at Chambishi, Roan Antelope and Nkana, but all inferior in value to Bwana Mkubwa. What hope was there for these? And all were overshadowed by the plenteous bounty of Katanga. On the credit side was a substantial lead and zinc deposit at Broken Hill.

In fact the mineral wealth of Northern Rhodesia lay deep down out of sight of prospecting eyes and was not to be revealed by the unscientific methods then in vogue. Prior to the advent of systematic prospecting (an innovation brought about by Dr Bancroft in 1927) a success or failure depended either on luck—and it is astonishing how high a percentage of Copperbelt mines were discovered by random stumbling upon ancient workings or mineralised outcrops—or on the goodwill of the local natives. It was therefore common for prospectors to carry samples of malachite, azurite and other easily identifiable ores in the hope that they would be recognised by the local inhabitants and similar outcrops indicated. Streams could be usefully investigated for their mineral content, and by following any such indication to the point at which it was no longer present, it was sometimes possible to isolate the source of the occurrence within the drainage area. It

27

may be noted that although to reveal the potential of the Copper-belt mines required intensive, scientific investigation, all the present operating mines—with the one exception of Chibuluma—were initially located by such elementary methods as those detailed above.

In view of the lack of substantial success, together with instability in the prices of base metals during 1907 and 1908, there was a decline in prospecting activities in Northern Rhodesia for the few years after 1906—a decline, however, which was checked by the Mining Proclamation of 1912. This laid down that, after the simple formality of taking out a prospector's licence costing only £1, anyone could search for minerals anywhere in Northern Rhodesia, except for those areas already pegged or assigned by previous agreements. If the prospector was fortunate enough to make a discovery he could stake claims in a stipulated area and subsequently protect them against encroachment by others by undertaking some annual development work. Unfortunately the stimulus which this gave to prospecting proved to be only temporary, for the outbreak of the first world war on 4 August 1914 brought investigations almost completely to a halt. Further, the influence of the war was not immediately beneficial to Northern Rhodesian copper. It did indeed demonstrate to the British government that in times of crisis it was undesirable to be too dependent on the United States for supplies of raw materials, and this factor undoubtedly helped to stimulate subsequent activity in Commonwealth countries, including Northern Rhodesia. But Katanga rather than Northern Rhodesia was the area to profit from the war-time price increases, and the post-war decline—to £62 per ton by 1922—meant a proportionate decline in interest in base metals as investment prospects. Nor was this all, for the twofold calamity of a minor famine in the area together with the post-war epidemic of 'Spanish 'flu' also added to the difficulties of investigation and subsequent development. Thus little prospecting work was undertaken from 1918 to 1922.

So far, apart from the work at Kansanshi, all the operations noted had been under the aegis of the Edmund Davis group of companies. Nevertheless, the mineral rights ultimately belonged to the British South Africa Company, with which friendly co-operation was essential. In return for disposing of mineral rights to other groups, it looked for recompense to income from royalties and share holdings in development companies. During the period of administration from 1889 to 1924, far from making a profit, the company had suffered heavy annual deficits. The shareholders had never received a dividend. Thus it was that the company negotiated with the British government, the negotiations resulting in the successful agreement of 29 September 1923 by which the Crown provided £3¾ million to recompense the company for its losses while it had acted as the governing body and agreed to take over the administration of Northern Rhodesia, which therefore passed to the Colonial Office as from 1924. This in no way affected the mineral rights, which were still held by the company.

Bwana Mkubwa
Although the immediate post-war years saw no revival of prospecting activity in Northern Rhodesia, some attention was given to the most likely prospect, Bwana Mkubwa. Early in 1918 the London firm of Minerals Separation Ltd, a company which specialised in metallurgical operations and held a number of patents for extracting metals from ore concentrates, was engaged by the Bwana Mkubwa Copper Mining Company to investigate the possibility of treating the lower-grade ores by a flotation process. The tests, which were completed in January 1920, showed that when the ore averaged more than 4·25 per cent copper, over 77 per cent recovery was possible. It was not clear, though, how the average grade of ore—an estimated 3,700,000 tons at 4 per cent[1]—would respond. Nevertheless, the mine was closed in March 1920 to enable preparations to be made for the new techniques involved in the treatment of the ore. In 1921 J. E. G. Williams[2] arrived as assayer, and in the following year Minerals

[1] The Emery report, 1 March 1920. A. B. Emery, an American, was the general manager of the Messina (Transvaal) Development Company. His report cannot be considered enthusiastic nor his estimate (relative to Katanga) startling.
[2] Mr Williams—known as 'Bugs' because of his interest in lepidoptera—provided me with much of the detail regarding work at Bwana Mkubwa in the 1920's. For obituary, see *Horizon*, May 1965, page 25.

Separation Ltd, with Preston K. Horner, an American, as consulting engineer and W. Perkins as consulting metallurgist, was commissioned to prepare the mine for the new 'Perkins process', which was designed to handle 1,000 tons of ore a day. This was an ammonia leaching as opposed to an acid leaching process, the idea being that the solvent would not be consumed by the carbonates in the gangue. In the event it was lost in other ways, and the entire process proved more expensive than had been envisaged.

Horner's decision to use steam shovels to remove the ore from the surface down to the water level was an error of judgment. It involved the removal of a great deal of barren overburden before any ore could be reached, and in addition caused the ore to be mixed with a substantial amount of waste material, which seriously affected the true copper values of the rock sent for treatment. In consequence, although Emery had estimated the average value of the ore as 4 per cent copper, much of the material sent to the plant averaged only 2 or $2\frac{1}{2}$ per cent copper.

The dilution in copper values brought about by the work itself was not the only cause of false values reported from Bwana Mkubwa. The manager, W. Broadbridge, had long suspected that the high values of the central lode had been influenced by large pieces of pure malachite occasionally intersected in the workings. On further investigation by the assayer, Williams, it was proved beyond doubt that particles of malachite were being found in bags of samples which had been taken in areas where malachite did not exist. When this knowledge was made public the Africans who handled the samples suddenly disappeared. It seems probable that at the instigation of some local native chief who wanted to see increased development taking place in the area, with consequent greater prosperity for the local population, the samplers were deliberately increasing the ore values by mixing malachite with the genuine samples. It may be, therefore, that the dilution of the ore in the actual mining process was not so serious as at first thought.

The error in estimating copper values, together with the unsatisfactory results given by the Perkins process, soon had the mine in financial difficulties. Its subsequent short and unhappy history is soon told. For the year 1928–29, although 5,550 tons of copper were produced, the operating loss was £41,000. The slump of the early 1930's proved fatal. The mine closed in April 1931 and has since been long neglected in favour of the more recent substantial discoveries on the Copperbelt. The company itself had been sold to Rhodesian Congo Border Concession Ltd in 1930 and subsequently became the property of Rhokana Corporation, which carried out a further investigation in 1956.[3] It is interesting to note that Bwana Mkubwa may yet rejoin the ranks of the producing mines on the Copperbelt.

One of the most important aspects of the first world war, as far as the copper industry was concerned, was the rise to dominance of the United States and Latin America, where in any case production was largely under United States control. Between them these areas accounted for approximately three-quarters of the annual world production by the end of the war. Inevitably, therefore, American engineers and metallurgists possessed considerable advantages in background knowledge and experience, and were greatly in demand in other parts of the world. American interests also enjoyed great financial strength and to a considerable extent determined the future prospects of the industry. Much as American skill and knowledge was required in Northern Rhodesia, it was a very debatable point to what extent the financial and other 'strings' attached, involving potential policy decisions covering more than local interests, were either welcome or desirable. These factors were to loom large, especially in the thinking of Ernest Oppenheimer and his Anglo-American Corporation of South Africa, which was soon to appear on the scene. This does not, of course, imply that in the immediate post-war years American mining interests were already anxious to invest in Northern Rhodesian projects. On the contrary, American experts were generally sceptical about the prospects in the territory, the Emery report on Bwana Mkubwa being typical of the type of thinking which envisaged only very moderate profits. But indivi-

[3]These companies are discussed below (pages 33 et seq.).

dual Americans were already interested and were soon to become prominent within the copper mining industry.

Two of these were Preston K. Horner, a former manager of the Union Minière du Haut-Katanga, and Alfred Chester Beatty, who had long experience of the Congo, having taken part in the initial negotiations on behalf of the Guggenheim group which led to the formation of 'Forminière', the diamond concern, as far back as 1906. Beatty had also considerable experience in American copper affairs, but had given up these interests to settle in England in 1913. Subsequently, in 1933, he became a British citizen. In 1914 Beatty had been the founder of a company known as Selection Trust which in 1920 he interested in Bwana Mkubwa, himself becoming a director of the latter company, on the board of which by this time were also P. K. Horner, Edmund Davis and W. Broadbridge. These four now put up half the capital of £5,000 required to form a new syndicate known as Copper Ventures Ltd, which was registered on 10 November 1921. The other half-share in this syndicate was held by Minerals Separation, and the function of the new company was to apply the Perkins process in the treatment of copper ores in Northern Rhodesia. As has already been seen, the fiasco at Bwana Mkubwa resulted, but by good fortune the other new activities of Copper Ventures soon rendered that failure of relatively minor importance.

Towards the end of 1922 the British South Africa Company abandoned its policy of granting individual prospecting licences in favour of giving exclusive prospecting rights to large concerns. Although the credit for this change of policy is often given to Edmund Davis,[4] who indeed did possess some influence with the British South Africa Company, becoming a director of it in 1925 and of Anglo-American in 1928, yet there was almost certainly more prompting this decision than his advice alone. The fact that the first action of the British South Africa Company was actually a reservation to itself[5] of an area of some 1,800 square miles

[4]See, for example, Sir T. Gregory, *Ernest Oppenheimer and the Economic Development of Southern Africa*, Oxford University Press, Cape Town, 1962, page 392.
[5]By Government Notice No. 73, dated 8 June 1922. See *Northern Rhodesia Gazette*, 21 June 1922.

known later as the Nkana concession, which contained three prospects, Nkana South, Chambishi and the Roan–Rietbok claims, in which oxides similar to those at Bwana Mkubwa had been found, suggests strongly that the chartered company was confident that the operations at Bwana Mkubwa were going to be highly successful. In fact this reserved area now contains the present Roan Antelope, Nkana, Mindola, Chibuluma, Baluba, Chambishi and Mufulira properties.

A further stimulus to the British South Africa Company was provided by P. K. Horner, who had already suggested to Copper Ventures in August 1922 that a large concession should be asked from it. The first major concession was therefore granted for a period of five years from 31 December 1922 to Copper Ventures Ltd. It consisted of 50,000 square miles stretching along the Congo border, west of the railway, to the border with Angola. By the terms of the agreement arrived at, £9,000 was to be spent each year on prospecting and the working capital was to be £45,000. One hundred and fifty thousand £1 shares were to be assigned to the new syndicate, which would actually undertake the work. Thus was formed Rhodesian Congo Border Concession Ltd to acquire the concession from Copper Ventures Ltd. The chairman, F. L. Gibbs, was also chairman of Minerals Separation Ltd, and the directorate included A. Chester Beatty and W. Broadbridge. The first manager was an American, Raymond Brooks.[6] Of the initial capital, 100,000 fully paid £1 shares were to be allotted to Copper Ventures Ltd, of which 15,000 were to fulfil the obligation to the British Africa Company. Subsequently the area of the concession was increased by a further 2,000 square miles, involving the allocation of a further 2,000 shares to the British South Africa Company and an increase in annual expenditure from £9,000 to £9,600.[7]

[6]For obituary and commentary, see the *Northern News*, 12 and 23 August 1960.
[7]For details of the negotiations, see P. K. Horner: 'History of the prospecting for copper in Northern Rhodesia, 1921–25', unpublished paper in the Rhodesian Selection Trust archives. Eventually the concession was extended for a further period to 1929 and then to 1940.

It is not absolutely certain, therefore, whether the British South Africa Company's decision to grant concessions was prompted by the advice of Edmund Davis, which implied that the enormous scope of the work involved, both financially and in terms of the actual area to be covered, was beyond the powers of individuals or small organisations; by the knowledge that Copper Ventures actually wanted such a concession; by continued faith in the value of Bwana Mkubwa, or by a combination of all three. The results, at least, were clearly summed up in 1939 by Sir Dougal Malcolm, the president of the British South Africa Company.[8]

The growth of the Northern Rhodesia copper industry has indeed, in the sphere of mining, been the most remarkable development which has taken place in the recent history of the British Empire. It is mainly to be attributed to the adoption by the British South Africa Company, some sixteen years ago, of what was then a new policy with a view to the development and exploitation of its minerals. The method adopted has been that of granting to large Prospecting Companies, well equipped with capital, the exclusive right, for definite terms of years over large defined areas, to prospect for minerals on the terms that the grantees were to spend during the currency of their rights such minimum annual sums as would secure that the whole of their areas should be adequately prospected. During the currency of their rights the Prospecting Companies were given the exclusive right within their areas of marking out mining properties to be held by them under the terms of the Mining Law of the territory and of a common form of Prospecting Licence. The practice has been for the British South Africa Company to stipulate that mining properties so marked out when worked for profit shall be worked through mining companies formed for the purpose in which the British South Africa Company is entitled to a share interest, its remaining interest in the properties being commuted for royalties, or agreed scales, on the minerals produced.[9] The great areas covered by

---

[8]Rhodesian Selection Trust archives, memo 5, pages 19-20.
[9]As an example, the agreement made with Rhokana Corporation in August 1931 was on the following scale: if price less than £55 per ton (copper) royalty to be 2 per cent; if price less than £55–£60 per ton (copper) royalty to be $2\frac{1}{4}$ per cent; if price less than £60–£80 per ton (copper) royalty to be $2\frac{1}{2}$ per cent plus 10 per cent on price over £60; if price over £80 per ton (copper) royalty to be 5 per cent plus 10 per cent on price over £80 (figures in Nchanga files). In 1960 the arrangement was a price of 13·5 per cent of the London Metal Exchange average prices

the grants of exclusive prospective were intensely prospected at a cost of many thousand pounds by thoroughly well equipped geological organisations. This policy during its continuance had the effect of shutting out the individual prospector, and small worker who in Southern Rhodesia produced so substantial a proportion of the gold output. But, as a mining country, Northern Rhodesia is not like Southern Rhodesia. The great deposits of copper-bearing ore found in Northern Rhodesia can be exploited only by great companies commanding abundant resources of capital. Operations on the scale of those which have produced the great results are not within the reach of the small man, and in fact, during all the years before 1923, when practically the whole of Northern Rhodesia was open to public prospecting by anyone who chose to take out a prospecting licence for £1 almost nothing resulted from exploration by individuals.

This latter remark is not, of course, strictly true. It would be invalid to argue that such men as Davis and Beatty were individuals, since they involved already organised companies enjoying substantial capital. On the other hand Moffat Thompson was purely an amateur when he was first shown the Nkana outcrop. Basically, though, the argument that no private individual, prospecting off his own resources and developing his finds with his own capital, has ever enjoyed success in copper mining in Northern Rhodesia is incontestable.[10] This applies equally to the post-1940 era, during which the areas not already covered by prospecting licences and special grants have been open to individual prospectors. Nothing noteworthy has resulted.

per ton for the month, less £8; e.g. if the average price was £300 then royalty was 13·5 per cent of £300 = £40·5, less £8 = £32·5 per long ton copper. In 1947 the British South Africa Company agreed to hand over all mineral rights to the Northern Rhodesia government on 1 October 1986. Meantime, the company was paying 20 per cent of its mineral revenues as tax, but in 1964, immediately prior to Zambian independence, the new government negotiated for a complete hand-over of the rights with immediate effect. For full details, see M. M. Williams, *The Mining Law of Northern Rhodesia*, British South Africa Company, London, 1964, pages 186–216.

[10]On the other hand, mica, bismuth, tin, gold and a little silver have been successfully worked by the small worker. See *A Prospector's Guide to Mineral Occurrences in Northern Rhodesia*, ed. T. D. Guernsey, British South Africa Company, Salisbury, 1952, page 9. (See also page 59 below.)

Nkana

At about the same time as the Nkana concession was established Donaldson and Sievewright took over Lee's prospects (see page 26), retaining him to carry on further work on their behalf. Lee concentrated on sinking a pump shaft some 3,500 ft north of the Wusikili stream. Although, at a depth of 100 ft, the flow of water was 3,000 gallons an hour, he still managed to prove the presence of an ore-body about sixty feet wide averaging 3·4 per cent oxide copper. Obviously the area had enormous possibilities; equally obviously, substantial financial backing was necessary to develop it. C. Gordon James, a mining engineer, who was asked by Horner to represent Copper Ventures in investigating the Nkana claims, therefore visited the property, where he found Lee in residence. Nine shafts had been sunk to a depth of 60 ft, the dumps of five of which showed signs of copper. James took samples from all the shafts and also from the cross-cuts, and, in view of the satisfactory results obtained, secured from Donaldson and Sievewright an option on the claims for the sum of £35,000 cash or alternatively for a small cash consideration and a substantial shareholding.

It soon became obvious to Horner that the original claims would not cover the actual area of the deposits. He therefore asked for and in 1924 obtained the exclusive right to prospect the Nkana concession for three years and to select three areas each of ten square miles, two possessing full land and mineral rights, the remaining one land rights only. This was the 'small' Nkana concession.[11] Almost at once, Copper Ventures, which did not itself possess the capital necessary for development, sold its rights to the concession, together with the eight blocks of

[11]For a first-hand account of the work at Nkana, see (*a*) letter from C. Gordon James to Krogh (Rhodesian Selection Trust) dated 10 December 1948; (*b*) C. G. James, 'Notes on the early history of the Copperbelt', 24 May 1959, unpublished (both in Rhodesian Selection Trust archives). It should be noted that the Nkana concession was granted to Copper Ventures on 21 February 1924, over a year after Rhodesian Congo Border Concession Ltd had been formed on 16 February 1923. This contradicts K. Bradley (*Copper Venture*, op. cit., page 80), who places them, without giving dates, in the reverse order.

claims already registered in its name at Nkana, to the Bwana Mkubwa Copper Mining Company for a lump sum of £60,000 together with 517,500 fully paid shares of 5s each in the latter company. A further 57,500 shares became the property of the British South Africa Company.

The Bwana Mkubwa company almost made a totally unexpected profit on this deal, for when J. E. G. Williams was making his heroic journey to Nchanga[12] he noticed, whilst shooting for the pot, that the boundary between the concession granted to Rhodesian Congo Border Concession Ltd and the Nkana concession did not coincide with the areas marked on his official map, with the result that part of the Nchanga area was indicated as being within the Nkana concession. Surveys were carried out by both sides before the matter was referred to litigation, in which Rhodesian Congo Border Concession Ltd was successful.[13]

Copper Ventures had worked very hard on the Nkana concession, having extended drives and cross-cuts at the level of the water-table, which lay 50–60 ft below the surface, at frequent intervals from a position some 800 ft south of the Wusikili stream to a point about 5,400 ft northwards. As might have been expected, only oxides were found. From 2,400 ft to 4,800 ft north of the Wusikili stream a syncline was discovered which gave rise to two parallel sub-outcrops, which, however, petered out into barren rock when explored by cross-cuts to the east and west. Unknown to the prospectors at the time, the ore-body dipped steeply to the north-west before rising again as the Mindola outcrop. A great prospect was missed at this point.

By 1924 a considerable amount of work had also been done on the eight Nkana claims themselves. Many feet of prospect shafts, drives and cross-cuts were excavated, all at ground-water level, except for the pump shaft, which was sunk to a depth of 113 ft. Then, in September, Bwana Mkubwa prospectors made a momentous discovery. About 8,000 ft north-west of the Wusikili stream lay an open glade, completely devoid of trees, which appeared to the prospectors as a typical 'copper clearing' such as

[12]See page 82.
[13]Personal information: J. E. G. Williams and L. Tucker.

had already been seen at the Roan Antelope and elsewhere. There was no obvious sign of copper. Nevertheless, the Bwana Mkubwa men tried the experiment of a prospect shaft, which, between depths of 10–25 ft, passed through micaceous ore averaging 3·6 per cent oxide copper. This was the southern tip of the very important Nkana North ore-body.

Further investigation disclosed that this ore-body, within a length of strike of 500 ft, varied from 35 to 39 ft in width and contained 9·7 per cent copper. There was no other surface indication of copper, and a great deal of further exploratory work was necessary before the continuation of the ore-body was located to the north-west. From the end of October 1922 until December 1923, under the supervision of the local manager, Raymond Brooks, sixteen shot-drill holes had been distributed along the line of the strike. Of these, six showed no copper and the remainder encountered ore dipping so steeply that accurate estimates of values could not be made. One, however, had penetrated a value of 2·9 per cent sulphide copper. In consequence of these results, obtained before 1924, it was concluded, erroneously, that several ore-bodies rather than a continuous one had been discovered at Nkana, the values of which were not as high as the ore-bodies at Bwana Mkubwa. The Bwana Mkubwa company itself was primarily concerned with starting production when it took over in 1924, and devoted very little attention to further prospecting.

Mufulira and Bancroft
Although a number of other concessions were granted during the following years, notably in the Loangwa, Serenje and Kasempa areas, 1923 was the vintage year for discoveries on the Copperbelt, during which all the honours went to Rhodesian Congo Border Concession Ltd. For in spite of the failure of the company adequately to appreciate the potential of Nkana, geological teams operating under the overall control of Raymond Brooks had within a few months discovered the three major mines of Nchanga, Mufulira and Bancroft. The fortunes of Beaton and Osterberg in the Nchanga area are detailed in chapter 5. The gist, if not the details, of this story has been known for many years.

Recently, though, its interest has been overshadowed by the fascinating corollary to the activities at Mufulira.

The original account of the expedition of James Moir and Guy Bell, as generally accepted by mining historians, was related by the chairman of the Rhodesian Selection Trust group, Sir Ronald Prain, when he unveiled the memorials at Mufulira and Luanshya in honour of their discoveries on 28 September 1960. Moir and Bell, he explained, had been sent out with instructions similar to those normally issued at the time, namely to follow streams and make enquiries among local Africans about the presence of malachite outcrops. This was, of course, before the introduction of systematic prospecting by Dr Bancroft in 1927. Having camped one evening in August 1923 by the banks of the Mufulira stream, they were excited to find evidence of copper mineralisation: a clump of peat moss stained green and, a short distance away, further green stains on a rock outcrop—both suggestive of the presence of copper oxides.

Immediately they took samples, which were despatched to the Nkana laboratory operated by J. E. G. Williams, where they were received by Lewin Tucker, who, twenty-three years later, was to become the general manager of Mufulira mine. The African runner who carried the now famous sack of specimens was still employed at Mufulira in 1960 and attended the ceremony along with Tucker. But although Guy Bell was known to have worked at Mufulira in 1934, no trace of either him or James Moir could be found.

Bell has still not been traced, but, alone in his shack in the Mkaradzi valley near Mount Darwin in Southern Rhodesia, the seventy-seven year old, almost blind James Moir heard Sir Ronald Prain's speech relayed by the Federal Broadcasting Corporation. Within a few days a number of people in the Mount Darwin area had written to the press verifying his whereabouts. As a result the Rhodesian Selection Trust directors agreed to offer him an annuity for life and soon afterwards he was visited by Lewin Tucker. Visits to leading eye specialists followed, but nothing could be done to alleviate Moir's almost total blindness. Nevertheless, he had not permitted this disability to interfere with his prospecting career, claiming to be able to identify by touch the specimens brought to him by his African servant. He refused to return to civilisation, preferring to continue his nomadic search for the fortune which always eluded him.[14]

The finding of James Moir, apart from its great human interest, is of importance to the history of the Copperbelt in that subsequent conversations with him have led to a complete revision of the original account of the discovery of Mufulira. Moir claimed that he was prospecting alone in the Mufulira area towards the end of 1922 and early in 1923, during which time he recorded a number of copper indications, including the peat moss which caused such commotion later. He had never at any time camped at this spot, as was commonly believed. Bell had been sent to assist him some months later, when the two men again visited the discovery in June. It must have been Bell, thought Moir, who later sent the samples in August.

Apparently, though, the find was deceptive, for when in 1924 prospectors from Bwana Mkubwa sank four prospect shafts to a maximum depth of 110 ft, the cross-cuts showed nothing greater than patchy areas of one per cent copper. The work was therefore abandoned and the area lay dormant until the Rhodesian Selection Trust began further investigations in 1928.

The third party to gain success for Rhodesian Congo Border Concession Ltd was that of Williams and Babb. By 1923 Williams had been transferred from Bwana Mkubwa to Nkana, where he first made the acquaintance of Raymond Brooks. Brooks and Horner had failed to find Beaton's discovery at Nchanga in July 1923,[15] and had later sent Collier to investigate the find. It was in the course of further trenching by Collier that the important Nchanga Dambo lode was discovered. Williams and Babb— who was later accidentally shot in a hunting accident—were also sent on an expedition, part of which involved the taking of

[14]For an account of James Moir's career, see the *Northern News*, 9 May 1961, and also an article in *Horizon*, December 1960. Moir died in Bindura Hospital on 4 May 1964. For obituary, see *Horizon*, June 1964, page 9.
[15]See page 80.

samples *en route* from the Nchanga discoveries. Having accomplished this, the two men continued along the line of the copper to the Kafue in the vicinity of Konkola. Here, whilst chasing a guinea-fowl for the pot, Williams tripped over a stone and fell sprawling to the ground. On looking round to ascertain the cause of his mishap he saw, to his amazement, that the dislodged stone showed traces of green underneath. The two traced the copper four miles through feldspathic quartzites to Kirila Bomwe. Samples were taken and, with a sketch-map, sent along to Brooks early in 1924.[16] Little attention was paid to the find and no further action was taken until the deposit was 're-discovered' in 1928 by two of the men carrying out the new systematic prospecting scheme devised by Dr Bancroft. Bancroft mine is situated in one of the few areas of the Copperbelt where ancient workings have not been found.

Economic developments: the Anglo-American Corporation and Rhodesian Selection Trust

On 25 September 1917, some two thousand miles away in Johannesburg, Ernest Oppenheimer finally formed his own independent company, the Anglo-American Corporation of South Africa Ltd, with the now apparently meagre capital of £1 million. After negotiations with an American, W. L. Honnold, who had formerly been managing director of the Consolidated Mines Selection Company and the Rand Selection Company, both gold mining houses, American financial interest was gained and the new company had a distinct American identity. Honnold became a permanent director and two other Americans also joined the board, C. H. Sabin of the Guaranty Trust Company and W. R. Thompson, through whom the Newmont Mining Corporation acquired an interest. The American financiers, J. P. Morgan and Company were also heavily involved. Apart from the American interest, Oppenheimer himself became a permanent director and other board members included H. C. Hull, the Minister of Finance in the first Union of South Africa government in 1910, and H. Crawford of the National Bank.

[16]Personal information: J. E. G. Williams.

The alternate directors were E. S. Langerman and F. R. Lynch, who was then managing director of the Consolidated Mines Selection Company.

Oppenheimer rapidly made himself a major force in South African mining circles and, ever anxious to widen the sphere of the Anglo-American Corporation's interests, sent his American consulting engineer, Carl R. Davis, and his brother-in-law, Leslie Pollak, to the Copperbelt area in October 1923 to see if there were any developments likely to prove of interest to his company. Apparently, as far as Northern Rhodesia was concerned, there were not, and it was Oppenheimer's old associate Edmund Davis who finally involved him in Copperbelt affairs, as Oppenheimer himself pointed out:[17]

. . . The corporation's original incursion into Northern Rhodesian mining was really the result of our diamond activities. After negotiations with the Belgian and Angola diamond companies, through the intermediary of Sir Edmund Davis, for the purchase of their diamonds, had been successfully completed, Sir Edmund Davis asked me as a favour to assist with Bwana [Mkubwa] finance and I agreed to participate in a small way on condition that we were appointed consulting engineers. We looked upon the deal as a share transaction; it was liquidated fairly promptly, actually with the assistance of Sir Edmund.

Later on, after negotiations with Mr Chester Beatty with reference to West African diamonds had brought us into closer relations with him, he asked the corporation to help in Rhodesian Congo Border Concession finance, which it did, again stipulating for the consulting engineership, which was readily granted. It must be recorded that at this time Bwana was in a state of continuous reconstruction, and nothing of any value had been found in the Rhodesian Congo Border Concession territory.

In due course the corporation became interested in other enterprises in Northern Rhodesia . . .

It is clear, therefore, that although the two companies, Rhodesian Congo Border Concession and Bwana Mkubwa, were linked through Chester Beatty, the involvement of the Anglo-American

[17]Memo of August 1930 from Sir Ernest Oppenheimer, quoted in Gregory, op. cit., pages 385–86.

Corporation in both of them was the result of two separate negotiations not connected by this common factor.

Oppenheimer's small participation involved the purchase by the Anglo-American Corporation of 100,000 Bwana Mkubwa shares and the election of himself to the Bwana Mkubwa board of directors. This investment seems to have been purely speculative, arising from Edmund Davis' pressure and the apparent optimism of the British South Africa Company. Subsequently, though, as the optimistic reports of Carl Davis on the Copperbelt and other concessions were presented to him, Oppenheimer's activities became increasingly widespread. By the end of 1925 the Anglo-American Corporation had acquired interests in all the concession companies and had become consulting engineers to them. In addition, Oppenheimer became a director of each. Within a year the network had been further extended by the appointment of Anglo-American to the position of consulting engineers to the British South Africa Company itself. These appointments were of vital importance, not merely in the degree of unification thus brought about, but also in that the Anglo-American Corporation now became possessed of the overall picture as it developed and could anticipate future prospects accordingly. Already, then, Anglo-American was a factor to be reckoned with in Copperbelt economics.

The rise of the Anglo-American Corporation in Northern Rhodesia in no way deterred Oppenheimer's colleague and rival, Alfred Chester Beatty. Although Copper Ventures Ltd, having satisfactorily completed its original purpose, had sold the Nkana concession to the Bwana Mkubwa company and then gone into voluntary liquidation in 1925, Beatty remained a director both of the Bwana Mkubwa company and of Rhodesian Congo Border Concession Ltd. He too was extremely optimistic about future copper prospects in Northern Rhodesia and anxious to continue operations on his own behalf in the development of some suitable property. He therefore put an intriguing proposition to Pollak and Wetzlar of Anglo-American to the effect that a syndicate consisting of himself (one-third), Anglo-American Corporation (one-third) and an American group (one-third), of the best credentials and with whom he is in touch, should secure options on two or three promising areas from certain properties such as the Gold Fields Concession, Congo Border, etc.; that the funds of the syndicate be used to prospect these areas and to take up the most promising one, assuming of course it is sufficiently attractive. Then a company should be floated to take over, develop and produce . . .[18]

This was the first mention of an American syndicate, as distinct from individual experts, taking an active interest in Copperbelt affairs and was a clear pointer to possible future trends.

Beatty obviously meant business. By April 1926 he had reorganised his original Selection Trust into the new Selection Trust Ltd, with its capital enlarged to £800,000 to cope with his future plans. And even before this he had satisfactorily concluded negotiations with two other companies, the Northern Rhodesia Company and the Rhodesia Copper and General Exploration and Finance Company. The first of these was yet another offshoot of the Edmund Davis group, which had been formed to take over the Roan Antelope and Rietbok claims from the Bechuanaland Exploration Company, the Bwana Mkubwa company and the Rhodesia Copper and General Exploration and Finance Company. This latter company held shares in it. In return for taking over these shares, together with other shares in the Northern Rhodesia Company, Beatty's Selection Trust was granted the option to take over the Roan and Rietbok claims until 31 March 1926. Under these circumstances Beatty proposed that a new company, 'The Northern Rhodesia Option Venture', should be formed with a capital of £200,000, and offered Anglo-American a 24 per cent share in the the scheme. The offer was accepted. Out of the subsequent operations developed the Roan Antelope mine. Similarly, when in August 1926 Edmund Davis and the Bwana Mkubwa company permitted Beatty to form the 'Muliashi Venture' to examine the

[18]For the text of Pollak's letter to Oppenheimer on this subject, see Gregory, op. cit., page 404.

Muliashi claims,[19] contiguous to the Roan Antelope area and since acquired by the latter, Anglo-American was offered and accepted a 15 per cent share in this enterprise also.

It is reasonable to suppose that Beatty was not unaware of the possibility that sulphide ores might be found at a depth below the oxides of the claims possessed by his company, of which the most noteworthy were the Roan Antelope and Rietbok. Thus a relatively junior engineer, the late Russell J. Parker,[20] was engaged to investigate the problem. One of his main tasks was to 'prepare the ground' for an examination by R. M. Geppert, one of the American engineers in the employ of Selection Trust. Accompanying Parker was S. H. Ford, the consulting engineer to the Northern Rhodesia Company, which had ceded the option on the claims to Selection Trust.

Parker arrived in September 1925 at a time when very little was known of bedded deposits and no substantial quantities of sulphide copper had been found either in Northern Rhodesia or in Katanga. On his arrival he found the original work which had been carried out by the Rhodesia Copper Company between 1902 and 1907, consisting of fifteen trenches and four inclined shafts on the Roan outcrops, together with a further five trenches which had been started on the Rietbok side. The trenches were about six feet deep and the shafts some sixty feet in length, with short cross-cuts after fifty feet.

As Parker later pointed out,[21] the original workers had missed the most important points, which were:

1 A gradual increase in copper values with depth.
2 An increase in the width of the mineralised shale with depth.

[19]Not to be confused with the adjacent Baluba deposit, to investigate and develop which a separate company was floated in 1954.
[20]Parker was tragically killed when a time bomb exploded in an aircraft in which he was a passenger, causing it to crash into the St Lawrence river near Montreal. For obituary, see *Transactions* of the Institution of Mining and Metallurgy, vol. LIX, pages 327–8.
[21]Letter to D. C. Sharpstone dated 11 March 1929. In Rhodesian Selection Trust archives.

5

3 The possibility of the two parallel reefs forming a synclinal structure.

He therefore immediately pegged the intervening ground between the Roan and Rietbok claims on behalf of the Bwana Mkubwa Copper Mining Company, the new claims being known as the 'Luanshia' claims, from which the present name of Luanshya derives.

Following on this action, Parker sank the two centre shafts to greater depths and put in further cross-cuts. No. 3 shaft, which was sampled at intervals of 5 ft, at once showed a great increase in chalcocite from depths of 50-110 ft. Parker then began to suspect the presence of a sulphide mine.[22] A senior director of Selection Trust, W. Selkirk, who was also a consulting mining engineer in London, then came out to examine the property and recommended a large-scale programme of shaft sinking and drilling to the extent of £27,000. This exercise commenced towards the end of April 1926.

The astounding results which followed, with the discovery of a belt of sulphide ore some 36.5 ft thick and averaging 3.87 per cent copper at a depth of 500 ft, greatly encouraged all those concerned with the other oxide deposits in the area. Not only would sulphides be much easier and cheaper to treat, but the much-vaunted Perkins process for dealing with oxides was already proving to be a failure. It was undoubtedly with all these factors in mind that Beatty approached Sir Edmund Davis in November 1926 with the request that Selection Trust should be permitted to undertake the prospecting of the hitherto unexplored areas of the Nkana concession, and for the same reasons that Davis retained for the Bwana Mkubwa company a one-third share in the enterprise, together with the rights over a large area of approximately 62½ square miles to the south of the Nkana workings. It was this foresight of Sir Edmund Davis

[22]Just before these events the manager of Nkana, C. O. Wraith, had drilled into sulphides there (personal information: L. Tucker). See also his letter to D'Eath (Rhodesian Selection Trust) dated 20 December 1949 in the Rhodesian Selection Trust archives. Raymond Brooks had also proved sulphides at the Nchanga Dambo lode in 1925 and had drilled a 2.9 per cent sulphide deposit at Nkana in 1923.

which accounts for the present Rhokana Corporation having a substantial interest in Mufulira and the other properties within the Nkana concession. Anglo-American was offered and accepted a $7\frac{1}{2}$ per cent share in the new company—Mineralized Venture—formed to carry out the work.[23]

A great deal of the credit for the demonstration of the potential of the Roan Antelope mine must go to Parker and his successor, Nicolaus. Parker had been sent to examine a considerable number of prospects in Northern Rhodesia, and he must be credited with being the first to appreciate the significant resemblance of the feldspathic quartzites in the areas of the major deposits—Bwana Mkubwa, Roan Antelope, Nkana and Nchanga—and for recognising the sulphide deposit at the Roan Antelope. It was Parker, too, who recommended to Selkirk that Selection Trust should endeavour to acquire the Nkana concession and thoroughly survey it: and it was through this that the sulphides at Mufulira were found. Although the original Copper Ventures never possessed sufficient capital to develop its findings, and never even intended to do so, there must certainly have been pangs of regret in the breasts of P. K. Horner and his associates at the thought of what they had unwittingly surrendered so cheaply to the Bwana Mkubwa company in 1924.

It is interesting to speculate that in 1924 the possibility of sulphide ore lying at depth below the oxides may have been completely overlooked. If such a find had been made, then it might have meant the ultimate survival of the Bwana Mkubwa company after the Bwana Mkubwa mine itself had been abandoned. When diamond drilling was started at Mufulira in 1928 by Rhodesian Selection Trust geologists under Parker, the very first hole proved a success, showing a width of 20·7 ft of sulphide ore averaging 9·49 per cent copper at a depth of 291 ft. There was, naturally, great excitement, especially as the surface deposits—which were no more impressive than at Nchanga—were in quartzite, and the only other known deposits in quartzite up till then were at Bwana Mkubwa and the Nchanga Dambo

[23]The interrelationship of the various companies may be followed on Fig. 9 (chapter 6).

lode. The tonnage at Bwana Mkubwa had already proved to be small, whilst at Nchanga the mixture of sulphide and oxide ore posed considerable technical problems. However, in this case a further width of 32·6 ft averaging 5·72 per cent copper as sulphides was found at a depth of 391 ft, and yet a third, this time 58·7 ft wide and assaying at 6·6 per cent copper at 491 ft. After an intensive drilling programme it was clear by 1934 that there were three superimposed ore-bodies showing a combined total of 116 million short tons of ore.[24] The Mufulira Special Grant of 9,344 acres was registered in January 1930 and a new company, Mufulira Copper Mines Ltd, formed early in February. During this same period another programme of pitting and drilling north-east of the Muliashi property had disclosed the extensive Baluba deposits, which are not yet being mined.

The advent of the American Metal Company as a colleague and partner to Beatty's Selection Trust is regrettably undocumented, at least on the eastern side of the Atlantic. This was explained by D'Eath of the Rhodesian Selection Trust when he was gathering material for its archives in 1949:

You must wonder how it is that I haven't got this information already in our files. The reason is that in the early days Mr Beatty, having a 90 per cent interest, ran these companies through 'Ventures' and, for reasons which you will understand, very meagre details were put in the minutes of Selection Trust, as they were private ventures, and the same applied to the keeping of the records. I think these must have been sent out as salvage during the war when the Government were pressing us for all waste paper.[25]

It is known, however, that the first connection of the company with Rhodesia was in 1925, when it made a loan to the Bwana Mkubwa company under a sales agency agreement.[26] It is known, too, that the vice-president of American Metal, Dr Otto Suss-

[24] In 1961 the published reserves were 182,205,000 short tons averaging 3·35 per cent copper (Chamber of Mines *Yearbook*, 1961).
[25] D'Eath to Hochschild (American Metal Company), 22 December 1949; in Rhodesian Selection Trust files.
[26] Hochschild to D'Eath, 14 December 1949; in Rhodesian Selection Trust files. Apart from this bald statement, no further information is available.

man, visited the Copperbelt in July 1927, when he examined
the Roan and Rietbok claims. He was deeply impressed and on
9 July was cabling Hochschild: 'Roan promises to become very
important. Probably annual production 100,000,000 lbs likely
in three or four years. Capital required $12,000,000. Advise you
to try to acquire an interest.'[27] This was done to the extent of
almost a half of the original development capital of £175,000
and was maintained at approximately one-third as the capital increased. Subsequently, in March 1928, two American Metal
Company engineers, A. D. Storke and P. Wilson, came to the
Copperbelt and examined the Bwana Mkubwa, Nkana, Nchanga
and Roan Antelope properties in July of that year, reporting on
them in turn to Hochschild. But as Roan Antelope Copper
Mines Ltd was floated in June 1927 with a 33 per cent American interest, it is clear that Hochschild had already made up his
mind to participate prior to his consideration of Storke's report,
and on the strength of Sussman's opinion alone.[28]

The new company, with an initial capital of £600,000, acquired the Roan, Rietbok and Luanshia claims, exploring them
to such good effect that by October 1927 reserves of approximately 20 million tons averaging $3\frac{1}{2}$ per cent copper had been
found.[29] The capital was therefore increased to £1 million in
April 1928, and again to £$1\frac{1}{4}$ million in April of the following
year.

The early development of the Roan Antelope was rapid. By
July 1928, when D. D. Irwin was appointed general manager,

[27]Copy in Rhodesian Selection Trust archives.
[28]Hochschild himself makes this point in his letter to D'Eath of 14
December 1949 previously referred to. (Unfortunately this contradicts the
statement made by K. Bradley, *Copper Venture*, op. cit., page 92, that
'As a result of their reports and another by Mr T. F. Field, Dr Sussman
was convinced of the magnitude of the discovery and staked his reputation
on it to the extent of persuading the American Metal Company and other
American interests to put up an almost 50 per cent share in the capital of
£175,000 needed for the early development work.')
[29]Statement by Chester Beatty to shareholders, 27 October 1927. These
reserves have been continually expanding through further prospecting,
and, after thirty years of mining, stood at 93,429,000 short tons averaging
3 per cent copper in June 1961 (Chamber of Mines *Yearbook*, 1961).

the construction of the plant area and the township had already begun and a pilot plant was actually in operation. The railway was extended from Bwana Mkubwa early in 1929, having already been extended to the Congo border as far back as 1908-9, and before the end of 1931 the smelter and concentrator were ready to commence operations. The first copper to be produced was marketed in October, although concentrates had been sent to the United States before this.[30] It was, in fact, the generosity of the American Metal Company, which paid in advance for the concentrates supplied to it, which enabled the Roan Antelope mine to weather the depression of 1931-32 and remain in production.[31]

During this period, in the late 1920's, feverish activity was taking place in many areas of the Copperbelt. In the extreme west there was a spate of exploratory work at Kansanshi from 1927 to 1932, when the economic depression forced the mine to close down for a second time. A great deal of surface diamond drilling and underground development, comprising vertical shafts, drives and cross-cuts, was carried out. To the north of the hill a three-compartment vertical shaft failed to penetrate water at a depth of 150 ft. To the south a similar shaft had reached a depth of 543 ft by April 1931, but through poor drilling conditions and failure to understand the structure of the ore-bodies and country rock, the figures quoted for the value of the deposit—11 million tons averaging 4.34 per cent copper— were wildly inaccurate.[32]

[30]It is interesting to note that the first smelting of copper at the Roan Antelope on 20 October 1931 was the first production from any of the companies still in operation. The wood fire had been ceremonially lit in the furnace fifteen days earlier by Mrs Lucy Cullen, the niece of Mr Irwin.
[31]Letter from Irwin to D'Eath in memorandum No. 14(D) in the Rhodesian Selection Trust archives. Quoted by K. Bradley, op cit., page 97.
[32]A figure of 4 million tons averaging 3.65 per cent copper is given in the Weldon report, dated 23 August 1938, written after sampling in 1937-38. This figure is also quoted without acknowledgment by K. Bradley, Copper Venture, op. cit., page 61. More recent exploration is almost certain to lead to further revisions.

A hundred miles to the east, Nchanga Copper Mines Ltd, a subsidiary of Rhodesian Congo Border Concession, which held 43 per cent of the capital, with the Anglo-American Corporation as consulting engineers, was busily engaged on the River and Dambo lodes of Nchanga mine (see chapter 5). Further investigations were being made in the Bancroft area (see page 58) and Mineralized Venture was beginning its work in the Nkana concession. The secretary of this new company was Lewin Tucker, and in charge of the geological operations was R. J. Parker, who had previously been at the Roan Antelope, with two assistants, T. F. Andrews and A. Gray. This team undertook to make a geological map of the entire concession area, from which special grants of 150,000 acres could be selected, the remainder of the concession being then abandoned. The work was carried out with such skill that almost all the copper-bearing deposits fell within the selected areas.

The area first selected for investigation in the Nkana concession in 1927 was Chambishi, the relevant claims being bought by Selection Trust Ltd from Donaldson and Sievewright in February 1928 for £3,000. (Subsequently these claims were transferred to Rhodesian Selection Trust Ltd and from that company to Mufulira Copper Mines Ltd in 1931.)

The decision by Parker and Gray that Chambishi should be the first area in the Nkana concession to receive attention was made partly because of its nearness to Nchanga and Nkana—it is approximately equi-distant between the two—and partly because the outcrop there was similar to those at Nkana and the Roan Antelope. It consisted of a sandy shale bed of a very porous nature, containing many small cavities in which were particles of limonite and malachite. It appeared to have been thoroughly leached, a fact which suggested to the geologists that there might originally have been sulphides present. Parker and Gray exposed the mineralised rock over 2,000 ft. The initial results were interesting—a 25 ft width averaging 4.27 per cent copper sulphides—certainly sufficient to justify the decision to continue further development.[33] It was soon shown that a valuable ore-body existed, but, in common with so many others, the mine was abandoned as a result of the economic depression of the early 1930's. Later, attention was devoted to developing Mufulira and the Roan Antelope, Chambishi being further neglected, even though the ore reserves stood at 35 million short tons averaging 3·37 per cent copper. Unfortunately, though, much of the ore was in an oxidised condition.

Exploitation of the Mufulira property, which began in 1929, was severely handicapped by the financial depression. Early in February 1930 the Rhodesian Selection Trust, the British South Africa Company and the Bwana Mkubwa company agreed to sell the Mufulira Special Grant to a new company, Mufulira Copper Mines Ltd, which was incorporated on 2 March with a capital of £600,000 (now £18 million). Then, as a measure to reduce the immediate capital requirements and at the same time increase efficiency by unifying the management, Rhodesian Selection Trust decided that as from 1 December 1930 all its mining properties in the Nkana concession and the claims at Chambishi should be transferred to the Mufulira Copper Mines company. Rhodesian Selection Trust then became an investment holding company having approximately a two-thirds interest in Mufulira Copper Mines Ltd.

By April 1931, when the combined ore reserves at Mufulira, Chambishi and Baluba totalled 162 million tons averaging 4·14 per cent copper, the depression brought prospecting to a halt. In January of the same year, also, by agreement with the British South Africa Company, the Mufulira company had been relieved of its development obligations for a period of five years, in return for 50,000 fully paid up Mufulira shares.

Meanwhile, although a concentrator to handle 1,500 tons of ore a day had been completed in December 1931, the introduction of the 'quota system'—the voluntary reductions in produc-

[33]For a full account and description, see R. J. Parker and A. Gray, 'Prospecting and geological survey (1927–29) of the "Nkana concession"', with comments by P. K. Horner, in *Transactions* of the Institution of Mining and Metallurgy, 1935–36, pages 317–364.

tion devised to meet the economic crisis—led to operations being temporarily suspended before actual production had even begun. The quota applicable to Mufulira was produced partly from the stockpile of ore there, which was carried to the smelter at Nkana by the newly built railway which arrived in April 1932, and partly from production at the Roan Antelope and Nkana. Some 49,000 tons of ore from the Mufulira stockpile which were treated at Nkana proved to contain the very satisfactory figure of 5 per cent copper.

Prospecting and Dr Bancroft
In April 1927 Dr J. Austen Bancroft arrived in the Nkana concession as consulting geologist to the Anglo-American Corporation. Already an outstanding geologist, and former professor in the subject at McGill University, he combined with his great scientific ability a most convincing air of his own infallibility. Both these aspects were to make their mark on the Copperbelt. Thus, as related in his own work and quoted by Gregory,[34] he was largely responsible for Oppenheimer deciding to back the developing Nkana mine substantially. Nevertheless, he remained an egotistical, intolerant and irascible man under whom few of his subordinates really enjoyed working. Further, his claims to fame on the Copperbelt are greatly exaggerated. It must be borne in mind that before he had even arrived in the Copperbelt area the major mines—Nkana, Roan Antelope, Nchanga, Mufulira, Chambishi and even Bancroft itself—were already known. Dr Bancroft, therefore, cannot be hailed as a discoverer of new mines; his fame rests upon two things—his genius for disclosing the potential of the already known desposits and his new scheme of 'systematic' prospecting. Even in this latter field he cannot claim to be the introducer of scientific techniques into Northern Rhodesia. From 1925 to 1927 electrical prospecting (see Appendix II) was attempted—without particularly impres-

[34]Op. cit., pages 401–2. It may reasonably be argued, though, that as reserves of over 24 million tons averaging 4·2 per cent copper were already known, Oppenheimer would not really have needed very much persuasion to participate in the venture.

sive results on the Copperbelt. In 1926 also, another intriguing technique had been tried:

An important feature of this year's programme is the carrying out of an aerial survey of the concession. This is, I believe, the first occasion on which aerial photography has been applied to mineral prospecting, but from the results obtained by the aircraft company in Burma, where they carried out a forest survey, there is every reason to believe that very valuable information regarding the potentialities of the company's property will thus be obtained.[35]

However, Oppenheimer proved to be wrong in this instance, the experiment being an expensive failure, partly through the heavy expense of constructing and maintaining the necessary chains of emergency landing fields in a region where termite hills can appear overnight, and partly because the continual dry-season haze of dust and smoke from bush fires effectively obscured the view of both aircrews and cameras. Nevertheless, operating from the main bases at Nchanga and Lunsemfwa, 12,000 square miles were photographed and another 3,000 square miles visually surveyed between May and December 1927, when the venture came to an end.[36]

Bancroft's technique, depending on field parties operating on foot, was more empirical than these, yet vastly more effective. It will be recalled that the old system as applied under Raymond Brooks from 1923 envisaged prospectors finding outcrops under native guidance or through routine testing for mineralisation in such likely places as streams. The prospectors were looking specifically for mines, without having any preconceived notions as to where or how they might be found. Normal practice, after discovering a hopeful area, was either to trench across the suspected line of the ore-body, if the soil cover was sufficiently thin to permit this, or to sink 'prospect pits' at regular intervals similarly. Both methods served to show the possibilities of ore being below ground without outcrops being visible and also

[35]Sir E. Oppenheimer, Anglo-American Corporation chairman's annual report, 1926.
[36]See G. L. Walker, 'Surveying from the air in Central Africa', Engineering and Mining Journal, New York, January 1929.

provided a rough indication of the scale of visible outcrops. The prospect pits were shafts, circular for strength, approximately 2·5 ft in diameter and some 60–70 ft deep. At the top a primitive form of windlass, constructed from rough hewn timber felled on the spot, served to hoist the bucket filled by the African labourer at the bottom of the shaft. Samples of rock were taken from the bottom and also at regular intervals from the side of the shaft by the geologist, for immediate analysis.

Bancroft's scheme was an enlargement and improvement upon these existing techniques. The object now was to search for any formations that might conceivably contain mines and then interpret them to decide whether or not they were worthy of a full investigation. The plan therefore involved virtually the mapping and cataloguing of outcrops within the entire concession areas. For this the district was divided into predetermined surveyed areas, for example *ABCD* in the diagram.

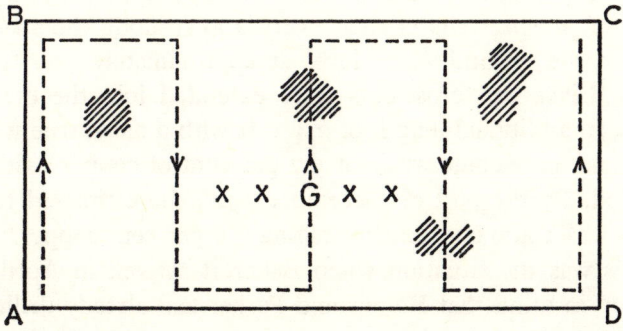

The geologist (G) travelled along a set track as indicated, measuring distances with a cyclometer. On both sides he was flanked by native 'outriders' (XX) so spaced that the entire area was covered. These 'outriders' were trained to detect outcrops, which would be accurately pinpointed on the surveyed plan.

Notwithstanding the skill and care of the prospector, the above methods could indicate nothing more than likely fields for more intensive investigation. This investigation could be carried out only by means of deep drilling, both to delimit the actual area of the ore-body and also to provide regular samples to determine its precise value and potentiality as an economic proposition. Not every prospector could afford the expense of the cumbersome steam-driven drills then in use (see plates 3 (a) and 4(a)), with the inevitable result that much that might have deserved immediate investigation had to be shelved until more economically sound syndicates or individuals could undertake the necessary drilling and core sampling. It becomes apparent, therefore, that prospecting is not merely a matter of chance. Although the discovery of an individual vein may be so, the actual determination of ultimate values involves skill, persistence and considerable expenditure. These were the assets which Beatty, Parker and Gray on one hand, and Oppenheimer and Bancroft on the other, provided for the emergent Copperbelt.

The immediate task facing Dr Bancroft when he arrived on the Copperbelt was to make an assessment of the Nkana claims themselves. The main development work, which had been to determine the possible extension of the Nkana North ore-body, consisted of prospect shafts sited every 400 ft along the strike and sunk to the ground-water level at approximately 100 ft, from which drives and cross-cuts were extended into the ore. As a result, an additional length of 2,400 ft with a mean true width of 30 ft and an average assay of 5·7 per cent of copper oxides was revealed. By the end of December 1926 the estimated tonnage of ore was 1,409,000 tons averaging 4·6 per cent copper.[37]

This was the situation when Bancroft arrived in April 1927. Bearing in mind that Brooks and Parker had already drilled into sulphide ore at depth (see pages 38, 46 and 91). Bancroft came to the conclusion not only that oxide might largely give way to sulphides at depth, but that the general dip of the ore-body to the north-west might indicate a synclinal formation. He therefore instigated an intensive search for outcrops, by means of parallel traverses, to the north-west of the Nkana outcrops, a search which brought to light not only the western end of the Nkana syncline

[37] Figures quoted at the annual general meeting of the Bwana Mkubwa Copper Mining Co. Ltd., 1926. Report in Rhodesian Selection Trust archives.

but also some copper staining in the Mindola stream, which in turn led to the discovery of the Mindola ore-body. This was the beginning of Bancroft's scheme of systematic traversing, which contributed in no small measure to his fame in Copperbelt mining circles.

By the end of 1927 the mine plus its extensions covered an area of 62½ square miles, and during the following year the ore reserves had been increased to 24,106,000 tons averaging 4·2 per cent copper.

Meantime, a major, three-compartment shaft, known as 'A' shaft, was being sunk into the foot-wall beds, from which it was proposed to extend cross-cuts, at the 300 ft and 450 ft levels, to obtain bulk samples of the ore. A temporary township began to appear, including workshops, a power plant, offices, houses and a hospital. These Kimberley brick and thatch buildings replaced the tents in which Horner, Brooks, Tucker and the others had lived.

The drilling programme on the North ore-body continued in spite of the difficulties of poor equipment and shortage of casing for the holes. The first hole, some 450 ft west of 'A' shaft, penetrated a width of 21·5 ft of ore averaging 5·82 per cent copper, mainly as sulphide. The second hole, a further 400 ft to the west, passed through 16 ft averaging 5·01 per cent copper, and the third encountered 38 ft averaging 4·52 per cent. The programme was now considerably intensified in view of these early successes. On 16 June 1930 the consulting engineers were able to report[38] that the reserves then totalled 70 million tons averaging 4 per cent copper, and were concentrated in three major ore-bodies, the Nkana South ore-body, 6,500 ft along the strike, with an average width of 20·5 ft, the Nkana North ore-body, 7,900 ft by 27·5 ft, and the Mindola ore-body, 4·2 miles along the strike and 15·5 ft wide. By the time drilling operations were suspended early in 1931, a total of forty-one holes had been drilled and 22,500 ft of ore had been developed. The reserves then totalled 127 million tons averaging 4 per cent copper.[39]

[38]Rhodesian Selection Trust archives, memo 12.
[39]J. A. Bancroft, op. cit., page 158.

The preparation of Nkana for the production stage coincided with the similar activity then taking place at the Roan Antelope. The initial output was to be 5,000 tons of ore per day, for which almost all the surface equipment—ore bins, crusher plant, power plant and so on—was ready early in 1931, and the first unit of the concentrator by the end of the year. The famous landmark of the 300 ft steel smelter stack was erected at the same time, the smelter itself being completed in March 1932. Preparations were also being made to extract cobalt from the ore, production beginning in 1933. The railway had already arrived in May 1930.

Nkana, like the other Copperbelt properties, was handicapped by the financial depression which coincided with the start of production. Output was severely curtailed and the staff drastically reduced. Although a little more shaft sinking was done, the total production during the three years from June 1932 to June 1935 was only just over 5¾ million tons of ore, which yielded 186,000 tons of copper selling at about £30 5s per long ton. The situation eased, however, from this year, when the new electrolytic refinery at Nkana came into operation, thereby obviating the expense of sending ore to the United States for treatment by the American Metal Company.

Dr Bancroft's activities ranged throughout the promising areas of Northern Rhodesia and were by no means confined to the Nkana area. Thus in 1928 two of his prospectors carrying out his 'systematic' prospecting scheme 'rediscovered' the Konkola deposits (see page 41). The two men, T. V. Wilson and A. H. Douw,[40] recognised the possibility of copper existing in the Konkola area, where the strata outcrop in an elliptical ring, some ten by five miles in extent, enclosing a dome-like structure of older rocks. The international boundary between Northern Rhodesia and the Congo Republic runs along the long axis of the ellipse, thus separating Konkola itself from Musoshi in Katanga. Douw and Wilson also rediscovered Kirila Bomwe to the south-east. Kirila Bomwe, which lies on the northern extension of the

[40]In 1962 Mr Douw was a consultant geologist resident in Bulawayo. I am indebted to him for much of my detail on early work at Bancroft.

Nchanga shales, was recognised as being part of the Lower Bwana Mkubwa series of rock formations, in which the main copper-bearing deposits were found. In addition to these finds, an anticlinal structure was located some four and a quarter miles distant from the Konkola dome and copper shales were discovered at Kakosa,[41] some eight miles north of Nchanga on the bank of the Kafue. These results were obtained by the systematic traversing and plotting methods introduced by Dr Bancroft, in whose honour the new mine was subsequently named. Keen interest and excitement were aroused, and an intensive programme of exploration and verification was instituted at both Konkola and Kirila Bomwe.

The investigations, which were carried out by means of prospecting pits, began early in 1929. At about the same time a number of widely spread diamond-drill holes, RLE (River Lode extension) Nos 1–8, were put down at intervals from Nchanga to Kirila Bomwe. Some of the most senior men available, including Brooks himself, W. Burns, D. Gilchrist, E. G. Bishop and D. H. Ellis, personally supervised these drilling operations. Their immediate hopes were doomed to disappointment: only fractional copper values were found, and with the financial stringencies occasioned by the depression, work was suspended altogether. This was most unfortunate, for one of the two holes which were stopped before reaching maximum depth was immediately over the rich Kirila Bomwe South ore-body, which it failed to intersect by only a few feet. This ore-body remained unknown until 1939.

Further economic considerations; amalgamation
It is abundantly clear from the remarks of Sir Dougal Malcolm (pages 34–35) that Northern Rhodesia was not envisaged as being a suitable area for the operations of the independent prospector or miner, and indeed this would seem to be eminently reasonable. The small worker has never been able to undertake any but the most elementary mining processes, which generally

[41]Kakosa is the site of a well known pioneer farm which was sold in 1963 to Nchanga Consolidated Copper Mines Ltd by its owner, the late Mr Percy Quinsee.

preclude the deep, sub-aquatic excavating necessary on the Copperbelt; he was unlikely to be able to find the substantial capital required for transport costs, shaft sinking, pumping, labour and the miscellany of equipment and stores necessary before work could even commence; it was practically impossible for him to finance and operate the metallurgical processes required in the concentrating of the ore and extraction of the metal —a vastly more complicated business than in gold mining; he would not normally possess the expert technical knowledge necessary to minimise the physical and economic risks; and he had no access to the capital markets in Johannesburg, London and New York. Although some individuals possessed a selection of the necessary requirements, even the wealthiest, such as Rhodes himself, found it essential to operate some kind of joint stock enterprise. The assistance of investors was a prerequisite to the successful exploitation of any substantial quantity of Northern Rhodesian copper.[42]

In certain circumstances, where risk appears small and the chance of gain substantial, it is possible for individuals to create separate mining companies, retaining a controlling interest for themselves and using the proceeds of the remaining shares as working capital, but in the normal conditions of prospecting and exploitation the risk of investment in a single property may seem far too great to entice the cautious investor. It is, therefore, obviously more desirable to spread the risk of a property failing by creating companies which would hold interests in several. Not only does this technique reduce the possibility of loss, but at the same time it greatly enhances the chances of securing ultimate financial control of all, and this at the minimum level of capital investment.

Such a system is also in the interests of the individual companies because of the administrative convenience of operating from a single centre and because of the savings possible through

[42]It is worth noting in this connection that although the initial capital of Rhodesian Anglo-American in December 1928 was £2½ million it had proved necessary to increase this progressively to £6½ million by January 1931.

Plate 1 Kansanshi hill, 1927. *Photo: J. C. Ferguson, courtesy National Archives of Rhodesia and Nyasaland*

Plate 2 (a) Electrical prospectors crossing the Lunsemfwa river, August 1926. *Photo: C. W. Scrymgeour*

Plate 2 (b) Living quarters of electrical prospecting party near Nchanga, August 1926. *Photo: C. W. Scrymgeour*

the centralisation of finance, sales, technical assistance and common necessities such as stores. Sir Ernest Oppenheimer has himself publicly summed it up:

The advantages of the system are manifold, but I will mention a few of the more outstanding features:

The financing of the individual companies is facilitated.

The parent company acts as a link between the various operating companies, and promotes co-operation in matters of common interest.

The services of a staff of highly skilled experts in all departments of mining and metallurgy are constantly available to the individual companies.

Administration is standardised, in itself a matter of premier importance in all secretarial and accounting work.

The stores and other requirements of the mines are bought to the best advantage and at a minimum cost for the service.

Where, as is the case on the Rand, there are many companies whose properties adjoin or are adjacent to each other, all engaged in the same class of work, the existence of a central organisation for the supply of expert advice and information on matters which must in the nature of things be of common interest, is clearly of incalculable value. It certainly ensures to the individual companies great economies compared with the cost which would have to be faced if each company were called upon to maintain a separate and complete staff.[43]

It is clear that the situation described relative to the Rand in the above paragraph applies with equal force to the Northern Rhodesian Copperbelt. Nevertheless, it is possible to over-centralise, with the result that maximum local advantage is sometimes lost. There is sometimes, therefore, a case for decentralisation to the extent of forming a sub-group to handle the affairs of a particular region. Such a situation arose in Northern Rhodesia, operations in which formed only a minor part of the interests of both Selection Trust and the Anglo-American Corporation. The initiative, though, came not from Oppenheimer but from Chester Beatty.

On 22 May 1928 Beatty registered his Rhodesian Selection

[43]Presidential address to the third (triennial) Empire Mining and Metallurgical Congress, South Africa, 1930.

Trust, with an initial issued capital of £500,000. The purpose of the new company was to develop the work of Mineralized Venture, from which it took over the exclusive rights in the Nkana concession, including the Mufulira properties. Selection Trust had now divested itself of its direct interests on the Copperbelt to Rhodesian Selection Trust and Roan Antelope Copper Mines Ltd, whilst continuing to dominate both through share holdings. And, as it proved impossible to undertake the full requirements of the British South Africa Company concerning the surveying and pegging of the entire area, this latter company issued twenty-one Special Grants to the Rhodesian Selection Trust in exchange for an interest in any resulting mines. In consequence, the chartered company held a minor interest in Mufulira and the other developments within the Nkana concession area.

This was not all. A further complication arose from the fact that the Anglo-American Corporation, a $7\frac{1}{2}$ per cent shareholder in Mineralized Venture, now held a 10 per cent interest in Rhodesian Selection Trust. There was, therefore, already considerable interlocking of the interests of the major groups.[44]

When Beatty formed his Rhodesian Selection Trust the Anglo-American Corporation—with its interests in Broken Hill, the

[44]For a detailed chart, see the *Economist*, 12 May 1934, and for the situation in 1962 see Figs. 9 and 10 in chapter 6. Further changes will ensue once the details of nationalisation have been finalised. At the time of writing (November 1969) the unconfirmed arrangements are that the two major groups, Anglo-American and Roan Selection Trust, will be reorganised into two companies to be known as Nchanga Consolidated Copper Mines Ltd (New Nchanga), which will incorporate the Anglo-American mines plus Rhokana copper refinery, and Roan Consolidated Mines Ltd (RCM), to absorb the Roan Selection Trust mines and the Ndola copper refinery. The present Anglo-American and Roan Selection Trust companies will be reformed as external companies which will own their minority holdings in New Nchanga and RCM together with their other interests which have not been nationalised.

The proposed financial arrangements provide for a Zambian government payment of approximately £122 million plus interest, which is substantially less than the book value (over £130 million) of their 51 per cent share. On the other hand, the companies have gained very favourable marketing and managerial contracts involving the receipt of $1\frac{1}{2}$ per cent of gross sales revenue plus 2 per cent of the profits of the nationalised companies.

amalgamated concession companies, Bwana Mkubwa, Nchanga, the Roan Antelope and various ventures in Southern Rhodesia —was fully as deeply involved in Copperbelt affairs as the Beatty group. With the need for co-ordination and the obvious future demands for ever-increasing capital, the amalgamation of the rival group merely crystallised the need for Oppenheimer to institute some similar proceedings. But, unlike the Rhodesian Selection Trust, Oppenheimer was determined that his further ventures in Northern Rhodesia should be under British control and dominated by British capital. Thus the new company was registered in London on 8 December 1928 with a chairman and deputy to be appointed by the Anglo-American Corporation,[45] and American participation—in practice the Newmont Mining Corporation—restricted to a minority role. Oppenheimer's position was clearly stated in a letter[46] from R. B. Hagart to C. B. Kingston:

Sir Ernest has asked me to mention to you that he would be glad if you would take the first suitable opportunity of giving the Governor an outline of the position of the new company. As you are aware, from the very outset of development in Northern Rhodesia, a great point has been made of the fact that there was being developed a big and practically the only copper-field in the British Empire, and the political importance of this fact has been emphasised on several occasions. This being so, we feel that this great national asset is passing into foreign hands. From the figures . . . you will see that the capital[47] of the new company is being provided almost entirely by British interests, the only American interest involved being the Newmont company, whose co-operation it was desired to obtain as it was felt essential that we should have on the technical side some large American copper group interested.[48] You will be able to assure the Governor, therefore, that the Rhodesian Anglo-American Ltd is a British company with almost entirely British capital and that we have not

---

[45]They were Sir Ernest Oppenheimer and Sir Edmund Davis respectively. Other board members were S. B. Joel, representing the Barnato interests (the Johannesburg Consolidated Investment Company), Sir Drummond Chaplin and Sir Henry Birchenough of the British South Africa Company, F. Searls Jnr. for the Newmont Corporation, L. Pollak, C. Davis and, later, S. S. Taylor.
[46]Quoted in Gregory, op. cit., pages 415–16.
[47]£2½ million initially.
[48]In fact an American, H. S. Munroe, became consulting engineer.

overlooked the importance of the political aspect in this respect. Incidentally, I might mention that the Bwana Mkubwa Copper Mining Company has recently had several extraordinarily attractive offers made to it in connexion with N'Kana and the N'Kana Concession by large American copper groups[49] and these have been unhesitatingly turned down on the ground that, apart from other reasons, the board is anxious that the vast potentialities of N'Kana should be developed by British capital. I might also mention that when the company was first under consideration we investigated fully the question of registering it in the first place in Northern Rhodesia, but for various reasons it was decided that the registration should be effected in London, and I am sure the Governor will appreciate our attitude in this respect.

Although Oppenheimer could not have been aware of the full facts at this time, the Americans were already seriously investigating the prospects in Northern Rhodesia. Already they largely controlled the Rhodesian Selection Trust, six of whose nine directors were American. Oppenheimer's natural fear was that if the Americans controlled the Copperbelt, being already a major force in the world of copper outside it, their manipulations of production markets in their own general interest might well act unfavourably on the specific interests of the Copperbelt itself. And the Americans were possibly already taking their future domination of the Copperbelt for granted.

In the matter of labor, the English feel their experience in the African gold and diamond fields will stand them in good stead in the Rhodesian copper fields, but the American group in London has the view that, inasmuch as there has always been talk of shortage of labor in the South African gold country as well as in the Katanga copper operations to the north, perhaps the shortage may be due to a policy of living conditions, which *the Americans can and will improve in*

---

[49]Possibly the American Metal Company, which had concluded a ten year sales agreement through its British associate, the Anglo-Metal Company, with the Bwana Mkubwa company in 1925 The latter was offered £1 million for a four-fifths interest in the Bwana Mkubwa holdings in Nkana, i.e. four-fifteenths of the total. The bidder therefore valued Nkana at £3¾ million. See A. J. Rosenthal & Co., 'Report on the copper district of Northern Rhodesia, Africa', 18 February 1929, page 31. This is an unpublished report prepared for the above by Rogers, Mayer and Bell, New York. In Rhodesian Selection Trust archives.

Rhodesia. Though native labor is cheap as to daily remuneration, the Americans do not look on it as low labor cost, in reality, and base their copper cost estimates on the American standard of unit prices.[50]

In fact this report considerably over-simplified the position. It is true that there was a shortage of labour in both Katanga and the Copperbelt, these areas being relatively unpopulated in the first instance,[51] but this was further aggravated, as far as Northern Rhodesia was concerned, by recruiting for the Katanga mines from within Northern Rhodesia itself. Thus in 1921, when the Copperbelt was only really beginning to develop, Northern Rhodesia supplied about 56 per cent of the Union Minière labour force. Yet by 1931 this figure had fallen to a nominal 0·7 per cent.[52] It is clear, therefore, that as the demand for native labour increased within the territory, so the Northern Rhodesian African preferred to remain within his own country. Even so, the manpower resources were strained to the limit. Merle Davis considered that as many as 60 per cent of the able-bodied Bemba men aged from 15 to 45 were away from their villages in 1931, most of them on the mines.[53] The figures quoted above indicate that most of these must have been employed on the Copperbelt, in spite of the fact that the death rate on the Copperbelt was appreciably higher than in Katanga[54] and living conditions were less attractive under a system of temporary labour, as opposed to the permanent conditions offered under Belgian auspices. Such was the demand for work on the mines that from October 1931 it was no longer necessary to recruit

[50]Rosenthal report, op. cit., page 2. My italics. For particulars of wages at the Roan Antelope in 1929, see Appendix V.
[51]In 1933 Merle Davis quoted a figure of 2·2 persons per square mile for the Ndola district: *Modern Industry and the African*, ed. J. Merle Davis, Macmillan, London, 1933, page 33.
[52]Ibid., page 159.
[53]Ibid., page 57.
[54]In 1931 the deaths on the Northern Rhodesian mines were 25·03 per 1,000 native employees as opposed to 8·01 per 1,000 in Katanga. Fatalities reached as high as 39 per 1,000 at Nkana (ibid, page 66), *Note:* these figures are not for accidents alone but include loss from disease and other causes attributable to poor living conditions; these rapidly improved as the pioneering era was left behind.

labour, as sufficient numbers were presenting themselves in person for employment. On the other hand, during this period of economic depression and retrenchment far fewer men were being engaged than previously.

Nor was the economic situation in terms of labour costs as straightforward as the Americans purported it to be. The Merle Davis Commission, which was actively investigating social conditions on the Copperbelt in the early 1930's, pointed out[55] that there was no accurate measurement of local purchasing power; yet it was clear that expenditure on welfare, medical attention, food and housing already greatly exceeded the actual cash remuneration of the African employees, itself approximately double that offered by the missions. Much of the necessary expenditure by the Northern Rhodesia copper companies on their employees was not paralleled by operations outside Africa; thus a comparison of actual cash incomes at once becomes invalid.

The first two years, 1929 and 1930, of the new Rhodesian Anglo-American company saw the onset of the years of depression which were to close all the Copperbelt mines except the Roan Antelope and Nkana. Amalgamation seemed the obvious means of increasing both capital and status to the level necessary to weather the storm successfully. Oppenheimer had long envisaged this on a grand scale, with the amalgamation of the interests of the two major groups—Rhodesian Anglo-American and Rhodesian Selection Trust—into one enormous combine which could more readily resist the potential domination of the world copper market by American interests and at the same time preserve Northern Rhodesia as a predominantly British sphere which could not be submerged or neglected through American self-interest. Although Oppenheimer's idea seems grandiose and unrealistic—for neither Copperbelt group would voluntarily take second place to the other, and it was unlikely that they would put themselves under the control of a third party such as the British South Africa Company, as Oppen-

[55]Merle Davis, op. cit., page 170.

heimer later suggested[56]—nevertheless Oppenheimer's fears about American ousting of imperial interests in the Copperbelt were certainly not without foundation. Two significant pointers had already been seen, even before the slump, the first of which occurred in 1928 when the Rhodesian Selection Trust proposed to sell most of its Bwana Mkubwa holdings to the American Metal Company. Anglo-American, also a major shareholder, was so antagonistic to the scheme for 'imperial and financial reasons' that rather than agree to it the corporation was prepared to abandon its Rhodesian operations altogether. The negotiations were therefore dropped.[57]

Much more serious was the conflict over the financing of Nchanga, in which Rhodesian Anglo-American held an interest. On 28 January 1929 the Nchanga shareholders received a circular letter containing proposals for obtaining finance from the American Smelting and Refining Company on terms which would have given that company control of Nchanga, including the major deposits of Nchanga West, which were to be handed over to Nchanga by Rhodesian Congo Border Concession Ltd. The result of this would have been American majority control of the entire Copperbelt, as the Americans were already strong in Rhodesian Selection Trust. In fact the only company to remain clearly under British control would be Bwana Mkubwa.

An outcry followed, which was commented on significantly by the authors of the Rosenthal report, but before the final decision had been reached:[58]

While this report is being written the [Nchanga] company has suddenly come into public notice, due to a surprise announcement that an

---

[56]Letter to S. S. Taylor dated 5 August 1938. Quoted in Gregory, op. cit., pages 442–6. Indeed, Oppenheimer himself later realised this. See below, page 71.
[57]For details of these negotiations, see Gregory, ibid, pages 412–15. One of the most important consequences was a break-off of discussions between Anglo-American and the American Metal Company and the opening of new negotiations regarding Rhodesian Anglo-American with the Newmont company, which was already a large shareholder in Anglo-American.
[58]Rosenthal report, op. cit., page 7.

option on Nchanga shares was given to the American Smelting and Refining Company, subject, however, to the approval of the shareholders at a meeting to be held on February 7th [1929]. Immediately the following comment appeared, being abstract from the *Financial Times* of London:

'By what can only be considered a clever coup, the famous American Smelting and Refining Company has secured, provisionally, the technical control and the reversion of the financial control for immediate payment of under £210,000 (118,750 shares at 35s each against a current market price of well over £4). For this miserably inadequate 'mess of pottage' they would have the right eventually to increase their holdings to 1,375,000 £1 shares out of a total of £3,000,000.

'What are our Kaffir houses doing to let the A.S. & R. get a throttle-hold on one of the best of the coming Rhodesian copper producers on such easy terms? Only the Anglo-American Corporation of South Africa, and to a lesser degree the Johannesburg Consolidated Investment Company, appear to have as yet shown anything like the same vision. Is it too late for one of the others to make a better bid than the Guggenheims have put forward?'

The foregoing is quoted to give evidence of the change of heart on the part of the English in connection with the Rhodesian copper situation, in that they now realise that they have in large measure parted with property which, from a national standpoint, they ought to have retained.

However, this conclusion was premature. A counter-offer came from the Oppenheimer group which resulted in the withdrawal of the American offer. After some months of discussion, financial support for Rhodesian Congo Border Concession and Nchanga came from the British South Africa Company, the British Metal Corporation, the Johannesburg Consolidated Investment Company, Minerals Separation, Rhodesian Anglo-American, N. M. Rothschild and Sons, the Union Corporation, the Anglo-Metal Company and Rio Tinto, which thus entered Northern Rhodesian mining enterprise for the first time. (It is interesting to note in connection with this company, which was closely connected with the banking house of Rothschild's, that the chairman in 1929 was Sir Auckland Geddes, who had formerly been the principal of McGill University. As Dr Bancroft had himself been a professor at McGill, there exists at least the possibility that Geddes was influenced to some degree from this source. It should also be noted that as Oppenheimer had recently invested £1 million in Nkana (see page 53) he now had an interest in every major venture on the Copperbelt.)

In terms of the agreement finally arrived at, Rhodesian Congo Border Concession shareholders were to be offered approximately 300,000 shares at £5, these being guaranteed by the concerns involved. From the proceeds RCBC was to subscribe for 100,000 Nchanga shares at £3, with a further 200,000 being offered to the Nchanga shareholders at the share price. The Nchanga shares were to be guaranteed by RCBC. In consequence of this influx of capital, the Nchanga company could proceed to develop and equip its own property and the Rhodesian Congo Border Concession company could conclude the intensive prospecting of its concession area. Chester Beatty supported Oppenheimer in the negotiations, which also resulted in the shedding by Rhodesian Anglo-American of its shareholding in Rhodesian Selection Trust (but not the holdings in the operating companies, where Rhodesian Anglo-American representation on the boards was still desired).

The increasing interest in Northern Rhodesia shown by the American copper concerns, together with the worsening economic depression, caused Oppenheimer to give serious thought to the question of further amalgamation within his own interests. Already he was a substantial shareholder in the Bwana Mkubwa company, and in May 1931 he proposed to increase the Rhodesian Anglo-American shareholding in Rhodesian Congo Border Concession Ltd from 169,000 to 200,000 as a means of redressing the imbalance between his holdings and those of Rio Tinto. Further, in view of his amalgamation schemes, substantial increases in Rhodesian Anglo-American capital were authorised. Discussions on amalgamating Nchanga and Rhodesian Congo Border Concession (which owned the Nchanga West area) took place throughout 1930 without any immediate developments. But by the end of the year it was clear that an even greater amalgamation was desirable.

It will be recalled that although the Bwana Mkubwa mine itself had proved disappointing, the Bwana Mkubwa company still enjoyed rights over the proven Nkana mine and over one-third of the Nkana concession. The discussions therefore began to centre around the possible amalgamation of all three companies. Oppenheimer wholeheartedly supported the move on the grounds that it would greatly help the financing of technical developments, would render borrowing easier in view of the greater security available[59] and would place the company 'in the same class as such groups as Kennecott/Utah, Anaconda, Phelps Dodge/Calumet and Arizona and Union Minière.'[60] Oppenheimer based this conclusion on his own calculation that by about 1935 the combined annual production of RCBC, Nchanga and Nkana would amount to approximately 195,000 short tons, or roughly 10 per cent of the world production in 1929. Not only would these economic considerations be greatly assisted by amalgamation, but Oppenheimer's fears of government intervention would also be substantially allayed.[61]

The formation of one large company would greatly strengthen the position *vis-à-vis* legislation and the Government authorities generally. There is a tendency among governments today to intrude themselves into the affairs of private enterprises and invariably when they do so it is with disastrous results. This disposition is probably most accentuated in regard to mining. In the nature of things, for profitable operation, mining has to be conducted today on a very large scale, which, for financial reasons, leads to the creation of powerful groups and combines. This naturally tends to place the control of large sections of the mineral wealth of a country in a few hands. On the other hand it is a popular argument in these democratic days that the

---

[59]It had already been estimated that an expenditure of at least £5 million and a delay of four years would be necessary before there would be any return on investments in any of the Copperbelt properties. (Memo No. 13, page 8, Rhodesian Selection Trust archives.)
[60]Letter from Oppenheimer to Sir Auckland Geddes read at the eighth annual general meeting of Rhodesian Congo Border Concession Ltd, 17 December 1930.
[61]Letter from Oppenheimer to Geddes, ibid.

mineral wealth should be the property of the nation. In their efforts to reconcile the irreconcilable, governments incline to exercise control over mining operations. This tendency to interfere finds fruitful soil in dissensions among rival mining enterprises, because it provides the government with an excuse to intervene ostensibly with the object of settling those differences but really with the aim of controlling the industry. It is improbable that any basis could be found for merging all the enterprises in Northern Rhodesia because the interests are too divergent. As between Bwana and RCBC–Nchanga, however, there is much common ground. The value of a united front as presented by these companies, as opposed to individual action and divided council in negotiations with the Government, cannot be over-estimated.

In the event, there was little that the government could do when faced with the enormous financial combines which arose and without which the Copperbelt could not have been developed at all. In fact the government largely failed to carry out even its legitimate functions on the Copperbelt, with the result that health, housing and indeed all aspects of welfare, particularly of African employees and their families, have been attended to by the companies themselves.[62]

The need for finance was rather more obvious, for Rhodesian Anglo-American's interests were already straining its resources. By August 1930 the company held a 54 per cent interest in the Bwana Mkubwa company and (as this latter owned approximately 30 per cent interest in all the Rhodesian Selection Trust properties in the Nkana area) a substantial minority share in the Chester Beatty interests. It held the first option for the purchase of the British South Africa Company's holdings in the Nkana grants and was in any case the largest single shareholder in the chartered company. It was the largest shareholder in Rhodesian Congo Border Concession, controlled the various concession companies, and acted as consulting engineers to all of them.

The estimates for developing these interests to the production

[62]Obviously, the decision taken in 1969 to nationalise the copper mining industry is going to involve the government in these matters to a much greater degree than in the past.

stage were enormous[63]—£3¾ million for Nkana and up to £5 million for Nchanga, where the mixed sulphide and oxide ores might require the erection of an expensive electrolytic refinery. Given an amalgamation of the two, the first to commence operations (Nkana) would be able to subsidise and act as security for the latter until it too became self-supporting.

There was, of course, no doubt that the proposed amalgamation would inevitably become an accomplished fact, for Rhodesian Anglo-American controlled the Bwana Mkubwa company and also, along with Rio Tinto, predominated in RCBC-Nchanga. Nevertheless there was some initial dispute both from the American interests and the representative of the British 'Union Corporation'. The points on which the two directors, R. E. McConnell and Sir Henry Strakosch, opposed the scheme were quite straightforward: they were not satisfied with the claims made on behalf of the Nchanga mine by the experts on the spot (who included Dr Bancroft and who were, of course, absolutely correct in their optimistic prognostications); second, at a time when RCBC and Nchanga did not need *immediate* finance, they objected to having to channel capital through these companies to bolster the Bwana Mkubwa company.

As anticipated, the objectors were outvoted and the merger took place, with Rhodesian Congo Border Concession increasing its capital from £750,000 to £2 million and then buying out the other two companies. This was accomplished by the Bwana Mkubwa shareholders selling their assets to Rhodesian Congo Border Concession for 550,000 £1 shares in RCBC. The Nchanga company was then liquidated and taken over by RCBC for 126,000 shares in the latter. The new company now held all the above interests, together with a one-third share in Mufulira. Finally the outside shareholders in the Bwana Mkubwa company exchanged their shares for Rhodesian Anglo-American at the rate of ten for three, and the Bwana Mkubwa company went

[63]Figures provided by Oppenheimer: letter to Geddes, op. cit. *Note:* as late as 1962 the entire revenue of Northern Rhodesia, including copper, was only £17 million (quoted in the context of education in the *Northern News*, 21 February 1962). Obviously the government in the 1930's could not even begin to compete with the private enterprise involved.

into voluntary liquidation in January 1935. The new company, with Sir Auckland Geddes of Rio Tinto as chairman and Oppenheimer and Edmund Davies as deputies, took the name of Rhokana[64] Corporation Ltd. Rhodesian Anglo-American now withdrew from its role of consulting engineer to the various concession companies in favour of Rhokana Corporation, to which company it transferred its consulting and mechanical engineering staff, the geologists going to the British South Africa Company.

This manoeuvre alone could not save the copper industry from the effects of the slump, which itself had not occurred by chance. It was, in fact, a direct reaction to a scheme designed to prevent such an occurrence ever taking place. In spite of the fears of many experts, the end of the 1914–18 war had not brought with it a major depression in the copper industry (although there was a minor one: see page 20), for the ever-increasing demands of the electrical and automobile industries maintained an unprecedented consumption of the metal. In October 1926 there was founded in the United States of America a combine known as Copper Exporters Inc, the purpose of which was to stabilise copper prices. All the main American groups, some of the main European concerns, Rio Tinto and the Union Minière, totalling some 90 per cent of the world's production, joined the combine. However, its attempts to eliminate the price fixing function of the London Metal Exchange by restricting supplies simply led to consumer resistance to the high prices demanded by the group, which in turn stimulated the operations of low-cost producers such as Northern Rhodesia and Katanga—and, even worse from the Americans' point of view, led to experimentation in the use of other alloys to replace copper in industry. These factors caused stockpiles to accumulate and ultimately, in late 1929, the collapse of the copper market, with the price slumping from 24 cents per pound in April 1929 to only 6¼ cents per pound by November 1931.[65] It

[64]An amalgam of Rhodesia and Nkana.
[65]Figures quoted in L. H. Gann, *A History of Northern Rhodesia*, Chatto & Windus, London, 1964, page 251.

may therefore be seen that the development of the Northern Rhodesian properties in 1930 and 1931 was guided by a spirit of optimism for the future rather than in the hope of immediate gain.

The only hope for the copper producers was to allow the natural law of supply and demand to operate in their favour by drastically reducing their output. A conference to consider this matter in November 1930—before the Copperbelt mines had begun to operate—failed to bring about any reduction, but a second conference in August 1931, which included Northern Rhodesian representatives, resulted in a general agreement to limit production during the first three months of 1932 to 26.5 per cent of the capacity of each mine. In April 1932 this was reduced to 20 per cent. The Northern Rhodesian companies, in view of this, decided to operate only from the Roan Antelope, in the case of the Rhodesian Selection Trust group, and from Nkana alone, in that of the Rhodesian Anglo-American interests. Bwana Mkubwa had already closed down in February 1931. The Anglo-American decision, which involved the closure of the recently flooded Nchanga—a much richer ore-body than Nkana —was taken not only because of the flood situation at Nchanga, but also in view of the lack of railway and treatment facilities there, and the difficulties involved in the actual extraction of the metal from the mixed oxide and sulphide ores at Nchanga. Nevertheless, although the decision was eminently reasonable, it evoked great resentment on the part of the Nchanga manager, G. C. R. Stewart, who remarked bitterly that the Rhokana quota could be produced entirely from the material extracted during the mere development of Nchanga West.[66]

[66]Personal information: N. M. Airey. Figures quoted in Bancroft, op. cit., page 139, give the value of ore dumped at Nchanga during the development operations prior to the flood as:

2,867 tons at	5.80% copper	—	166,286 tons copper
996 ,, ,,	26.00% ,,	—	258,960 ,, ,,
1,739 ,, ,,	9.39% ,,	—	161,727 ,, ,,
5,602 ,, ,, av. 10.16%		—	586.973 ,, ,,

N. M. Airey, who was employed at Nchanga at the time, states that each 8 ft × 8 ft drive was advanced by six 6 ft rounds on each day shift and

Table 2

Year	Northern Rhodesian copper production (long tons)	Average price per long ton (£)
1927	3,289	59·5
1928	5,930	67·1
1929	5,465	83·5
1930	6,269	59·8
1931	8,764	37·4
1932	67,887	25·6
1933	103,516	32·4
1934	137,897	38·8
1935	143,501	40·2
1936	142,333	43·6
1937	208,172	60·7*
1938	213,031	46·1
1939	211,668	50·6
1940	262,394	63·6
1941	228,254	62·4†

*Re-armament.
†Official control price.

Copper Exporters Inc collapsed in 1932, when many of the original signatories, including the Union Minière and the producers in Canada and Chile, withdrew because the United

similarly on each night shift, and that this amount of progress permitted the removal of 384 tons of ore per day, which was the maximum hoisting capacity of No. 1 shaft. In the light of the copper values quoted above this would realise approximately 38 tons of copper per day, say 1,200 per month, which at the selling price of around £30 per ton would realise £36,000 per month. During this period Nkana was raising 30,000 tons of ore per month at an average of 5·17 per cent copper, i.e. 50 tons of copper per day, say 1,500 tons per month. This is considerably more than the Nchanga potential. Further, during the next three years the Nkana production rose to around 6,000 tons per month (although during the period of quota restrictions only 4,200 tons per month were marketed). It is probable that if the flood problem at Nchanga had been immediately tackled and solved, the mine could have equalled the Nkana production—especially if No. 10 shaft had been re-opened, so increasing the hoisting capacity—but with the necessity of having to rail the ore to Nkana for processing. In the light of the current economic depression it is highly improbable that the very high dewatering and capital development expenditure required for Nchanga would have been forthcoming.

States introduced a protectionist tariff of four cents per pound in favour of its own producers. Britain had also imposed a tariff of 2d per pound on all copper coming from outside the empire as a result of the negotiations which took place at the Ottawa conference. A further conference held in New York in December 1932 broke down over the request of the Roan Antelope for an increase in its quota, and in 1933 unrestricted competition returned. Although further quota agreements were made in 1934 and 1935, the failure of the Geneva disarmament talks obviated any further collapse during the 1930's, the position of the mining groups being consolidated by the outbreak of war in 1939. Table 2 indicates these trends. The rise in prices was sufficient to permit Mufulira to re-open in 1933 and for the constitution of Nchanga as Nchanga Consolidated Copper Mines Ltd to be a feasible proposition by 1936. This new company, formed with a capital of £5 million in March 1937, was bigger in scope than the original Nchanga company in that it also included the Nchanga West and Chingola mining grant areas, the latter now being the site of the Chingola open pit.

Meanwhile, Belgian prospectors had begun to investigate the North or Congo side of the Konkola dome, (see page 58). In October 1935 they discovered an outcrop of copper ore on the slope of the dome and, on further investigation by drilling, an ore-body 37 ft wide, containing 3·17 per cent of mainly sulphide copper, was found at a depth of approximately 150 ft. Twenty-four shot drill holes were put down during the next two years, by which time the Musoshi ore-body, 26,000 ft long, 25·5 ft wide and averaging 2·6 per cent copper had been discovered.

The excitement of this find stimulated further activity on the Northern Rhodesian side of the dome. In May 1936 the field manager, Dr Brock, was able to report to Dr Bancroft at Nkana that prospect pitting on the eastern side of the Konkola dome had exposed a sub-outcrop of shales containing copper ore. In the following July diamond-drilling began under the immediate supervision of J. J. Lambertsen.[67] Twenty-five holes were drilled

[67]Mr Lambertsen has provided some of the data on the early exploratory work at Bancroft.

Plate 3 (a) Oxen hauling boiler, Lunsemfwa, 1927. *Photo: J. C. Ferguson, courtesy National Archives of Rhodesia and Nyasaland*

Plate 3 (b) Mimbula camp, 1927. *Photo: J. C. Ferguson, courtesy National Archives of Rhodesia and Nyasaland*

Plate 4 (a) Diamond drill, Mimbula, 1927. *Photo: J. C. Ferguson, courtesy National Archives of Rhodesia and Nyasaland*

Plate 4 (b) Class A single quarters, Nchanga, 1926. *Photo: J. C. Ferguson, courtesy National Archives of Rhodesia and Nyasaland*

at Konkola, followed by a further twenty-two in the Kirila Bomwe area, beginning in January 1939. One of these latter holes finally intersected the Kirila Bomwe South ore-body in December of that year. At a depth of 900 ft it had a width of almost 32 ft and averaged 5·30 per cent copper. Another well mineralised ore-body designated as Kirila Bomwe North was also found before work was discontinued in December 1940 for the duration of the war. It was already clear that the area showed considerable promise, but insufficient was known to justify the opening of a new mine at this stage. Special Grants totalling eighty-eight square miles were secured for further investigation.

Unspectacular progress was also taking place throughout the Nkana area during the same period. Mufulira began operations again in October 1933, a decision having already been taken to erect a smelter on the mine and increase production to 70,000 long tons of copper a year once all restrictions on production were removed. After this had taken place in October 1937, Mufulira steadily progressed to become the largest copper mine in the Commonwealth, in respect of the tonnage mined underground.

On the Nkana mine itself, until quota restrictions were lifted production was limited to little more than 4,000 tons per month. Development meantime took place at Mindola, where the vertical shaft begun in 1933 reached a depth of 1,943 ft by mid-1936. The ore reserves were continually being increased by further exploratory work, reaching over 123 million tons averaging 3·45 per cent in 1937,[68] and continuing to expand, in spite of continuous removal, up to the present time.[69] As in the case of the other mines, the real impetus to production came with the outbreak of war in 1939. During the war years 251,789 short tons of blister copper were produced, along with a further 6,154 tons of cobalt.

[68]Annual report for year ended 30 June 1937.
[69]The figures for 1961 (annual report, 30 June 1961) were:
Nkana North: 24,328,000 short tons averaging 3·06 per cent copper.
Nkana South: 14,913,000 short tons averaging 2·65 per cent copper.
Mindola: 81,106,000 short tons averaging 3·15 per cent copper.
Total: 120,347,000 short tons averaging 3·07 per cent copper.

7

5 The exploration and development of Nchanga mine

The change in policy of the British South Africa Company and the formation of Rhodesian Congo Border Concession Ltd have already been discussed in the previous chapter. With the approval of the local manager, Mr Raymond Brooks, five young mining engineers were recruited in England along with six experienced mining prospectors. A sixth young engineer, James Beaton,[1] who was actually studying land surveying at the time, was also engaged. In April 1923 a base was set up at Ndola, and from this headquarters six teams (including those operating for Copper Ventures Ltd), each consisting of an engineer and a prospector, were sent out to prospect in pre-defined areas.[2] The fortunes of one of these teams, James Moir and Guy Bell, have been described above (pages 39–40).

Early in May 1923 Beaton and his companion Andrew Osterberg set out on foot north-westward towards Elizabethville, their plan being to proceed up the north side of the Kafue river and return by the south. In view of the general trend of the Bwana Mkubwa series of rocks which had already been surveyed, the logical continuation of the ore-bodies appeared to lie in this direction. The prospecting was of the simplest nature. The limited field of operations and continued travel along river banks meant that the only feasible possibilities were either the accidental discovery of an outcrop or the hope that some native *en route* might be able to supply the necessary guidance. To this end, Beaton and Osterberg carried with them a sample of malachite, which, they hoped, might be recognised by the Africans through whose villages they passed. Osterberg's equipment was of the

[1]Lately Director of Public Works, Salisbury.
[2]I am indebted for much of this information to personal statements from Mr Beaton himself.

simplest—merely a prospector's hammer and the chemicals necessary for the tests to determine characteristic mineral re-actions.[3] 'It was,' wrote Brooks,[4] 'a system of search best suited to the conditions. Little specialised training was required for this type of prospecting, and so it is that Nchanga owes its first dis-covery, not to a professional prospector but to a man trained as an architect.'[5]

Their optimism was not shared by officialdom. Brooks himself requested help from the Governor in the making of roads in the area, to be met by the somewhat dampening response that the latter based no part of Northern Rhodesia's future development programme on the 'doubtful possibility of finding mineral de-posits of importance.'[6] In view of the rich copper deposits known to exist in the neighbouring Haut-Katanga for many years, this was an incredibly short-sighted decision.[7] Nevertheless, the gene-ral uncertainty of the venture persisted for some time, as the fluctuations in the share prices indicated. From £7 in 1925, these sank to 25s in 1927, varied between 17s 6d and £2 during 1928 and stood at £4 5s early in 1929.[8] The company was obliged to plan and cut over six hundred miles of road itself in its first year alone.

Beaton and Osterberg, however, travelled on foot with African porters. They were provided by the company with a generous supply of camping equipment, including a large double-flap tent, camp beds, table, chairs, bath, bedding and cooking utensils. A monthly ration of tinned foodstuffs, flour and other goods was also provided in addition to their basic salary, these extras being sent out monthly along with their mail, pay, food for the porters,

[3]Information by J. J. Beaton.
[4]'How the Rhodesian coppers were found', *Engineering and Mining Journal*, New York, 1944. Reprinted in *Northern Rhodesia Journal*, 1950, vol. 1, No. 2.
[5]Brooks appears to have overlooked Osterberg's and also Beaton's training in surveying in this unnecessarily disparaging comment.
[6]Brooks, op. cit.
[7]See the *Livingstone Mail*, 26 December 1908 and 12 August 1911 (quoted above, page 11).
[8]Figures quoted in the Rosenthal report, op. cit., page 38.

instructions and other requirements.[9] The porters normally carried loads of approximately fifty pounds for up to twenty miles a day.

The expedition travelled up the north bank of the Kafue to its source without success. No outcrops of mineral deposits were observed and the display of the sample piece of malachite met with no response. Similar failure greeted the return journey towards Ndola until the party reached the village of Chief Chipopo, on the Mushishima stream about seventy-five miles from their base, and near to where the main Chingola-Solwezi road crosses the stream. Here the headman had a vague recollection of seeing an outcrop of rock similar to that carried by the explorers. Even then, it was not until his memory was stimulated by a gift of £2 and some native blankets that he led them some eight miles to a point where the Nchanga river, then a clear, narrow, fast-flowing stream, flowed across a rocky outcrop in its bed. 'There,' said Beaton, 'just below the surface of the water we could see clearly what was obviously a fine copper vein.'[10]

This was certainly a piece of the greatest good fortune, for not only is there no other malachite outcrop near the surface for miles around, but the Nchanga stream also by chance flowed right over it, so washing away the soil and dead vegetable matter and revealing the green rock underneath. Beaton himself openly acknowledges the element of chance in his wonderful discovery.

Reaction was swift. Brooks and Horner set out in July to find the discovery, but failed. Brooks himself wrote to Collier early in August, instructing him to investigate Beaton and Osterberg's find. Beaton, returning to Nkana with his carriers, met Collier on the footpath, but returned with him to the Nchanga outcrop. The two cleared the bank of vegetation and exposed about thirty feet of the outcrop, from which Collier took samples. Beaton left for Nkana on the following day, whilst Collier started a trench on the west side of the stream, the ground to the east being swampy.

[9]Personal information: J. J. Beaton.
[10]Beaton has stated to the writer that this was, in fact, the only time in his experience in which a native ever identified a malachite outcrop in this way. On every other occasion there was no response at all.

The trench on the west side, which was situated on higher ground, was still in a very soggy area requiring lining with poles. Eventually, at a depth of 4 ft Collier found some reddish copper oxide in the mud, from which he at length took samples over a width of 140 ft. The ore, subsequently known as the River Lode, proved to contain $4\frac{1}{2}$ per cent copper. 'This,' related Brooks later,[11] 'created the first confidence in the real possibilities of Northern Rhodesia and was goodness indeed to the men who had to raise the capital.'[12] Brooks immediately visited the site to arrange for food supplies and a shot drill to be provided. Collier also transferred about this time from his original grass hut to a more permanent mud and wattle one, and, with the arrival of his wife, the European population was increased to two.[13]

The hard-working Collier, who was noted for his patience and skill in handling native labour,[14] now began an investigation of a *dambo*[15] parallel to the River Lode about 1,000 yards to the south. He put in a long trench, some fourteen feet deep, which showed no visible signs of copper, but yet proved to contain small amounts when assayed. By this time the drill had arrived and the camp began to grow in size, especially after Rhodesian Congo Border Concession's headquarters was transferred there from Nkana.

[11]Brooks, op. cit.
[12]It is interesting to note that the RCBC had set up a system of bonuses for discoveries, ranging from £100 for a workable prospect to £1,000 for what proved to be a rich discovery, the assessment to be decided by the company, after development and assay testing. All employees were to participate in these bonuses on the basis of 75 per cent of the bonuses to be paid to the joint discoverers and 25 per cent to go into a common pool. The Nchanga mine was subsequently assessed at £500, Beaton and Osterberg being paid accordingly. (The mine is now the richest in the British Commonwealth, with an authorised capital of £28 million in 1959, subsequently increased to over £32 million in July 1964.)
[13]There is an original note by Collier on his work dated March 1931 in the Rhodesian Selection Trust archives. See also letter from Mrs Collier to D'Eath (RST) dated 2 May 1959 in the Rhodesian Selection Trust archives.
[14]Personal information: Lewin Tucker.
[15]*Dambos* are open areas, sometimes watercourses, which flood in the rainy season.

It is obvious that although prospect pitting, soil analysis and the other weapons of the prospector may in themselves determine the presence or otherwise of copper, the ultimate decision regarding the workability of the prospect, its area and the gross tonnage of copper present can be reached only after long and exhaustive examination, for which comprehensive diamond drilling is essential. With the interest shown by the Anglo-American Corporation, which bought 2,000 reserve shares for 55s each in May 1925, the floating in 1926 of Nchanga Copper Mines Ltd, favourable reports from Carl Davies for Anglo-American and P. K. Horner for Minerals Separation in 1926, and finally the appointment as consulting geologist in 1927 of Dr J. Austen Bancroft, the future seemed reasonably assured.

The River Lode

Meanwhile, Williams had been given the contract of moving the first shot drill from Ndola to Nchanga, a distance of seventy-two miles, for only forty of which a track was in existence. The Kafue river also had to be crossed. The heavy steam-driven drill, forming together with its boiler a load of five tons, was dragged by oxen and manhandled by Williams' 128 Africans for no less than twenty-six days before the convoy finally arrived at Nchanga.[16] Williams has related how the most difficult parts of the journey were downhill, when the heavy load would run away from the handlers and bury itself in soft ground. Then at the Kafue the original pontoon of oil drums and planks sank under its burden. Two pontoons had to be constructed and lashed together before the party could cross. The route from Ndola to the Kafue had been 'scuffled'—that is, the vegetation cut down by hand—but from there the party had to carve its own way through the bush.

Once in operation, the machine quickly demonstrated that the River Lode was more or less vertical, with a dip that decreased in depth, as shown in the diagram. The use of vertical and diagonal drill holes speedily delineated its shape, thickness and direction, whilst analysis of the copper present gave some indication of the

[16]Personal information: J. E. G. Williams.

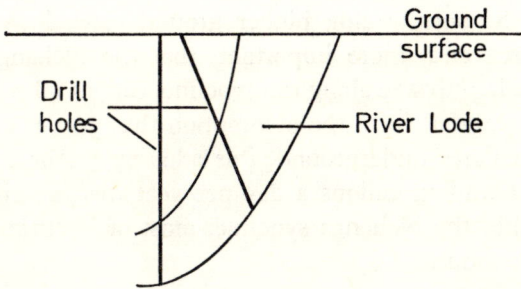

percentage and quantity of copper available.[17] Already, even at this early stage, a grave obstacle to future mining in the area had become apparent. During an average rainy season on the Copper-belt approximately fifty to sixty inches of rain falls during the short period of five months. Of this water, some evaporates and some drains into the Kafue river and so the sea. However, a large percentage of it percolates below ground, where it lodges in certain well defined 'water horizons' immediately above the more impermeable rocks, below which are generally to be found the copper ores.

One may approach this problem from several angles [wrote Dr Bancroft], from each of which one is forced to the conclusion that a very large total volume of water is involved and that safe, efficient and economical mining of the ore-bodies at Nchanga will in very major measure depend on the operation of requisite pumping capacity.[18]

He goes on to analyse the geographical and geological situation. The Nchanga syncline is a structural trough with high ground to the north and south, underlain by comparatively impervious rocks. An area of about twenty-five square miles, plus the fifteen square miles of the syncline itself, discharges its water into that portion of the syncline within which the ore-bodies are located. The rocks of the syncline itself are often so permeable as to permit the underground circulation of large amounts of water.

During the rainy season it is noticeable that much of the rain

[17]According to the Chamber of Mines Year Book for 1959 it contains at present 2,280,000 tons of ore of 4·21 per cent copper.
[18]Memorandum dated 15 October 1931, in Nchanga 'Dewatering' File.

falling on the surrounding higher ground runs down into the Nchanga area and, more important, that the Nchanga stream, which flows lengthwise along the syncline, carries off only a small part of this rainfall.[19] On the assumption that 30 per cent of the rainfall percolates underground, this adds up to the astonishing figure of 24 million gallons a day per year disappearing underground within the Nchanga syncline, most of it during a period of about five months.

No one can say [continues Bancroft] just how much of this water will enter mine workings. As the workings are extended, an increasingly large proportion of this volume will have to be coped with.

When, however, one considers this phase of the problem in conjunction with the permeability of the rocks, one arrives at the conclusion that sufficient water is entering the basin to maintain the steady circulation of an important volume of water through all of the various waterbearing horizons that will be intersected by mining operations, and that eventually, when the workings are sufficiently extended, a major proportion of this volume of water from rainfall will gain access to the mine.[20]

A cross-section of the strata at Nchanga is shown in Fig. 3 (see also Figs. 5 and 8). As will readily be seen, water is fairly universal within the strata concentrating particularly at certain water horizons above impervious layers of rock. A heavy flow of artesian water from some of the drill holes, a very low core recovery through certain groups of strata (having in some places, for example, a consistency of liquid mud) and the universally porous nature of much of the rock indicated plainly not only that the Nchanga syncline contained a large amount of water, but also that at certain levels or horizons the rocks were sufficiently permeable and fissured to permit the ready circulation of water.

For purposes of discussion and commentary, the water-bearing strata may be divided into three groups:

[19]Subsequently, two weirs were installed on this stream to measure the seasonal rise and fall of the flow. Even without these it is plain that the stream cannot account for the substantial rainfall which occurs every year.
[20]In February 1931 Bancroft estimated that at least 15 million gallons per day would have to be handled. By October 1931 he had revised this estimate to a figure very close to the truth—$17\frac{1}{2}$ million gallons per day, an amount which was still being pumped until recently.

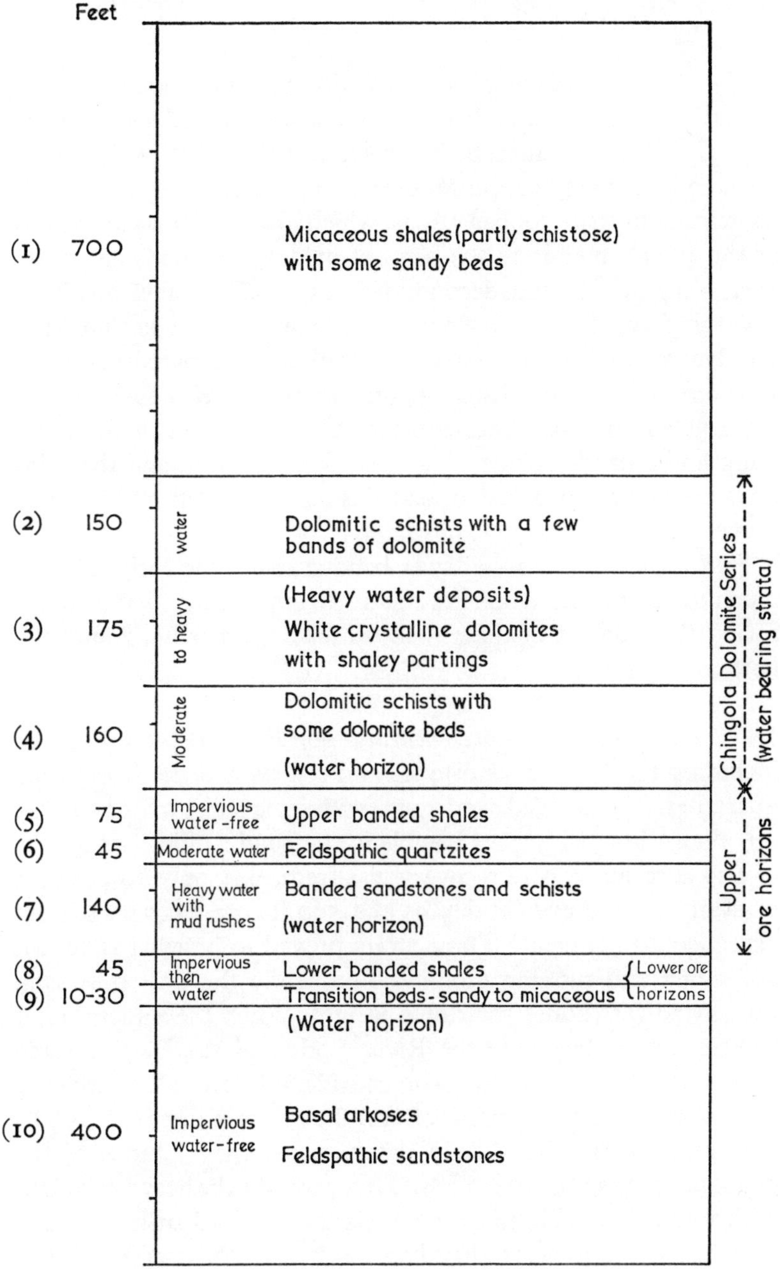

Feet

(1)	700		Micaceous shales (partly schistose) with some sandy beds
(2)	150	water	Dolomitic schists with a few bands of dolomite
(3)	175	to heavy	(Heavy water deposits) White crystalline dolomites with shaley partings
(4)	160	Moderate	Dolomitic schists with some dolomite beds (water horizon)
(5)	75	Impervious water-free	Upper banded shales
(6)	45	Moderate water	Feldspathic quartzites
(7)	140	Heavy water with mud rushes	Banded sandstones and schists (water horizon)
(8)	45	Impervious then	Lower banded shales ⎰ Lower ore
(9)	10–30	water	Transition beds - sandy to micaceous ⎱ horizons
			(Water horizon)
(10)	400	Impervious water-free	Basal arkoses Feldspathic sandstones

Chingola Dolomite Series (water bearing strata)

Upper ore horizons

Fig. 3 Cross-section through the Nchanga syncline, showing strata and water horizons

1. *The footwall water-bearing horizons,* which include the top of the arkose, the transition beds and the lower banded shales (10-8 Fig. 3). These transition beds, twelve to fifteen feet in thickness, form an important horizon for circulating water. They frequently contain high-grade copper values, which also are found at the top of the arkose, mainly in the form of oxides. The beds are, however, very porous and decomposed, except for a few relatively small impervious patches where the copper is found as sulphides. Dr Bancroft, when discussing these points,[21] compared these impervious patches to islands within an ocean. However, in the more general porous areas considerable thicknesses of the overlying lower banded shales have also been oxidised and the minerals leached out in solution. Cavities have been left which are so numerous that water circulates freely.

Further up through the lower banded shales the rocks become much less mineralised and are relatively impervious. Water therefore gathers on top of these rocks to form a water horizon at the bottom of group 2.

2. *The intermediate water-bearing horizons* (7-5 on Fig. 3), including the banded sandstones and schists and the feldspathic quartzites. The banded sandstone (with its layer of mica half-way up) almost invariably gave trouble in diamond drilling. At depths of 600 ft or more, core recovery was frequently only 10 per cent or even less, and even at depths of 1,500 ft core recovery seldom exceeded 20 per cent.[22] These strata proved to be what is known as 'caving and running ground'. Frequently the drill rods sank for several feet under their own weight. When the underground workings were begun in the River Lode and the Dambo Lode it was these beds which gave considerable trouble there and necessitated the abandoning of No. 8 shaft at a depth of 256 ft. The realities of mining fully substantiated the evidence of the diamond drilling in these beds. They proved to be heavily charged with water and liable to develop spasmodic 'mud-rushes'. When Bancroft wrote in 1931 they had not been fully penetrated, but

[21]Memo dated 27 October 1931, in Nchanga 'Dewatering' file.
[22]Ibid.

even then it was evident that their presence immediately above the ore-bearing lower banded shale would constitute a serious handicap to mining at Nchanga. Bancroft was adamant[23] that they would have to be fully drained before economical and safe mining could be carried out, and warned that it was quite probable that they would have to be drilled and pumped before they discharged all their water. On the other hand, the feldspathic quartzites are much less heavily water-charged and present no mining difficulty.

3. *The Chingola dolomite series: hanging wall water-bearing horizons* (4–2 on Fig. 3). Resting directly upon the upper banded shales is a group of beds approximately fifteen to twenty-five feet thick so decomposed that the core recovery from them was actually nil in places. This is an important water-bearing horizon. Immediately above is the group of dolomitic schists, also heavily charged with water. Here too the drills often sank under their own weight. The middle part of some 175 ft thickness of the dolomite series, the white, shaly dolomites, is overlaid with sandy dolomites so decomposed that they may be described as 'running sands'. The rock is honeycombed with fissures and much artesian water was found there while drilling.

When Dr Bancroft opposed the sinking of No. 2 shaft—which was in fact stopped at 292 ft—he did so on the basis of his knowledge of the precarious state of this part of the Chingola dolomite series. A Layne & Bowler pump, introduced into a nearby drillhole of 14 in. diameter, where it pierced the water-bearing horizon, had been used to pump 1,440,000 gallons a day from the area continuously from March 1931 to 5 October, when it was finally withdrawn. During these seven months the pump made no appreciable impression on the water level in the hole, although it did cause the artesian flow to cease at another hole, $1\frac{3}{4}$ miles to the eastward. This, of course, was a most unsatisfactory feature, implying as it did that the water-bearing horizons were interconnected over a wide area. The micaceous shales above the Chingola dolomite series also contain considerable water, although not to the same extent as the beds below.

[23]Ibid.

Throughout the syncline, therefore, considerable water would be encountered in a well defined area. This known hazard, however, did not indicate the real danger which was ever present, namely that at some point, whilst apparently working in perfect safety, the minners might pierce an unknown cavity connecting one water horizon with another. Such cavities undoubtedly existed, and the puncture of one of them would result immediately in a gush of water—a flood which could have deadly consequences. Great care would be necessary to ensure that before any development took place pilot holes were pushed forward to make certain that the ground was safe.

The earliest development on the River Lode was mainly exploratory, four shafts being sunk to the 50 ft level in the orebody. The technique was, of course, very primitive, being simply a version of the prospect pitting already described (page 55). The shafts, each measuring 8 ft × 6 ft, were dug by hand, the earth being removed in buckets by means of a simple windlass at the top. As the shafts deepened, so they were 'timbered'—lined with round timber props each six inches in diameter. This timbering was a masterpiece of precision work which has scarcely been equalled even at the present time. All the materials, both for lining the shafts and for the construction of the windlasses, were hacked from the surrounding bush.

At the 50 ft level the workings were extended to join up the four shafts. At intervals of 125 ft exploratory cross-cuts were driven into the ore-body and samples removed for analysis. The first three shafts were then sunk further, down to 150 ft, with similar connections between each, and the same exploratory cross-cuts as before. Water difficulties were encountered and, with the likelihood of more profitable development being available further to the west in the Dambo Lode, the workings were abandoned.

A further vertical shaft, River Lode No 8, was started towards the end of 1926. This too was abandoned in May 1927 at a depth of 256 ft. Having passed through the feldspathic quartzite it penetrated heavily water-laden running ground at about 225 ft. This running ground was the same mica schists in the banded sandstone as were also to give trouble in the Dambo Lode incline shafts.

Soon after No. 8 shaft was abandoned a further attempt to develop the ore-body was made. Another vertical shaft—River Lode No. 9[24]—was begun in the footwall arkose, where good, firm rocks could be expected. This indeed proved to be the case, and the shaft was rapidly sunk to the 300 ft level, when a cross-cut was extended southwards to the ore-body. This was explored for a total length of 1,500 ft, with further cross-cuts at intervals of 125 ft as before. From the faces of some of these cross-cuts, horizontal drill holes were inserted to a maximum depth of 160 ft, again with regular samples being taken for assay.

The strata here proved to be complicated. They are almost vertical, with considerable crumpling along both the strike and the dip. The lower banded shale is generally distinctive but has occasionally changed to mica schists as a result of the folding processes. Further, before the footwall arkose is gained there is also a band of conglomerate some seven to eight feet thick.[25]

The shaly schistose beds below the conglomerate were found to be slightly water-bearing. Locally also, especially in the crumpled areas, the lower banded shales were also water-laden. It was, however, the hanging wall beds—banded sandstones and schists—which proved to contain very large quantities of water. These beds had already been shown to be treacherous, running ground during the previous work on the levels above (River Lode shafts 1–4). In general, therefore, it was decided to stop developing the cross-cuts into the hanging wall before these beds were reached. It would not be possible to work these beds before they had been drained.[26]

During the course of this work on the 300 ft level the miners encountered two fissures, or water courses, which clearly demonstrated the correctness of Bancroft's theory that these features can

[24]This was a three-compartment shaft measuring approximately 19 ft × 10 ft.
[25]For a full account, see Dr Bancroft's memorandum dated 28 October 1931 in the Anglo-American Corporation files.
[26]Bancroft estimated that a minimum of 3 million gallons per day would have to be pumped when this was done; op. cit.

and do traverse shaly and schistose rocks, permitting the ready circulation of water. One of them, towards the western end of the workings, caused the ground to cave and forced a deviation in the progress of the workings.

Early in 1929 almost a million gallons of water a day were being pumped from River Lode No. 9 shaft. At this stage, the workings on the 300 ft level were sealed off with a watertight door. The shaft was continued during April and May 1929 to a depth of 614 ft, with further workings extended from it. Although no serious trouble from water was encountered in the shaft itself, the leakage through the watertight door amounted to no less than 1,500 gallons an hour. Then, with the discovery of the extremely rich Nchanga West ore-body, the workings were abandoned indefinitely and the shaft allowed to flood.

The miners moved on; the water crept up until it was only a hundred feet from the top of the shaft. The headgear deteriorated, uncared for. Only the mine farm flourished, irrigated by water from the shaft. Rust and decay prevailed. Termites destroyed the woodwork, the fierce vegetation of the tropics smothered the surface equipment. For more than a quarter of a century the mine lay neglected.

Salvation for No. 9 shaft did not come until 1957, when the company determined to reclaim the shaft and re-sample the ore-body in order to gain an accurate picture of the quantity and value of the ore reserves in the area. Pumps were installed and the shaft emptied to the 300 ft level, new timbering being inserted as the work progressed. A pump station was established at this level, and for the first time in thirty years the watertight door was opened. The timber had been well preserved under the water. In fact, to everyone's astonishment, the materials previously abandoned underground all proved to be in remarkably good condition.

Greatly encouraged, the miners now hastened to reclaim the remainder of the shaft, setting up another pump station on the 600 ft level. Towards the end of 1959 all was ready: the miners began to drive in a southerly direction towards the ore-body, which was reached after about five hundred feet. Two drives east and west, each measuring 8 ft × 8 ft, were now extended into the ore-body. The east face collapsed in February 1960, owing to bad ground, and had to be abandoned. It was replaced by a similar tunnel nearer to the south cross-cut, the venture this time being successful. By September 1960 the west drive had been lengthened because of the extremely unstable nature of the strata originally traversed. Diamond drill holes were being inserted at regular intervals to provide specimens for sampling.

Thirty-three men,[27] including twenty-two Africans, were then involved in the enterprise, which came under the same management as the Nchanga open pit. 'Wilkie's Lonely Mine',[28] as the notice at the gate proclaimed it, seemed to have a most interesting future.

The Dambo Lode

During the investigations into the River Lode, Raymond Brooks had pursued his drilling programme farther to the west to discover the richer Dambo Lode, which undeniably demanded further attention.

Although the first three drill holes put down on the Dambo Lode were disappointing, the fourth was far more satisfactory. After Collier had disregarded[29] Horner's instructions to stop the hole at a depth of 480 ft, a belt of sulphide ore averaging 5·2 per cent copper was intersected between depths of 575 and 650 ft. This discovery late in 1925 was claimed by Brooks to be the first major discovery of sulphide copper in Northern Rhodesia and the stimulus which led to searches at Roan and Mufulira by R. J. Parker.[30] It should be pointed out, though, that although this discovery of sulphide ore may have been the first of commercial value in Northern Rhodesia, the inference that Parker was in-

[27] An account of their work appears in the *Nchanga News*, 2 September 1960.
[28] Named after Mr Neil Wilkie, then Open Pit Manager. In fact subsequent decisions have recently (1969) been taken to develop the River Lode as another open pit.
[29] According to R. Brooks, 'How the Rhodesian coppers were found' *Northern Rhodesia Journal*, vol. 1 No. 2, 1950.
[30] Ibid.

fluenced by it in his own investigations has been hotly denied by Parker himself, whose own view of the direction of Rhodesian Congo Border Concession by Horner was not complimentary.[31]

As a supplement to the drilling of the Dambo Lode, two incline shafts, Nos. 1 and 2, were begun in 1926 and sunk roughly parallel to the footwall of the ore-body, with inclines of 22° and 25°, to depths of 682 ft and 740 ft respectively. Having reached a depth of 600 ft—equivalent to 250 ft of vertical depth —a 'drift' was extended within the lode for a length of 1,200 ft and four cross-cuts were inserted north to south. Although most of this development was within the feldspathic quartzites, the overlying upper banded shales were also explored by the cross-cuts for a horizontal distance of 75 ft—a true width of about 25 ft—and the underlying banded sandstones and schists for a horizontal distance of about 100 ft—a true width of about 35 ft.

The upper banded shales proved to be generally impervious. Nevertheless, they were traversed by joint planes, from some of which water dripped continuously. Further water was also found in certain areas of the feldspathic quartzites, but not in any important quantities.[32] On the other hand, the banded sandstones and schists were found to be treacherous, water-laden ground, especially in the strata containing mica, where mud-rushes occasionally developed. On several occasions a temporary decrease in the flow of water from a face for a few hours was followed by a rush of mud and water which would quickly flood the workings to a depth of four or five feet, in spite of the use of all available pumping power. During one of these mud-rushes in April 1928 no less than a hundred tons of mud was washed in this way from the beds of mica schist.

The Nchanga West workings
Encouraged by the successful results of the work undertaken in the River Lode and Dambo Lode areas, Brooks continued to ex-

[31]For Parker's views on his own and Horner's work, see his letter to D'Eath dated 2 September 1949 in the Rhodesian Selection Trust archives.
[32]For a fuller account, see Dr Bancroft's memorandum on the subject dated 28 October 1931.

Plate 5 (a) Shafts on the River Lode, Nchanga, 1927. *Photo: J. C. Ferguson, courtesy National Archives of Rhodesia and Nyasaland*

Plate 5 (b) No. 2 incline shaft, Nchanga, 1926. *Photo: J. C. Ferguson, courtesy National Archives of Rhodesia and Nyasaland*

Plate 6 No. 2 incline shaft, Nchanga, 1927. *Photo : C. W. Scrymgeour*

pand his drilling programme in the area.[33] Six further holes to the west proved barren, but the seventh, NE 5,[34] just touched the edge of what is now known as the Nchanga West ore-body. One of the richest copper ore deposits in the world had been discovered.

Previous to this drilling programme the 'New Discovery' area had been surveyed electrically in 1926 by the equipotential line method (see Appendix II) by a party consisting of J. C. Ferguson and S. H. Shaw. A weak indication was received in the area, but potholes and a 70 ft shaft sunk on it failed to reveal anything. Broughton Edge, who was in charge of the electrical prospecting for Minerals Separation Ltd, wanted to put down a drill hole on the site, but was prevented by financial stringencies. This decision not to drill probably robbed Edge of a resounding success.[35]

During the early stages of the drilling of NE 5 nothing of particular interest was expected from the hole. The purpose of the drilling to the west of the Dambo Lode was to investigate the possibility that the continuation of the feldspathic quartzites, in which the Dambo Lode lay, might be found to contain copper further west also. Since ore was never found in the Dambo Lode below the banded sandstones and schists, it was customary for all holes to be stopped once they had reached the lower banded shale horizon, which provided a convenient and easily recognised indicator. NE 5, together with all the other holes between it and the Dambo Lode, passed right down through the Dambo Lode beds without intersecting any copper. But, unlike the others, NE 5 was not immediately stopped once it had entered the lower banded shale. The 'core catchers', N. M. Airey and A. J. Liebenberg,[36] reported the mistake to A. Royden Harrison, but they and the

[33]To the disgust of a further prospector, C. G. A. Jackson, who was denied the money and equipment to carry out a programme of drilling of his own discovery in the Chiwempala area, three and a half miles south of Chingola. See his report dated 7 June 1929 in the Nchanga files.
[34]The NE (Nchanga Extension) holes were on Rhodesian Congo Border Concession property.
[35]Personal information: the late J. C. Ferguson. Ferguson was the Director of Geological Surveys (Southern Rhodesia) and Dr Shaw is (1963) Director of Colonial Geological Surveys.
[36]I am indebted to these two for first-hand accounts of the proceedings.

drillers continued working for another day or two while, for some inexplicable reason, the orders for Harrison to cease work on it did not arrive. By this time the hole had gone down some twenty feet into the shale to a total depth of 815 ft. The core was extracted as usual and lay for some days before a chance examination of it by one of the geologists in the camp showed the presence of fine particles of bornite. On assay, a value of 6 per cent sulphide copper was found. The excitement was naturally intense, and increased when a further deepening of the hole continued to show excellent sulphide ore in the lower banded shale, with considerable amounts of malachite in the transition beds (sandy micaceous schists) and chalcocite in the arkose below.

It is difficult to over-estimate the significance of this fortuitous discovery.[37] The future of Nchanga was still very much in the balance at this time. The River Lode ore-body on the North Limb, which was being developed from No. 9 shaft, was not particularly impressive—it would certainly not evoke much interest if newly discovered at the present day. Further, the Dambo Lode was badly delineated and difficult to work because of the excessive water encountered. If the drillers of NE 5 had ceased work immediately after the error was discovered and the drill had penetrated the lower banded shale to a depth of only five feet or so, it is probable that the core would have simply been thrown away and not examined at all. Even if it had been examined it would not have impressed, for the copper values greatly increased with depth. It was also the greatest good fortune that the chance examination of the core was made before the drill was dismantled and the casing of the hole removed. Although the core would certainly have yielded its secret in due course anyway, much time would have been wasted and expense incurred in redrilling the hole. Most striking of all, perhaps, is the fact that when all the other holes were deepened in turn, none of them showed any copper values in the lower banded shale or below.

[37] Nchanga legend has it that it was the result of an excess of zeal and/or alcohol on the part of one of the drillers, who exceeded his instructions. It has not been possible to verify this.

An intensive investigation by means of drilling from the surface was now begun. The results were astounding. Dr Bancroft, investigating the area around where Nchanga West No. 1 shaft (see Fig. 4(*a*)) was later to be, estimated by personal sampling that there was approximately 6,300,000 tons of copper ore averaging 17 per cent copper there—an extremely high figure.[38] Later, the Nchanga resident geologist estimated that in the area surrounding Nchanga West Nos. 1 and 2 shafts there were about 50 million tons of high-grade ore to a vertical depth of over 2,200 ft.[39] However, no estimates were made below 1,200 ft because of the financial depression of 1929–32, as only eleven holes were drilled below this level during that time.[40] It required a further twenty-seven holes to delimit the ore-body to the 1,200 ft level. 'In fact,' wrote Bancroft, 'had not the twenty-seven holes been drilled, serious errors would have been involved in the calculation.'[41]

Unknown to any of those concerned, serious error had already crept in. The method used in preparing samples for assay was later found to be faulty, with the result that the quotations given for copper values were actually exaggerated by as much as 13 per cent. In addition, the old records were badly kept and often inaccurate. From August 1931 the estimates had to be revised as follows :

	OLD ESTIMATES		NEW ASSAY RESULT[42]
	Old Nchanga (*River and Dambo lodes*)	*New Nchanga* (*Nchanga and West*)	
Sulphides	6·4% Cu.	6·0%	5·6%
Oxides	25·25%	26·0%	21·4%

[38]Quoted in the Gilchrist report, January 1933.

[39]Memorandum dated 12 September 1931.

[40]Wheeler (manager of Rhokana area) to managing director, Nchanga Consolidated Copper Mines Ltd, London, ref. J.L.32.A/46, dated 24 June 1946.

[41]Quoted in above letter. Wheeler himself believed that good ore would be found at greater depths when the necessary drilling capacity was available.

[42]See memorandum on Nchanga West mine by Gilchrist dated January 1933, in Nchanga 'Mining' file.

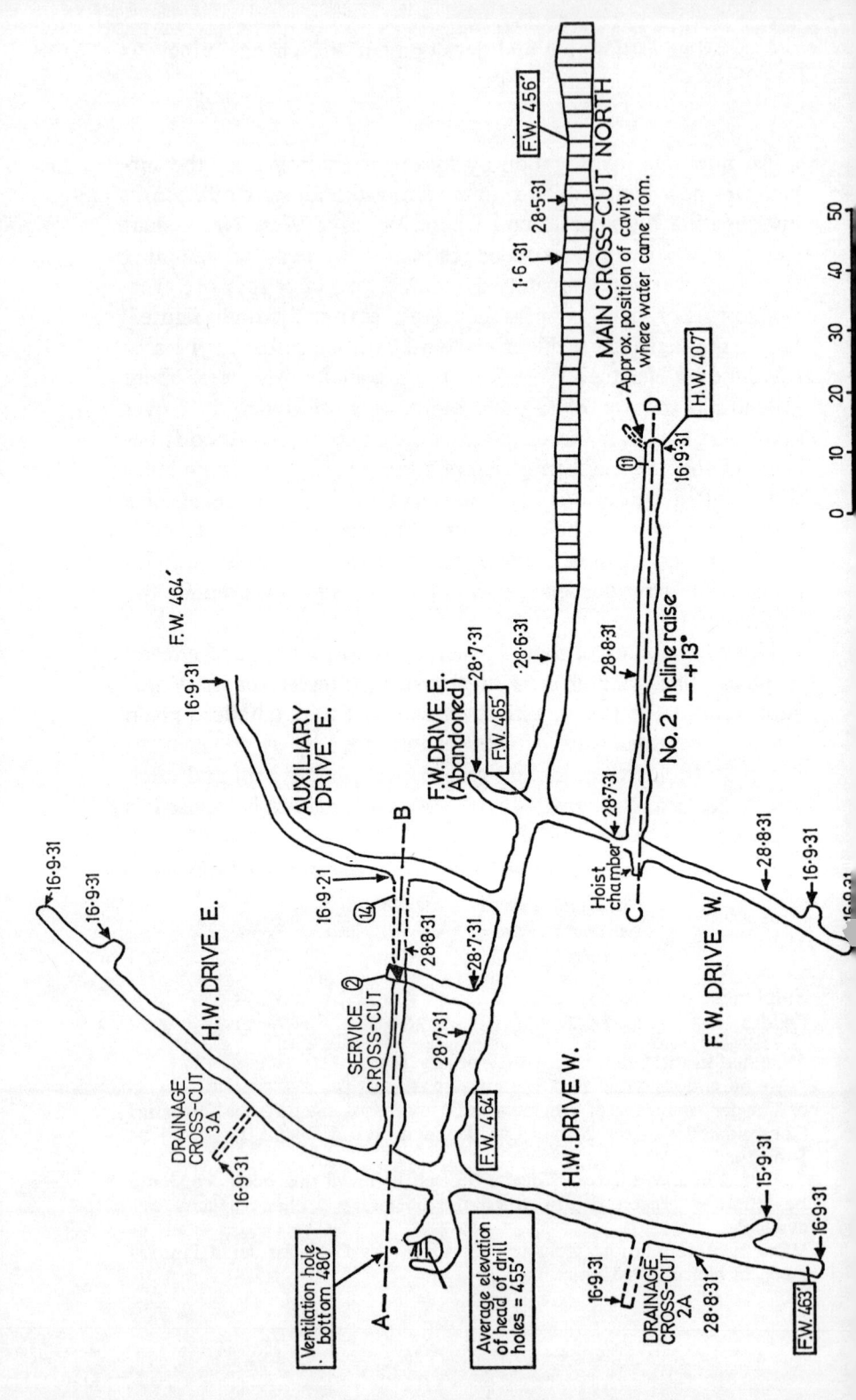

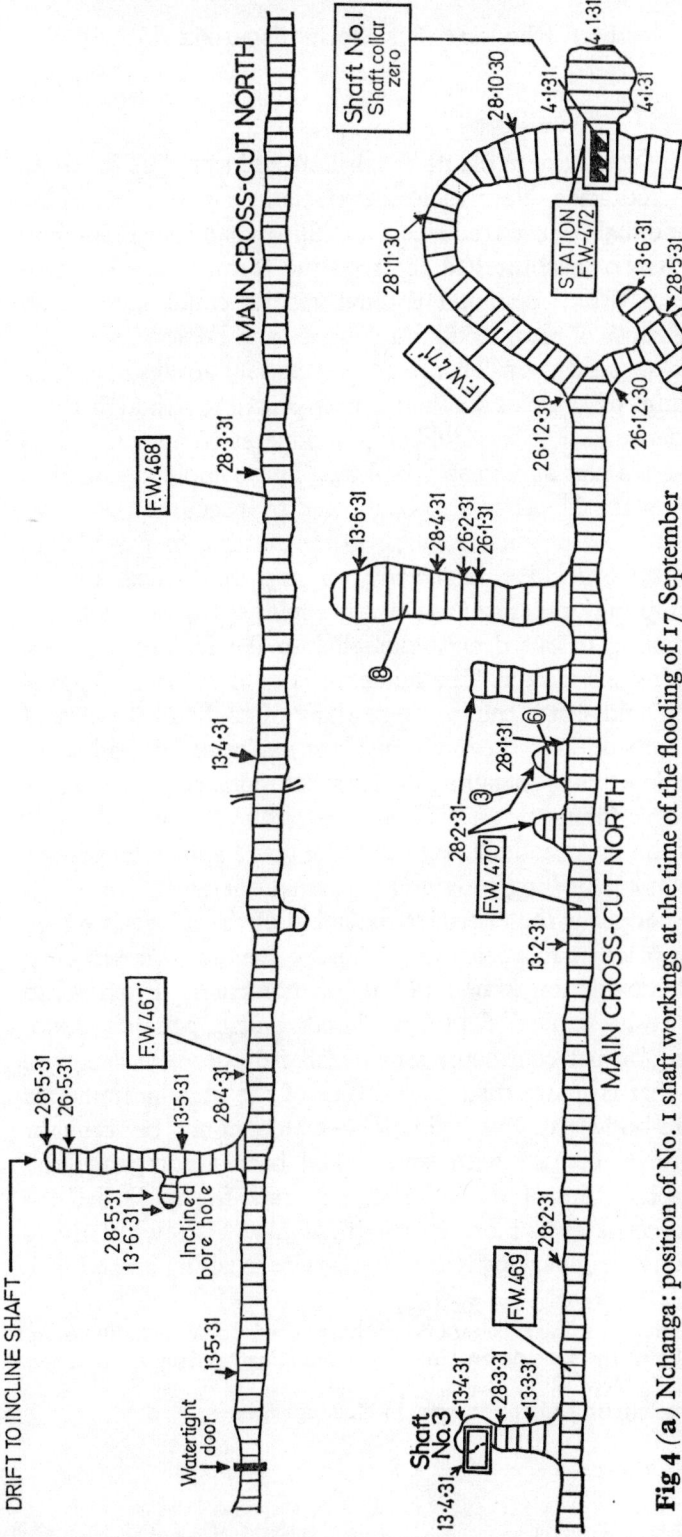

Fig 4 (a) Nchanga: position of No. 1 shaft workings at the time of the flooding of 17 September 1931 (from original survey plan in Nchanga files). Elevations are referred to No. 1 shaft collar = 0 ft. The main cross-cut lies on the 480 ft. level. The footwall of the ore-body was struck at the footwall drives. It was intended to hoist the ore to the surface in cages. Points 3, 6 and 8 (encircled figures) refer to the criticisms as regards pumping made by Dr Bancroft (see pp. 101 ff.).

It would be very easy to blame the drillers and samplers for these serious inaccuracies. Nevertheless, even though in 1931 a turbine air machine had been introduced for drilling shallower holes, and a petrol-driven machine had replaced the former very cumbersome steam drill,[43] diamond drilling results could still be an unwitting cause of error. Skill, intelligence and honesty, the attributes of a successful driller, are not necessarily always available. The 'salting' of samples was not a new practice, although there is no evidence that it was deliberately done at Nchanga, as it is said to have been at Bwana Mkubwa. The complex geological formation of the Nchanga area could lead to inaccuracy, as could the basic laws of physics (relating to the settling of particles in water) and the relative inefficiency of any mechanical device. When sampling underground, error could occur through the sampler failing to cut deeply enough into the face of the rock before taking his sample. The outer surfaces of the rock exposed to blasting and other mining operations often had particles of minerals embedded in them as a result of explosions or had acculated rich deposits of metallic salts from solutions carried in water dripping over them.[44]

One of the most notable features to be made known as a result of the diamond drilling programme carried out on the Nchanga West ore-body was the excessive oxidation of the minerals which had taken place at relatively great depths. Bancroft himself considered this oxidation to be a unique phenomenon.[45] From 2,140 to 2,200 ft in vertical depth, a diamond drill penetrated ore averaging 3·09 per cent copper, of which 1·64 per cent occurred as oxide, that is, more than 50 per cent of the metallic minerals in the ore-body. As this oxidation—which could be brought about only by contact with water—had been accompanied by partial leaching out of the sulphide minerals, the rocks had inevitably become even more permeable. Only in a few relatively small areas, and at varying depths, was there local impermeability

[43]Nchanga geologist's report for 1931.
[44]There is an interesting account of how these effects could be deliberately brought about by speculators in H. P. McKinstry *Mining Geology*, Prentice Hall, New York, 1948.
[45]See memo dated 15 October 1931, in Nchanga files.

resulting in the minerals remaining as sulphides. It was plainly evident, as a result of this drilling, that considerable quantities of water were circulating to great depths almost universally within the ore-body.

By October 1930 Nchanga West No. 1 shaft had been sunk to the 480 ft level and preparations had been made for the tunnelling of the main cross-cut north (see Fig. 4(a)). To speed up the unloading of the trucks of ore and waste, this cross-cut described a circular path below the shaft, so permitting continuous one-way traffic. The tunnel itself, which was 8 ft high by 9 ft wide, together with a ditch, was driven by a drill-column carriage on which were mounted four drifter machines and a scraper slide (devices for tunnelling and removing waste). The average progress through the arkose to the footwall of the ore-body was fifteen feet a day when three shifts were operated. but sank to twelve feet when only two shifts were employed. Much of the cross-cut was timbered. As large quantities of water dripped down from the timber roof, this particular area soon became known amongst the miners as the 'rain-forest'.[46]

The first drive along the footwall was to the east. After about fifteen feet of progress it was found necessary to timber the tunnel, which began to penetrate badly caved ground and to encounter large quantities of water which appeared to come from

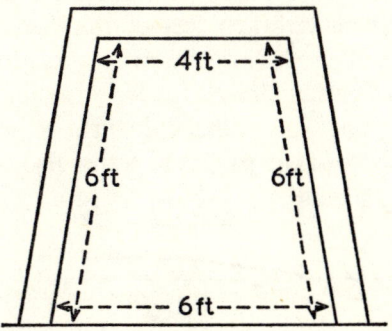

[46]The more usual 'rain-forest' is the area immediately facing the main Victoria Falls near Livingstone. As it is subjected to continual spray from the Falls, the vegetation there is luxuriant.

an underground watercourse. On 28 July 1931, therefore, this drive was abandoned in favour of an attempt to penetrate to the west. This footwall drive west was not exactly rectangular, but was cut and timbered throughout as shown in the diagram. The ground proved to be soft and waterlogged, requiring very little drilling or blasting for progress to be made into the footwall of the ore-body. On the average only four holes per round were used, three in the ore-body as lifters and one shaping hole in the back. As progress continued, a watercourse was encountered which caused the roof to cave in to a height of fifteen feet.

From the footwall drive, No. 2 incline raise, of 8 ft × 6 ft cross-section, was pushed up. No timbering was necessary, for the ground, although soft, held up well provided that the back of the tunnel was arched. Several small streams were struck which all stopped flowing on the morning the large water-fissure mentioned below (page 102) was pierced.

The auxiliary drive east which passed through the transition beds was designed to avoid the caved ground encountered in the footwall drive east. The drive followed the strike of the beds through soft ground, although very little timber was used. Only three or four shot-holes per round were necessary to maintain progress, and in one or two exceptional places the use of ordinary pick-axes was sufficient.

The small drive east to join the service cross-cut passed through the lower banded shales. Ten feet of this had to be timbered where the roof collapsed, but otherwise the ground was good. Similarly, although water flowed freely in the raise to the service cross-cut, the ground was sufficiently firm to offset the use of timber (see Figure 4(b)). A stream of water also ran continuously

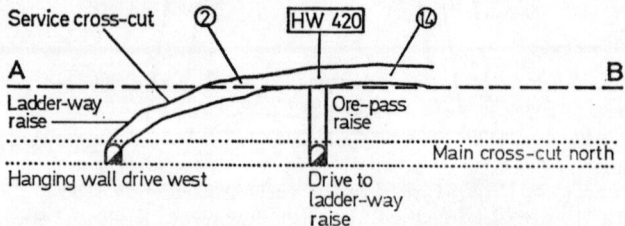

Fig 4 (b) Section through *A–B* on Fig. 4 (*a*)

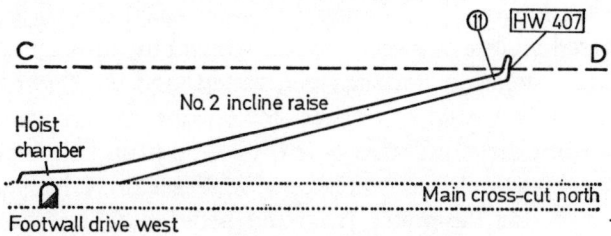

Fig. 4 (c) Section through *C–D* on Fig. 4 (*a*)

from the shale beds penetrated by the service cross-cut. It is interesting to note that a pilot hole drilled upwards from the ladderway raise struck the hanging wall of the lower banded shale only seven feet above the raise. A great quantity of light brown mud flowed from this hole, to be followed, after it had cleared, by a continuous stream of water.

On the other hand, the hanging wall drives, east and west, were completely safe. The west drive was timbered in parts where it widened to almost eighteen feet, but only a small amount of water came through. The east drive was practically dry throughout its length.[47]

The Nchanga disaster

Steadily the work at Nchanga proceeded. The hanging wall drives, east and west, made good progress. The initial flow of water had been small, because the cross-cut had intersected a small area of relatively impervious rocks, but as the drives were extended the rate of flow increased appreciably. Only No. 2 raise appeared comparatively dry, although even here further water was expected higher up, where less impervious rocks were known to exist.

The ventilation hole drilled nearby (see Fig. 4(*a*)) started below soil level in decomposed calcareous strata representing the basal beds of the Chingola dolomite series, and at a depth of about 150 ft passed into upper banded shales followed by felds-pathic quartzites, banded sandstones and schists, and the lower banded shales. When the miners tried to locate this hole from

[47]Information originally supplied by A. R. Harrison.

underground by means of numerous horizontal drill holes they encountered a large volume of water which obviously came from all the water-bearing horizons penetrated, and chiefly from the top of the feldspathic quartzites downwards. When water was pumped from the ventilation hole it became plain that there was a direct connection with water-bearing strata in Nchanga West No. 3 shaft, for the water from the beds overlying the lower banded shales ceased to flow.[48]

There were at the foot of Nchanga West No. 1 shaft five pumps giving a total pumping capacity of 2,500 gallons a minute, or 3,600,000 gallons per day. A further safeguard in the form of a watertight door had been placed in the cross-cut. As the mine was generally believed to be safe, at least by the rank and file, there was much speculation amongst the miners regarding the purpose of this door, which lay between the workings and the pumps. The atmosphere was light-hearted and even the meagre precautions which had been taken were ridiculed as being quite unnecessary.[49] Nevertheless, the geological staff, who were more aware of the potential danger, kept a wary eye on the water situation. On the orders of the manager, G. C. R. Stewart, a shot-drill hole was put down from the surface to intersect the 470 ft level horizon near the end of the cross-cut from No. 1 shaft and a daily check kept on the water level in it.

At 1 a.m. on the morning of 17 September 1931 No. 2 raise had been blasted in readiness for the day shift coming on duty, after which a small cavity near the left hand corner of the raise was seen to be releasing yellow mud but no water.[50] By 9.45 a.m., when the raise was inspected, the flow had increased to about 200 gallons a minute, the cavity being now about fifteen feet long and two and a half feet wide (see Fig. 4(d)). That morning shaft No. 3 was dry, indicating a direct communication between that shaft

[48]For a full account, see Dr Bancroft's memo dated 30 October 1931, in Nchanga 'Dewatering' file.
[49]Only two men—Guy Spires and Bill Mullins, both then in senior posts —remained at Nchanga in 1965 from the staff of 1931. Their accounts are remarkably similar.
[50]This was seen by N. M. Airey, who reported it when going off shift at 7.30 a.m. Personal information.

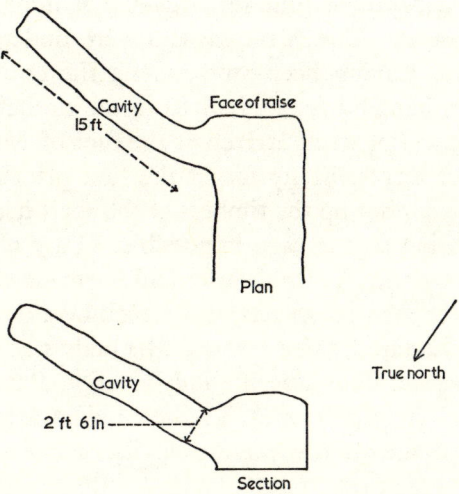

Fig. 4 (d) Sketch plan and section of the face of No. 2 incline raise, with approximate position of cavity

and the top of No. 2 raise. Only ten minutes after the two European inspectors had left, the cavity suddenly collapsed, releasing over two million gallons of water in less than an hour. 'In my opinion,' wrote Bancroft, [51] 'the cavity was being enlarged and carried further into the wall by the flow of water, which, gnawing headwards, suddenly tapped some fissure which probably interlaced at least those water-bearing horizons below the upper banded shales . Apparently the barrier between the top of the cavity and this fissure was broken down within ten minutes after the two white men left the raise.'

Fortunately, there was no 'mud-rush' in the sense of the rushes of mud and water previously encountered in the two incline shafts. If there had been, it is unlikely that any of those near the workings could have escaped. Nevertheless, the effect was awe-inspiring. A tidal wave flooded down the cross-cut and into the side drives, carrying all before it. Although all the workmen, including the 123 Africans who were on shift, managed to pass through the watertight door, silt and mud had already piled up

[51]Memo dated 30 October 1931.

against it to a depth of four feet, making it impossible for the miners to close it.[52] The Africans who were underground generally panicked. Having been swept along the cross-cuts by the flow of water, hanging for their lives to the timber props lining the passage, most of them arrived at the foot of No. 1 shaft in a state of abject terror. Many forgot the first principles of safety and began to clamber up the timbers of the shaft itself, so rendering the operation of the cage impossible. Many of these finally fought their way to the ladderway and so reached the surface, but one, slower than the others, was struck by a descending cage and fell into the rapidly rising water. His body was not recovered for several weeks. This was the only fatality. But for the cool-headedness of the cage tender, V. Corser, who delayed until the last possible moment, many more similar accidents must have occurred.

On the other hand, instances of African bravery took place. A European who had lost his helmet was given one by an African immediately before he set off up the ladders to safety. A falling wrench struck him and, even with the helmet on, caused him to require two stitches in a head wound. Without the helmet he must have died.[53] Haste was essential. All the underground workings were flooded and the water had risen over four hundred feet up No. 1 shaft in only thirty-five minutes. That no more lives were lost was a miracle, the credit for which certainly did not lie with the responsible authorities.

It is a reasonable supposition that in every organised mine or other industry, adequate precautions are taken and safeguards instituted to ensure that the normal danger inherent in the work is either obviated entirely or at least reduced to a minimum. There is no evidence to suggest that this was not done at Nchanga. There was, however, always present the danger referred to previously—namely, that the workings would intersect a water-filled fissure which would cause a flood. This was well

[52]Those who risked their lives trying to do so included Messrs Harrison and Botha.
[53]It is pleasing to note that the African was well rewarded later by his grateful colleague.

known to Dr Bancroft and his immediate staff. Shortly before the disaster, the resident geologist at Nchanga—Ellis—had informed Guy Spires in private conversation that the one watertight door in existence was completely inadequate in the event of flooding and that a minimum of three were necessary.[54] It is inconceivable that if he believed that there was a serious risk of flooding he would not have urged the manager to take such further pre-cautions as were necessary. Nevertheles, Stewart had also stated publicly at a 'sundowner' party a fortnight before the flood that the danger from water underground was negligible and that even one watertight door was a luxury![55] This was after Bancroft had mentioned the possibility of a fissure being encountered to Ellis on 29 August. Bancroft himself states, however,[56] that he care-fully avoided being an alarmist, and it is possible that Ellis, and therefore Stewart, was not made fully to realise the gravity of the situation. However, in view of the fact that Stewart had already instituted a daily check of the water level and had arranged to install a Layne & Bowler pump from Mufulira, which he hoped, might be placed in a watertight compartment, it is fairly certain that he appreciated the risks his men were running.

The mine captain, Tyack,[57] was not informed of the danger under which he and his men were working until 13 September, and the manager, Stewart, did not hear Bancroft's views until 16 September, the day before the tragedy.[58] Even then he was able to reassure Dr Bancroft by informing him that as a prepara-tion for the forthcoming draining of the ventilation hole he had obtained from Mufulira a large pump of 2,000 gallons per minute

[54]Personal information: G. Spires. This argument is clearly illogical since if one watertight door is going to fail under a given pressure then others in series will also fail in turn. It would appear that Ellis' words were either misinterpreted or distorted by the passage of time.
[55]Personal information: G. Spires.
[56]Memo dated 31 October 1931.
[57]Bancroft (op. cit., page 138) also notes that Steve Tyack was informed verbally by himself of the danger—but does not explain why he said nothing either to Dan Buttner, the underground manager, or, as the consulting geologist would normally do, report direct to Stewart, the manager.
[58]Bancroft himself admitted this in his memo dated 31 October 1931 (in Nchanga 'Dewatering' file) in which he also quoted Stewart's remarks.

capacity and was proposing to install a further pump of 1,000 gallons per minute capacity within the vent hole. 'I am through with small pump units at Nchanga,' he said—a very different statement from the one allegedly made only a few days previously.

Bancroft himself has stated after the event[59] that he had hoped a pumping capacity of at least 15 million gallons a day would have been installed before any serious removal of the ore was begun. Even this, of course, would have been inadequate to deal with the flow of 2 million gallons an hour which entered the mine. However, this additional pumping capacity would greatly have relieved the situation and the mine might not have been lost. Stewart estimated that when the flood took place about 1,200 gallons were entering the mine each minute from the drill holes penetrating the ventilation hole. When the water had covered the shaft station at the foot of No. 1 shaft it was then rising in the shaft at the rate of eighteen inches a minute. As two raises were also being filled at that moment, the inflow cannot have been less than 4,000 gallons a minute. After the ventilation shaft had been plugged with cement, thus blocking the drill holes, the inflow was soon limited to 2,800 gallons a minute. Pumping indicated that all the water-bearing horizons, at least below the upper banded shales, were now linked. The full pressure of this enormous body of water had entered the mine.

Although Dr Bancroft, the consulting geologist, explained all this at great length in his memorandum of 31 October 1931— written, of course, after the event—he admits that he deliberately omitted the question from his previous memorandum of February of the same year. Nor, in fact did he refer the matter in writing to any of the administrative and engineering staff responsible, although he claimed to have mentioned it many times in conversation. It is interesting to note, too, that in a letter to the consulting engineer of the Rhokana Corporation at Nkana on 5 November 1931,[60] in which he enclosed the memoranda previously referred to, he stated:

[59]Ibid.
[60]An original of the letter is on the Nchanga file. Further copies were sent to Johannesburg, Salisbury and London.

These notes contain some features pertaining to Nchanga that we have discussed but have not placed on record previously because we felt that nothing could be gained in having them so widely distributed that they would become 'common knowledge'.

If we accept that Bancroft feared for the safety of the mine for several months before the disaster, and that both the manager, Stewart, and the resident geologist, Ellis, were aware of his views, as the belated security measures indicate, then even if we discount all casual conversations as invalid evidence, the fact remains that several months elapsed during which no safety precautions designed to meet the specific threat, either by pumping or by sealing-off arrangements, had been instituted. It is easy to conclude that Stewart was careless in not acting to the limits of his own authority. Yet on the other hand, it is difficult to accept that the consulting geologist would deliberately 'play down' an issue involving immediate risk and potential disaster—and there can be no doubt that any major decision, involving, for example, the temporary closing of the mine whilst safety measures were instituted, was clearly the function of the consultants rather than of the local management. Neither before nor after the Nchanga flood was Bancroft's efficiency ever challenged by his employers and, indeed, his reputation continued to grow until his retirement and death.[61] There is no record of the various conversations between Bancroft and the local staff, no indication of any clash of opinion, no evidence of motive. Nevertheless, there were clearly gross errors of judgment in the build-up of the situation leading to the disaster, for which the ultimate responsibility must lie with the consultants. Stewart was not held to blame. He had already built up a brilliant record as a mining engineer, a record which was subsequently enhanced in his later appointment as the assistant general manager of Rhokana Corporation, in which post he was largely responsible for developing the mining techniques used to exploit the Nkana ore-body.

Bancroft reacted quickly to the grim news. Within three weeks

[61]For obituary, see *Transactions* of the Geological Society of South Africa, vol. LXI, 1958.

a memorandum[62] had been circulated to the head offices of the Anglo-American, Rhokana and British South Africa companies setting out his views, offering guidance for the future and stating plainly:

Nchanga is not a property that can be operated on a shoestring. Inadequate pumping installations and insufficient precautions during the progress of work resulted in the flooding of No. 1 shaft. When the present workings are de-watered, there can be no justification in resuming mining under the conditions existing to date.

Continuing, Bancroft asserted that to make mining safe and economical and to gain the profits which the high-grade ore warranted, initial expenditure should be directed towards draining the ore-bearing horizons and the hanging wall formations to the top of the middle portion of the Chingola dolomite series and at least to a depth equivalent to the deepest levels on which ore is being mined at the time, and preferably to one level below. This, he declared, should be done for several reasons:

1   The high-grade ore occurs in ground so badly decomposed that any system of mining involving the leaving of pillars would be a failure.
2   Immediately above the ore-bearing lower banded shales lie the banded sandstones and schists in which mud-rushes occur.
3   There will probably be subsidence and consequent rupturing of overlying strata—which must therefore be dry.
4   Further fissures may be encountered.
5   'To drain the intermediate water-bearing horizons a cross-cut should be extended for a length of 2,000 ft into the hanging wall from the vicinity of the ventilation hole. In driving this cross-cut, diamond drill holes should be progressively fanned out from the face. A watertight door which hinges in the roof in such a manner that it may be dropped quickly should also be installed in this cross-cut.'

[62]Dated 4 November 1931. *Note:* all further references to shafts in this chapter, unless stated otherwise, are for Nchanga West.

Plate 7 (a) Main vertical shaft, Nchanga, 1926. *Photo: J. C. Ferguson, courtesy National Archives of Rhodesia and Nyasaland*

Plate 7 (b) No. 7 shaft, Nchanga, 1927. *Photo: J. C. Ferguson, courtesy National Archives of Rhodesia and Nyasaland*

Plate 8 Shot drill, Nchanga B, 1927. *Photo: J. C. Ferguson, courtesy National Archives of Rhodesia and Nyasaland*

6 There is a possibility that a fissure might be met which would connect the workings with the enormous volume of water in the Chingola dolomite series.

7 '. . . . in future, when the workings are deep and much extended, a volume of water in excess of 15 million to 20 million gallons per day will have to be pumped'.[63]

'No mining methods should be permitted that will bring about any subsidence of hanging wall measures until assurance can be given that the hanging wall measures have been de-watered.'

The rehabilitation of the Nchanga mine

After a number of futile attempts to dewater the flooded workings, culminating in severe damage to the pump, Nchanga mine was abandoned indefinitely. The general economic depression of the early 1930's, coupled with the enormous difficulties apparently facing the company and the much more immediately obvious promise of profit from the Nkana and Mindola deposits, were the main factors influencing this decision. All development, including drilling, had been completely suspended by April 1931 (see page 74).

This, however, was merely the end of the beginning. Gilchrist[64] and others were concerned with the problem of making the mining of the valuable ores an economic proposition, and as the depression slowly lifted so did their dreams become a reality. By 1936 the decision had been taken to go ahead with the development of the property on a much greater scale than ever before and the preliminary work began in November of that year.

On 8 March 1937 Nchanga Consolidated Copper Mines Ltd was floated with a capital of £500,000 in £1 shares to acquire from Rhokana Corporation the mining rights over four areas previously selected by Dr Bancroft. These areas, known as Chingola (including Nchanga West), Nchanga, Kakosa and Mimbula,

[63]The present figure is around 15 million gallons, having previously been as high as 18 million.
[64]The Gilchrist report, January 1933. Copy in Nchanga 'Mining' file.

totalled approximately 38½ square miles in extent.[65] Further prospecting rights over the Chingola extension and Luano were also given by Rhokana Corporation to the new company.

The new board of directors, under the chairmanship of Sir Ernest Oppenheimer, and the local staff, under the management of W. A. Pope, were soon in action. The immediate problem was the dewatering of the old workings, accompanied by the need to provide new shafts, as none of the existing ones would be large enough to handle the greatly increased production which was envisaged.

The scheme for dewatering involved the sinking of two incline shafts measuring 20 ft × 7 ft at an inclination of 15° and at a position about 1,550 ft south of the old No. 1 vertical shaft. These two shafts, together with a new six-compartment vertical shaft known as 'C' shaft, were designed to pass through the footwall strata into the basal arkose and granite at the 480 ft level. The surrounding surface was cleared in case caving occurred, and the plant area moved to the south.

Of the two incline shafts, that known as 'A' shaft was designed for pumping, whilst 'B' shaft was intended for general mining operations. By the end of March 1939, 'A' shaft had reached a vertical depth of 520 ft, at which point a pumping station was established with a capacity of approximately one million gallons per hour. A cross-cut was driven below the old flooded cross-cut and drainage provided to the pump chamber. When all was ready, forty diamond-drill holes were extended under control conditions of high-pressure valves into the old workings. The valves were opened on Christmas day, 1938, the pumps began to operate, and within a week the mine was practically dry. On 2 January 1939 the wall of rock separating the new workings from the old was blasted down and the way lay open.[66]

The question of what was to take place next had been receiving theoretical consideration for some years. As early as 1933 Gil-

[65]At present the company has acquired Special Grants totalling fifty-nine square miles and possesses the surface rights over another nine square miles in addition.
[66]Much of the above is personal information from N. A. Wilkie.

christ had stated[67] that the immediate object after dewatering No. 1 shaft must be the connection between No. 1 and No. 3 shafts (see Fig. 4(*a*)). This, he considered, would present no difficulties, and as the connection would pass through high-grade ore, an immediate source of revenue would be available. After this, three possible schemes presented themselves.

'*A*' scheme (see Fig. 5). By this scheme an incline was to be sunk from the 470 ft level in No. 1 shaft to No. 2 shaft, which was to be continued to depth. Water would be removed through drill holes sunk from the surface near the north-west and north-east corners of the shaft. The largest quantities of water would almost certainly be encountered at the 450 ft level (near the top of the Chingola dolomite series) and from 775 ft to 875 ft in the dolomitic schists, where core recovery had been as low as 11 per cent. Once heavy pumps had been installed, development could proceed in ore below the 470 ft workings, the ore being transferred to the main inclined haulage through cross-cuts and ore passes.

The main incline would then be continued to the bottom of the syncline, where it would be connected by a cross-cut to 'C' shaft, which was envisaged as a large shaft driven to about 2,700 ft in the footwall rocks of the north limb of the syncline.

This scheme brought a pointed comment from G. C. R. Stewart:[68]

The bitter experience of the flooding of No. 1 shaft teaches that every precaution should be taken to prevent, if possible, its recurrence, and all necessary equipment collected and every preparation made to deal with the situation should it arise again in spite of all our precautions . . . I would add that conditions similar to those encountered before the flooding are likely to be met with again, and sudden bursts of large volumes of water must be expected at any time throughout the development of the mine.[69]

[67]The Gilchrist report, January 1933.
[68]Memo on the Gilchrist report, attached thereto.
[69]That this was no false prophecy is shown by a telegram from Nchanga to the consulting engineer, Nairn, dated 18 August 1939, which states that a pilot hole in 'A' shaft had started to liberate 200 gallons per minute. It took four days to seal off this water from 'A' shaft.

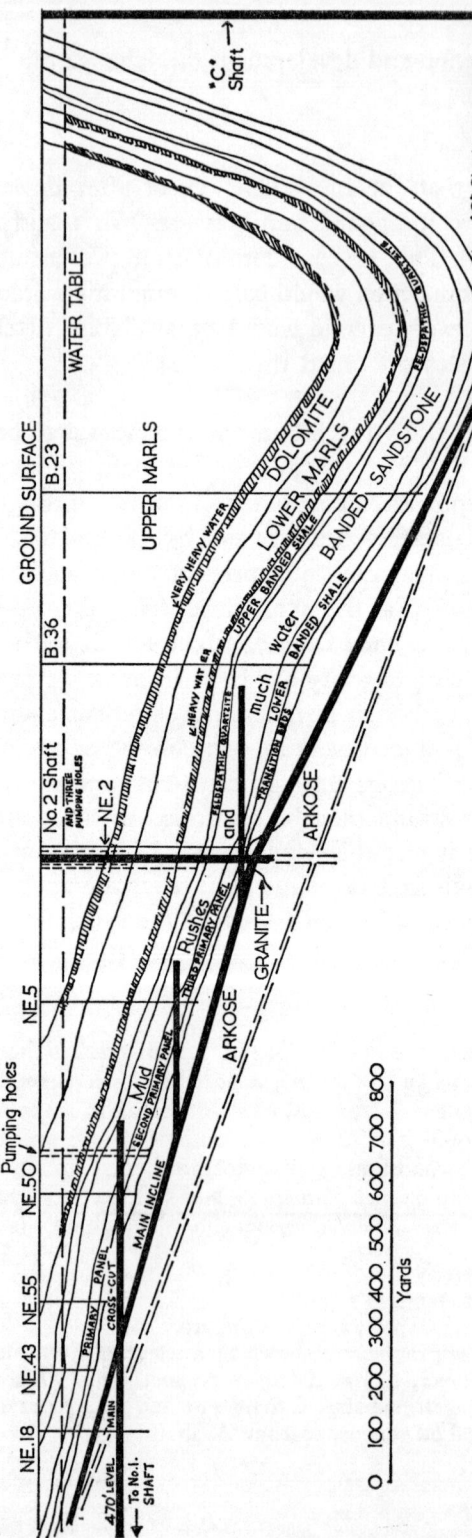

Fig. 5 Scheme A: diagrammatic cross-section (from original diagram dated 18 August 1932, Rhokana Corporation, Nchanga division). Diamond drill holes are shown as (e.g.) NE 18. *Note:* C shaft here is not to be confused with the existing C shaft

Working to the above scheme, Stewart then proposed his own more detailed method of tackling the problem. First, No. 1 shaft should be dewatered with the existing pumps capable of operating at about 3,500 gallons per minute at the 470 ft level. No. 3 shaft should also be drained, sunk to the 470 ft level and equipped with pumps to give a combined capacity with No. 1 shaft of 9 million gallons a day. The water between the two could then be drained and work could be done on the No. 2 inclined raise, raising from the 470 ft level and sinking from No. 3 shaft. 'No further development along the strike of the ore-body should be attempted,' he warned,[70] 'until the hanging-wall water is drained by means of . . . pumps from the surface.' He also criticised the unsatisfactory nature of the watertight doors then in use and suggested that a 'drop' type be installed. Pumping holes from the surface would be drilled as the normal means of dewatering in preparation for development.

With the fitting of the watertight door in the 470 ft level cross-cut completed, it would be possible to start lateral development in the footwall some fifty feet below the ore. Cross-cuts would be developed to join the pump holes, which, after drainage had been completed, could be supplied with fans on the surface and used for ventilation. Each cross-cut would contain a watertight door. After draining the hanging-wall beds, the work of mining the footwall ore could proceed in safety.

The main shaft which was to be sunk in the footwall of the north limb of the syncline would be connected to the incline by a cross-cut of large enough section to act as a reservoir in the event of uncontrolled flooding. This would allow time to close the watertight door of the pump chamber.

This comprehensive scheme, which would decide the final layout of the mine, would require about two and a half years before production could begin.

'B' scheme. As an alternative to the above scheme, it was also suggested that two vertical shafts be sunk between Nos. 2 and 3 shafts with a cross-cut extending northwards from one of them

[70]Comments on Gilchrist report, 1933.

to a pilot drainage hole near the other. This could be done in controlled stages, coupled with the drainage of the surface *dambos* over the syncline by means of ditches. This would also be of value in the anti-malaria campaign.

'C' *scheme*. This was a modification of the 'B' scheme to avoid sinking shafts through the hanging-wall beds. The main shaft should be sunk in the hard, impervious granite of the footwall.[71] Pumping and hauling facilities would be provided at three levels. From two proposed internal shafts, cross-cuts would be extended to the ore-body at intervals of 120–140 ft. The main footwall haulages would be placed below the ore-body some forty feet from it. In all other respects this scheme was similar to 'B'.

From a study of these schemes it is obvious that none of them was perfect. In the 'A' scheme, the linking of the main incline and the cross-cut from the proposed 'C' shaft could only be anticipated in the distant future. Further, the actual siting of the 'C' shaft was not ideal. However, it might be possible to develop No. 2 shaft as the main shaft or even continue the incline to the surface, where it would form the main entrance to the mine.

The 'B' scheme, although it offered fairly quick access to the first and second primary panels[72] and would give more time to solve the mining difficulties below, still involved both shafts passing through the heavily water-charged hanging-wall beds.

'C' scheme would obviate this difficulty by having the new shaft in solid rock near the old No. 1 shaft, which would then be too small to handle the increased production. However, much more cross-cutting would be involved before production could begin. A great advantage in the interests of safety would be that all pumping would take place underground at one large shaft, from which the surplus water could be delivered to the Nchanga

[71]When the main 'C' shaft was begun in May 1937 it struck solid granite at a depth of only 82 ft.
[72]Approx. 17 million tons of ore averaging 7 per cent copper (drilling estimate). *Note :* a later statement by L. A. Allen reviewing the progress of diamond drilling to date reveals that Gilchrist over-estimated the tonnage by 12 per cent—not much, under the circumstances (memo, L. A. Allen, 12 November 1940).

stream well to the north where it left the syncline. It might also be possible to connect this new shaft to the old No. 2 shaft.

The general considerations which would influence the final decision would be dictated largely by the financial position. Although it was reasonable to assume that nothing would transpire during the economic crisis of the early 1930's it was already known that:[73]

1 The main power supply would have to come from Nkana. At an estimated rate of £1,700 per mile, this would cost £60,000.

2 A pilot flotation plant capable of concentrating 500 tons of ore per day would cost £110,000. It would be unwise to exceed this tonnage during the initial few years of operation.

3 Railway rates to Nkana were then at 1s 9d per ton.

4 The concentrating costs added up to approximately 9s per ton plus 25 kWh per ton.

5 Nkana was already producing 8,000 tons per day.

6 If 20 per cent of the ore mined at Nchanga was sent to Nkana for direct smelting two more furnaces costing £300,000 each would be required and in addition the smelting charges would be £1 10s per ton.

7 The capital expenditure involved would be £500,000 (£600,000 if the pilot plant was constructed).

8 The work would take up to three years, with production commencing in under two.

In his report, Gilchrist produced an estimated balance sheet:

	£ per long ton copper
Mining, at 12s 6d per ton ore, including 4s per ton ore pumping etc.	6·95
Concentrating, at 9s per ton ore	5·00
General charge	1·31
	£13·26

[73]These figures are extracted from Nchanga mining files

Smelting	1·50
Royalty (at a price of £50 per ton)	1·00
	£15·76
Railway and Beira charges	5·45
Cost per long ton blister copper at Beira	21·21
Other realisation and general charges	2·60
Cost at market	£23·81

Copper produced per day: 45 long tons
Copper produced per year (45 × 300): 13,500 long tons

Annual profit at £40 per ton: £220,000
Annual profit at £50 per ton: £350,000

In view of this, he concluded that with an estimated capital expenditure of £5,600,000 it seemed that during the early stages of re-opening the Nchanga mine there would be sufficient return on expenditure to enable the mine to be rather more than self-supporting while the final layout of the mine and plant was being carried out.

The development of the modern mine
In practice, the procedure ultimately followed was very similar to the 'C' scheme. Throughout operations, all concerned were pre-occupied with the problem of preventing flooding, with the result that this aspect must loom large in the narrative of what took place.[74] Regardless of the method eventually used to remove the ore, it would be impossible to avoid fracturing the hanging-wall beds, and it was therefore of fundamental importance that these beds be thoroughly drained before mining operations began. Further, as mining continued so had the water level to be lowered progressively to keep pace with the mining development. The only way to do this was by drilling considerable numbers of diamond-drill holes into the porous beds and allowing them to drain under control to the pumps.

[74] Throughout this section reference should be made to Figs. 6 and 7.

The plan involved the driving of cross-cuts from the inclines into the hanging wall until they penetrated the feldspathic quartzites, taking care that they did not penetrate too far into the impervious upper banded shales immediately below the dolomite schists on which the dolomite rests. Any accidental penetration of the water-logged dolomite would have had most unpleasant consequences. When ready, holes were drilled into the dolomite through valves to control the rush of water. The main difficulty lay in preventing these comparatively narrow diameter holes from silting up with mud. Dr Bancroft suggested[75] that this mud should be allowed to drain freely into the cross-cut to avoid silting up the drainage holes. However, this would involve the problem of how to deal with the sudden mud-rushes which would inevitably occur into the cross-cut and probably fill it behind the watertight doors. It would be necessary to withdraw the water, open the watertight door—which should be constructed in two halves, the top opening first—and then dig out the mud. This would undoubtedly involve considerable delays. Further, the scheme would require the provision of substantial supports to prevent the collapse of the cross-cut: not timber, behind which mud could accumulate, but a steel grid embedded in concrete, strong enough to stand up to the shock of blasting. Alternatively, the even slower method of complete cementation, leaving a channel for drainage, would be necessary. The idea of drainage holes being drilled from the surface was not then favoured because they would be extremely difficult to locate from underground and in any case might link up the water reservoirs at different levels.

By the end of March 1939 the pumps were dealing with over 6 million gallons a day. During this time the pumping incline had been extended considerably.[76] It reached a vertical depth of 1,100 ft during 1942, at which depth a pumping chamber was established, from which pumping was steadily increased until,

[75]Mentioned in a letter from R. J. Nairn, consulting engineer, dated 9 September 1939, in Nchanga files.
[76]Under conditions of great safety and elaborate precautions. See memo from mine manager to mine captains and shift bosses dated 8 January 1938.

after pumping ceased at the 500 ft level early in 1947, it eventually reached a total of 18 million gallons a day. Meanwhile, Dr Bancroft was writing[77] to his Nchanga colleague, G. T. Walters:

. . . from the 1,050 ft cross-cut it is planned to drive within the lower banded shales in both directions along the strike and to extend diamond-drill holes at intervals into the hanging wall to drain at least the hanging-wall beds (banded micaceous sandstones with overlying feldspathic quartzites) between the top of the lower banded shales and the bottom of the upper banded shales.

The lower banded shales have an average true thickness of 45–50 ft. Presumably, from the drive within the lower banded shales it is planned to extend short cross-cuts at intervals towards the hanging-wall of these shales, which will just give sufficient room for the diamond-drill holes to be extended towards the upper banded shales. *I very much hope that none of the cross-cuts from which diamond-drilling is to be done will have less than a cover of 15 ft true thickness of the lower banded shales left intact over them.* [Bancroft's italics.] This should afford a reasonably safe barrier through which drilling can be extended into the immediately over-lying more or less soft, muddy banded micaceous sandstones.

Although valuable, the advice was not really necessary, as every possible precaution was already being taken.[78] The general manager was able to enumerate these measures within a few days.[79] The main features of the work on the 1,050 ft level he listed as follows:

1 Pilot holes of 12 ft are drilled before blasting, which does not take place if water flows under pressure from the holes.
2 Diamond-drill holes are drilled through stand pipes and high pressure valves.
3 All diamond-drilling will be done from cross-cuts driven north and south of the main drive. The southern cross-cuts are into quartzite.

[77]Letter dated 1 November 1943.
[78]Memo W. A. Pope, the general manager, dated 6 November 1943.
[79]Letter from W. A. Pope to assistant consulting engineer, Anglo-American, dated 13 November 1943.

4 In the dewatering drives the track is carried on short piers below which is a drain of cross-section 6 ft 8 in × 3 ft 0 in —sufficient to carry all normal water.

5 The survey and geology departments keep a close watch over the area.

'Unless unforeseen difficulties arise,' he was able to claim, 'the work now being undertaken should be carried to a successful conclusion without trouble and at reasonable cost.'[80]

The management's views could then be summarised. No difficulty was anticipated in lowering the water-table in the ore-body itself or in the beds immediately above it. However, it was possible that the water in the dolomite might not be affected by operations in the lower ore-body. It could only be hoped that sufficient fractures existed in the upper banded shales to allow at least some of the dolomite water to drain into the lower beds. Failing this, deliberate puncturing of the upper banded shales would be undertaken from about the 1,050 ft level.

It was considered that caving[81] could safely be started on the 625 ft level irrespective of the level of the water-table in the dolomite, but below that level any mining operations would necessitate attention to this water, as the caving procedure could conceivably fracture the containing rocks, permitting the large volume of dolomite water to enter the workings. It would not, however, be necessary to work out the procedure for draining this water until such a course became necessary. In any case, nothing could be done until the banded sandstones, quartzites and schists had themselves been sufficiently drained to below the level of where the necessary access cross-cuts would have to be placed. Even without considering the dolomite beds, at least 5 million gallons a day would have to be pumped to lower the water-table in the ore-body, and immediately above it, to any great extent.

It was at this stage that the Nchanga geologist, Dr Marais, produced a new scheme to aid dewatering which was given considerable prominence by the acting manager, H. F. Grace, in his

[80]Letter from general manager dated 13 November 1943.
[81]This is explained below in the section on mining techniques.

correspondence with the consulting engineer.[82] According to Dr Marais, one of the main difficulties of drilling up from the 1,050 ft level was that the holes were too long, had to be cased in soft areas and therefore finished up with too small a diameter. Instead of them he proposed that shot-drill holes should be drilled from the surface. These could be spaced as necessary and would have a final diameter of six or eight inches. The depth of the water-table could be controlled by the depth at which these holes were made to intersect the upper banded shales and feldspathic quartzites. This plan would not only reduce the volume of water that would have to be pumped, but would also ensure more regularity in the supply of underground water used on the plant and for domestic purposes. Further, and of even more importance in planning ahead, it would provide a definite indication at any given time of where the water-table actually was.

Marais therefore suggested that an experimental diamond-drill hole should be put down from surface at a point just north of the intersection of the 1,050 ft cross-cut and the 1,050 ft dewatering drive, to reach approximately twenty-five feet above the 1,050 ft level. Then, if there was an increased flow of water, a row of large diameter shot-drill holes should be drilled along the strike in such a position as to intersect the upper banded shales at the point A (on Fig. 6), that is, at a point a little below the position where the most northerly possible fracture plane induced by caving operations on the 760 ft level intersects the upper shales. This would ensure that the water-table was always lowered to a point below that at which the subsidence caused by caving could fracture the retaining rocks and release the water. Later a second row of holes could be drilled to intersect the upper banded shales at B, which would extend the range of operations to the 970 ft level. An important point was that this work did not all have to be done at once, the holes being extended along the strike only as far as was necessary to ensure safe conditions for the workings below. They would never at any time need to extend far beyond the end of the operating sub-haulage, their actual spacing being determined by trial.

[82]In particular, see letter dated 29 September 1944.

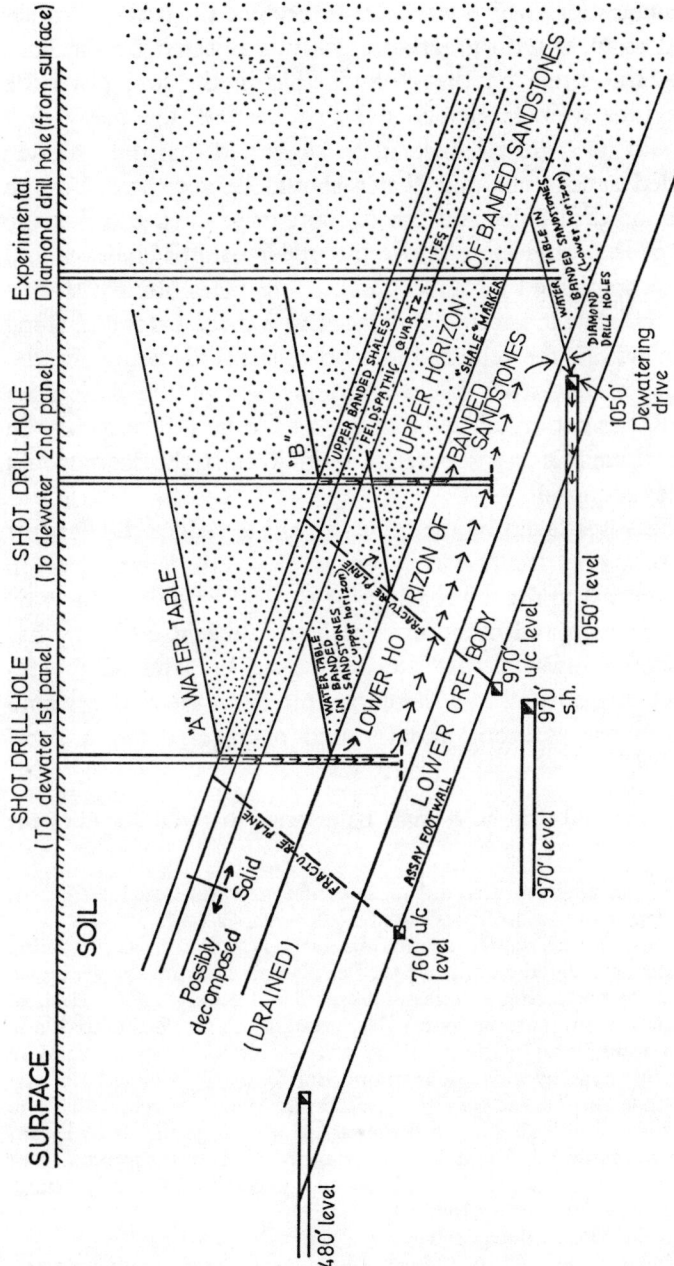

Fig. 6 Diagrammatic section showing the proposed method of dewatering the flooded strata of Nchanga West above the lower banded shale by means of shot-drill holes. (From original in Nchanga files)

This suggestion, which was later to become the accepted practice[83] and to meet with great success[84] was rejected by Dr Bancroft[85], at this time, on the grounds that in the first place the water cavities were lenticular and that, second, too many drill holes would be required. Instead he suggested that the water in the banded sandstones and shales should be removed through underground drill holes and one or more cross-cuts, and that the removal of the water from above the upper banded shales would best be accomplished by underground drill holes fitted with discharge valves, which would be placed in a drive extended along the strike within the feldspathic sandstones. This being the decision, the sooner work could start, in view of the difficulties envisaged, the better.[86] The cross-cut was to be 6 ft × 9 ft with the lower three feet as a concreted drain. Watertight doors would be fitted as required.

The measures taken by the management to reduce the dangers from flooding in the 1,050 ft water cross-cut north were in marked contrast to the approach prior to 1931, and illustrate well the extreme care and attention which the present company has always shown towards the interests of safety. The official requirements were listed in a memorandum from the underground manager to the assistant underground manager dated 4 April 1946:

1 Pilot diamond-drill holes must be inserted to 100 ft ahead of the face.

[83]By a decision taken at a round table conference and noted by W. A. Pope in a letter to the directors dated 24 November 1948.

[84]Memo from acting underground manager, N. A. Wilkie, to acting assistant manager dated 14 June 1950. See also memo from the geologist, McKinnon, to the acting general manager dated 6 July 1953: 'Each of these inflows from surface boreholes brought about substantial and permanent reductions in the dolomite water-table level far in excess of that brought about by any underground holes . . . This experience has indicated that the fastest way to dewater the dolomite reservoir is to drain the crystalline dolomite, and the fastest way to do this is by means of surface boreholes. If these can be extended to drainage points in or near the normal extraction workings, the necessity of costly, time-consuming cross-cutting is obviated.

[85]Letter to Dr Marais dated 4 January 1945.

[86]Consulting engineer, W. A. Odgers, to manager, dated 4 January 1945.

2 If water in quantity or under pressure is struck, further diamond-drill holes must be drilled to effect drainage.

3 If a full bore of water persists and no further holes are possible, the face must be stopped until the water runs off, even if a long period of time is required.

4 Immediately a diamond-drill hole is drilled the water pressure must be taken.

5 The maximum advance must never be less than 40 feet from the the end of the pilot hole.

6 If no water in quantity is encountered:

(a) 8 ft × 15 ft holes shall be drilled for cementation as indicated.

(b) Cement is to be pumped at a pressure of at least 1,000 lbs per sq. in.

(c) After pumping, a 5 ft round, including 2 ft × 12 ft pilot holes, should be drilled and blasted electrically.

(d) During blasting, the watertight door must be closed.

(e) The mine captain must be present during blasting, must verify (d) above, and report any increase in water or mud liberated by the blast.

(f) Before lashing [removing the debris] takes place, the top half of the door must be opened first to allow observations of the conditions behind the door.

(g) The lasher is to be accompanied by an official to examine conditions before lashing is commenced.

(h) All pilot holes and cementation holes must be measured by the shift boss and mine captain, and logged.

(i) The sump under the watertight door must be kept clear, and the door tested at least once a day in the presence of the mine captain.

(j) If the door requires closing, the bottom half must be closed first.

7 This memorandum is to be signed by all those concerned in the operation, the penalty for breaches of the instructions being instant dismissal.

Although no one can deny that such mining as this will always be a difficult and dangerous operation, the measures enumerated above go far towards making it a feasible proposition with a minimum of risk for those actually involved. It is ironical that the labour was largely in vain, for in spite of drilling numerous holes from this cross-cut and carefully keeping them open, the amount of water pumped from the mine during the three months from April to June 1947 showed no material increase.[87] It was this, no doubt, which brought about the decision to try drill holes from the surface.

Despite all precautions, the bottom of 'A' shaft flooded early in December 1949. Although no damage was done, the shock brought forth a severely critical letter from the managing director in London, Mr C. F. S. Taylor,[88] which was firmly dealt with by the general manager, W. A. Pope, in his correspondence with the managing director in Johannesburg.[89] After summarising the difficulties experienced with small diameter diamond-drill holes and the cross-cuts, and noting the successes obtained from them, he continues:

All the ore needed to run the proposed extensions to the plant to the end of 1953 will be obtained. There is sufficient above the 970 ft level to ensure this . . . After 1953 the requisite 300,000 tons per month for the plant can be mined from the Nchanga ore-body from levels above the water-table.

He goes on to comment on Mr Taylor's remark that, concerning the flooding of 'A' shaft, he had 'heard opinions expressed that we were fortunate that the results were not worse'. There was never any danger of flooding vital areas at any time, he declared. The watertight doors on the 1,100 ft level were intended to confine any flooding to 'A' shaft and protect the pump chamber. In fact it was not necessary to close the doors. The capacity of the fixed pumps in the pump chamber was more than adequate to deal with the situation, and although the mobile pumps were unable to cope, the watertight doors existed because of this very possibility. The pumping equipment was always adequately safeguarded by watertight doors, whilst the regular testing of the water-table before any mining operations was a perfectly satis-

[87]Memo from the geologist, McKinnon, to the assistant manager dated 4 July 1947.
[88]Letter L.J.60–A/50, dated 21 April 1950.
[89]Letter M.J.169/50, dated 11 July 1950.

factory method of ensuring that a major flood would not take place.

In any case, Mr Taylor's implied suggestions that there was no real policy regarding the dewatering problem, that opinions differed among the experts and that there was doubt whether future tonnage commitments could safely be met, were all unfair criticisms. The records clearly show that everything done had been the result of the most complete consultation and agreement between the mine management and the consulting engineers, and had followed the basis of a definite policy. Further, this policy was the one initially proposed by Dr Bancroft himself in 1944, although modifications had been made owing to the many unavoidable delays in implementing the original scheme.[90] Dr Bancroft continually urged haste but never complained about the method of approach, which was, fundamentally, his own. There seemed little doubt, at this point, that the future tonnage requirements would be met, provided progress was maintained.

It will be recalled that Dr Bancroft had rejected the idea of shot-drill holes from the surface, for what then appeared to be sound reasons (see page 122). Instead, his intention was to dewater the banded sandstones and schists by drilling through them from the 1,050 ft contour drive. Between this water and the water in the dolomites lie the impervious upper banded shales, in which he proposed to place another contour drive from which it would be possible to drill into and so release the water in the dolomite. However, in order to get into the correct position for this second contour drive, a cross-cut had to pass through the banded sandstones and schists.

It was here that the trouble arose, for these beds were soft in places, contained much water and were subject to mud-rushes. In view of the fact that the 1,050 ft level was the one from which the dewatering of the banded sandstones and schists was to take place, by means of holes drilled steeply upwards, it becomes obvious that the 1,050 ft level cross-cut must pass, throughout its length, through undrained ground. In retrospect it seems unfor-

[90] E.g. wartime difficulties in obtaining such items as drill-hole casing.

10

tunate that such a choice of site for it should have been made.[91] Early in 1945, when it had reached a point about thirty feet below the bottom of the lower water horizon, it encountered a flow which reached 2 million gallons a day, was abandoned and was subsequently used as a drainage point for this water.

It is not certain to what extent the decision not to proceed further with the cross-cut was dictated by necessity, or expedient. However, although technically the work might be possible, the danger was extreme. The ground was so soft in places that drill rods from the surface sank through it under their own weight and the probable water pressure was going to be about 100 lbs per square inch. There would be little opportunity for closing the watertight door if an inrush occurred, and in general the element of chance was too prominent for the attempt to be justified.

In 1947, after work had been suspended for two years, the general manager, W. A. Pope, and the consulting engineer, C. P. Nichols, fully discussed the matter and agreed that notwithstanding the urgency of the dewatering problem they could not risk advancing this face.[92]

As an alternative the decision was taken to attempt drainage of the dolomites by drilling through from the surface to the 1,050 ft contour drive, casing the holes below the upper banded shale. A number of these holes successfully penetrated the workings. The danger, of course, was that previously raised by Dr Bancroft—that a collapse of the casing could release water into the lower water horizon—and it was therefore agreed that any hole which was not apparently producing a normal flow should be immediately plugged at the upper banded shale horizon.

At the same time the process of drilling up from the 1,050 ft contour drive had been continued. The flow from these plus the heavy draw-off from the abandoned cross-cut was lowering the lower water horizon at an appreciable rate. Obviously, if more cross-cuts could be started from the 1,050 ft level to try and get

[91]See comments of C. P. Nichols (consulting engineer) to managing director, Anglo-American, Johannesburg, dated 2 August 1950.
[92]Discussed in a letter from Nichols dated 2 August 1950 to managing director, Johannesburg.

through to the upper banded shales, the process would be considerably accelerated. However, the considerable fall of the water-table already noted suggested to those concerned that if a cross-cut was driven at a higher elevation it might penetrate ground which was already partly drained. This would greatly decrease the probable difficulties of the venture. A cross-cut on the 970 ft level was therefore started. Although this cross-cut did, in fact, encounter water and soft ground, the water was under no great pressure and did not prove an insuperable obstacle. The cross-cut attained its objective; east and west drives were opened, and holes drilled up into the dolomite water. To hasten the completion of the project, large-diameter holes were also put down from the surface, several of which were highly successful, giving a yield of over 2 million gallons a day each.[93]

The fall of the dolomite water-table continued steadily. From mid-1947 to mid-1950 it fell 120 ft in hole M 1, 160 ft in No. 2 borehole, and over 125 ft in M 3, which had dried up by August 1950.[94] It appeared reasonable to suppose that if this reduction was maintained there would be little difficulty in maintaining the water level below the fracture line of the cave. Nevertheless, Nichols sounded a warning:[95]

We wish to repeat our firm opinion that the rate of extraction from the Nchanga West ore-body should be reduced from the 240,000 tons per month required for the Third Stage Expansion as soon as the Nchanga ore-body[96] can be brought into production. The possible maximum fracture line of the beds, when caving to the 1,085 ft level sub-haulage, intersects the upper banded shale at about 680 ft below the surface [the present intersection of the dolomite water horizon and the upper banded shale, over the centre of the workings, is about 420 ft below surface] and while we may reasonably assume from the evidence available that the dolomite water level can be brought below this point at the required date by intensive drainage on the 970 ft level, we do not think it safe to estimate on continued rapid extrac-

[93]Paper by M. W. Rushton and K. E. Mackay, general manager and manager respectively, in the *Journal of the Institution of Mining and Metallurgy*, December 1960.
[94]Figures from Nchanga files.
[95]Letter dated 2 August 1950, op. cit.
[96]Now the 'Open Pit'. This is discussed in a later section.

tion from the Nchanga West ore-body until we are firmly established as regards drainage from the 1,600 ft level pump chamber. Apart from the dewatering aspect, we do not consider it good policy[97] to concentrate all mining on the Nchanga West ore-body, but we have emphasised the dewatering aspect here to make it clear that it is not only policy that has to be considered.

He then goes on to concur with the general manager's comments on the critical letter from London:[98]

. . . we would also point out that criticism of the loss of the face of a shaft, sunk under the conditions in 'A', or of the consequence of this loss, can only be justifiable if it can be shown that there were precautions that could have been taken and were not taken. In this connection we feel it right to remind London that Nchanga have sunk many thousands of feet of shaft and driven a considerable distance of dewatering developments under extremely difficult conditions. The 970 ft cross-cut in particular called for a considerable degree of skill and judgment.

We trust that we have made it clear that the mine management and ourselves are giving the problem all the attention it deserves.[99]

By mid-1953 the position was becoming relatively clear.[100] The dolomite water problem was virtually solved, and the question of the water in the banded sandstones and schists and in the arkose was of far more immediate concern. The uppermost reservoirs had been so reduced that caving from the 1,085 ft under-cut could be started, although this was not scheduled to begin until June 1957. This was not the case, though, with the two lowest reservoirs, which were still too high for the work to begin. The main danger was the arkose reservoir, in which the level was still 300 ft above the 1,500 ft main cross-cut. There was a risk that the valley in the basement rocks (see Fig. 7) which had caused the flooding of 'A' shaft could extend to the 1,500 ft main haulage and cause an inflow which might overwhelm the pumping capacity in 'C' shaft unless adequate precautions were taken.

[97]The implications of this are discussed later. See below, pages 160-1.
[98]From C. F. S. Taylor, op. cit.
[99]Dr Bancroft also agreed with these comments; see letter J.L.140–A50, dated 8 August 1950, from the assistant manager, Phillimore, to the managing director, London.
[100]McKinnon to the acting general manager, dated 8 July 1953.

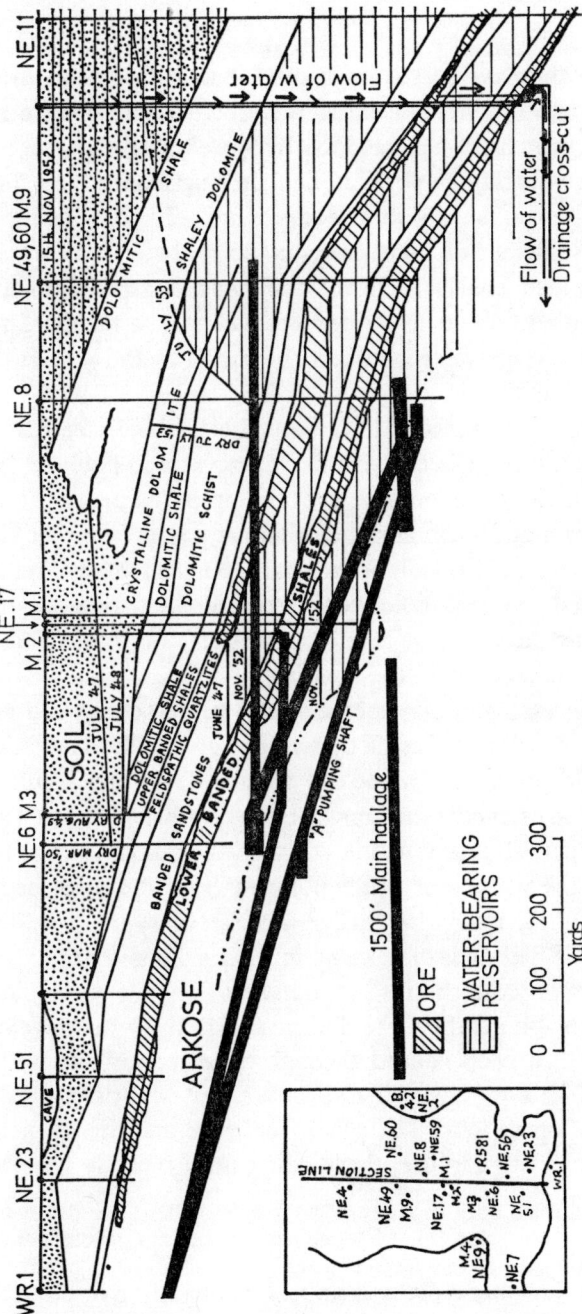

Fig. 7 Nchanga mine: transverse section on the north-south line shown on the key plan, showing the lowering of the water table. (From original in Nchanga files)

*NE 49, NE 60 and M 9 are in approximately the same position when projected stratigraphically on the dolomite beds.

McKinnon then produced a scheme for consideration during future planning. The first essential was obviously to reduce the arkose water, which should be done by developing the 1,550 ft sub-haulage as quickly as possible and drilling from there. This was dependent on the 1,600 ft level pump chamber being in operation.[101] Sufficient of these holes could be extended through the lower banded shales to lower the banded sandstones and schists reservoir to about the 1,050 ft level and so facilitate the mining of a drainage raise between the 1,050 ft and 970 ft de-watering cross-cuts.

In addition, three surface dewatering holes should be drilled to the lower banded shales near the 2,130 ft sub-haulage (see Fig. 6). The centre one would be over the proposed 2,130 ft level dewatering cross-cut north and the others at 500 ft on either side along the strike. Additional holes could be drilled as circum-stances dictated. As each hole would require about nine months to drill, and as the 2,130 ft level sub-haulage was scheduled to start in September 1956, the drilling should not be delayed longer than necessary. This scheme would permit controlled and safe dewatering, with the result that caving of the Nchanga West ore-body could proceed down to the 1,620 ft level under-cut.

The schedule of events may now be brought briefly up to date. Dewatering operations are well in advance of mining, so much so that in 1959 the volume of water pumped from the mine began to decrease, until, from the earlier average of over 17 million gallons a day it had dwindled to 15 million gallons a day.[102] The removal of water from the underground workings is a two-sided problem. Although much of the danger and difficulty of develop-ing the mine has been caused through an excess of water, the availability of this water on the surface is an essential factor in the scheme of operations. The plant, the mine and the township relied on it for everyday use, there being until recently no other

[101]An estimated maximum capacity of 10 million gallons per day would be required from the 1,600 ft level pumps and 30 million gallons per day when the pumps were at the 2,190 ft level.
[102]The present pumping capacity from underground is over 40 million gallons per day.

source of supply. Further, all the available supply was used.[103]
Faced with this dilemma, the management erected a pump
station on the banks of the Kafue river, some five miles away.
This station, with a capacity of 6 million gallons a day, came into
operation in 1960. It was not then supplying anything like that
amount, so that there was plenty of scope for handling any future
increase in demand.

Mining techniques at Nchanga (I)
Once the dewatering procedure at Nchanga was seen to be an
outstanding success, the question of production began to loom
large on the horizon. During these years in the late 1930's far-
sighted men, including some of the mining fraternity, began to
notice also the gathering clouds of war. With the ever-increasing
menace of Nazi Germany a harsh reality, all the indications were
that a maximum output of copper would soon become not merely
a desirable economic possibility, but a vital factor in the war
effort. Paradoxically, though, the motive for providing a maximum output might also be the means of preventing it from becoming a reality, for the outbreak of war would almost inevitably
involve considerable reductions in the quantities of the essential
materials and equipment required for the maintenance and operation of the mine which would have to be obtained from overseas.
As early as March 1938, eight months before the Munich conference, it had been suggested that the permanent hoists and
headgear for the vertical shaft should be ordered as soon as possible rather than wait until the shaft was completed.[104] The worry
in the minds of the engineers was not an idle one, for the exigen-
cies of the war years did actually delay the dewatering programme (see page 125).

To advise on the best method of removing the ore with the
maximum efficiency and expediency and minimum cost, an

[103]The differential flotation plant alone uses 10 million gallons a day, and
the average total consumption of mine and township is 17 million gallons
a day.
[104]Personal letter from R. Parker at Nchanga to the consulting engineer,
R. J. Nairn, dated 12 March 1938. The vertical 'C' shaft did not in fact
pass the 1,200 ft level until the end of 1939.

American expert, Mr W. E. Romig, was engaged by the Anglo-American Corporation. Romig very soon began to justify his position. His first step was to list the available information on the ore-body.[105] It was very limited:

1   A cross-cut on the 360 ft level had passed through the footwall into the ore-body, but had not contacted the hanging wall.
2   A cross-cut on the 480 ft level had been extended similarly.
3   There were other workings—cross-cuts and drifts—on the 480 ft level which did not contact any wall.
4   Flat diamond-drill holes from the 480 ft level had penetrated both the hanging wall and the footwall.
5   Diamond-drill holes had been put down from the surface.

It is plain, then, that the footwall had been exposed at only two points, and the hanging wall not at all. At this time, the water-table was only slightly below the 360 ft level.

Work had meantime been progressing on a pilot plant designed to treat 500 tons of ore a day. This was due to commence operation on 2 August 1939[106] but in fact was commissioned on the following day. This plant was finally closed down on 27 January 1946 when the new concentrator, which was able to handle 3,000 short tons of ore a day, came into operation. A temporary assay laboratory was also opened.

During the preceding weeks, Romig's task had been to produce a plan of operations. Two possible methods were open to him: (a) 'top-slicing', and (b) 'caving' (see pages xvi f.). He soon came to the conclusion that a system of caving would be the most desirable. Not only was the ore-body of a soft nature highly suitable for the process, but the strong arkose footwall would ensure good mining conditions. On the other hand, the hanging wall, which consisted in places of shale overlain by mica schist and banded sandstone, was also soft and would readily follow down the ore-body as it caved. Romig was confident that the method would

[105]Report from W. E. Romig dated 3 July 1939; Nchanga mining files.
[106]Letter from Pope to Nairn dated 1 August 1939.

succeed.[107] This did not mean, though, that the plan was not fraught with difficulties. A possible one was that after a considerable amount of caving had ben carried out the collapse of the overlying ground might cause such pressure on the workings that they would be crushed and the maintenance of the scraper drifts and finger raises (see pages 136 ff.) seriously handicapped. Only actual experiment would provide an answer. Further, the mud in the sandstone and schist of the hanging wall would have to be thoroughly drained. (This would, of course, apply equally to the 'top slicing' method.) In his report[108] Nairn explained the steps which had already been taken. The draining of the hanging-wall beds was proceeding satisfactorily and had reached almost to the 470 ft level in the area immediately overlying the ore-body. The drilling of a series of holes, each about 600 ft long, to the dolomite above the upper shale horizon had already been started, the idea being that although the flow to the pumps would be increased, the possibility of a sudden inrush of water to the workings would be considerably reduced.

Romig had by now produced his estimates of costs: 5s a ton for the caving method and 8s to 10s a ton for top slicing. An area at the extreme south end of the ore-body had been set aside for experiments in top slicing; otherwise a system of 'continuous caving' would be operated, extending both east and west and down dip simultaneously from the centre of the ore-body. This is a modification of the 'block caving' technique in which the ore-body is divided into segments for removal.

The more obvious 'cut and fill' method was not considered suitable here because of the considerable thickness of the ore-body—50-100 ft—and the likelihood of serious subsidence of the overlying ground. The cost would be high—over 20s a ton; the supporting pillars of ore left behind would have to be thick and close together, so causing considerable waste; and there was a lack of suitable material with which to fill the gaps between them. The method could be considered only if serious difficulties

[107]Report from Nairn to the Anglo-American Corporation dated 27 August 1939.
[108]Nairn, op. cit.

were encountered in draining the hanging-wall beds. In fact, though, some open stoping was actually undertaken before the caving system came into operation.

As the ore-body was limited in width, the footwall development was being so arranged that the scraper raises would be developed between levels, which themselves would be 160 ft apart. Finger raises would be pushed up to the ore-body from the scraper raises. On the various levels, the ore scraped from the raises would be loaded into trucks and hauled by locomotive to bins which would be connected to the main hauling level leading to the shaft.[109]

The complicated techniques of this method of mining required extreme safety precautions. In addition to the measures to be taken against flooding, the problem of possible collapse of the workings owing to pressure from above as caving proceeded had to be dealt with. Very probably the finger raises would require timbering, and for this, together with the actual drawing of ore from the raises, highly trained, experienced men would be required. They were not available locally. By arrangement with Messrs. Pope and Nairn, therefore, Romig arranged to make tentative enquiries in the United States for suitable experts to come to Nchanga. Two timbermen, a mine captain to take charge of withdrawing ore, and an assistant underground manager were envisaged.

In addition, further safeguards would have to be devised to prevent an increase of accidents to the African employees in the unfamiliar conditions of caving. Suitable training for Europeans and Africans alike would take some considerable time, during which production could not be expected to be high. Expenses would also be substantial initially. For a production of 1,000 tons of ore per day the costs from July 1939 to March 1940 would be approximately £1,161,550.[110] The intention, as previously seen, was to start at the extreme south end of the ore-body near No. 1

[109]These technicalities are explained below.
[110]Romig's estimate. One of the criticisms frequently made against Romig by those who worked with him was his failure adequately to translate his own concepts of large-scale operations to the relatively small-scale ore-body at Nchanga.

shaft. This would reduce ore loss to a minimum, but as the ore was comparatively poor there, the initial results from the pilot plant would not appear promising. It would have to be remembered that these results were certain to improve.

There was yet another factor which had to be considered. In some areas the Nchanga ore-body overlaps the deeper and richer Nchanga West ore-body. What was to happen to the 1,700,000 tons of ore above the 970 ft level if caving of the lower ore-body took place underneath it? The problem had not escaped the notice of the planners. The consulting engineer, Nairn, clarified the position to his directors[111] by making some telling points. This tonnage was actually comparatively low, the grade of ore was poor and the mining of it would prove difficult and expensive. In the lower ore-body itself above the 970 ft level the reserves indicated a life of twenty to twenty-five years at a removal rate of 4,000 tons a day.[112] In view of the low profits which would be made from the upper ore-body, he recommended that this ore be left out of the planning at that time.

The Nchanga West ore-body, which is the subject of the caving operations, is on the flatter, south limb of the Nchanga syncline (see Fig. 2). It dips at an angle which varies from 15° to 25° north and has an average thickness of eighty feet, although the maximum and minimum widths range from 200 ft to only a few feet in the narrowest parts. The ore-bearing rocks include the arkose, the transition beds, and the lower banded shale. Beneath them there is a hard granite in which, together with the arkose, the actual workings are sited. The ore-bearing rocks, together with the banded sandstones on top of them, are soft and easily caved. In places, however, the copper minerals penetrate down into the arkose for as much as eighty feet. Where this occurs a different caving technique becomes necesseary.

Mining techniques at Nchanga (II)
The method of mining the Nchanga West ore-body, as intro-

[111]Letter dated 5 April 1941.
[112]Bancroft's Nchanga West estimate had been 46½ million tons. By October 1940 it was 103,200,000 tons. This high figure was not generally publicised at the time.

duced by W. E. Romig, is known as a 'continuous longwall caving system'. Basically, it consists of excavating in the footwall of the ore-body, from below, a number of evenly spaced draw points known as 'finger raises'. These finger raises lead to collecting points known as 'scraper drifts', along which the rock is mechanically scraped to the service raises and sub-haulages.

When the finger raises are ready, the layer of ore immediately above them (the bottom layer) is broken up by blasting and allowed to collapse into the finger raises. When this is drawn off, the ore above caves, through gravity, and may be removed through the finger raises at a controlled rate. This process is repeated down the dip of the ore-body.

There are, of course, both advantages and disadvantages to this method of mining. By allowing gravity to do the work of breaking up the ore, expensive drilling and blasting is obviated. On the other hand, the initial development is costly, so that the method is uneconomic unless the ore-body to be worked is a thick one. Further, it is impossible to be selective when undercutting, and a dilution rate of 5-15 per cent of waste rock is inevitable.

When the continuous caving system came into operation it was essential that costs be kept to a minimum, bearing in mind that the maximum anticipated output of ore was not expected to exceed 120,000 tons per month. Hence the scale of development was relatively small. The haulages, 9 ft × 8 ft in cross-section, were driven along the strike some 35 ft below the footwall and about 150 ft apart. The vertical height between each was about 40 ft. The scraper drifts were pushed up from one haulage to the next at 30 ft intervals and the finger raises were 15 ft apart, placed alternately on either side of the scraper drifts. After the finger raises had been mined in an orthodox manner, the ore was induced to cave and scraped down the scraper raises into four-ton Granby cars.[113] The direction of caving was along the line of strike, working out to the limits of the ore-body. Those 'old timers'—and there are several—who were involved in this experiment all recall

[113]Specially designed wagons embodying a tilting arrangement for unloading the ore as required. Later, Lawrence Allen introduced a larger, ten-ton car. Now, 25-ton cars are used.

that although there was an immediate return of ore for processing, there were many disadvantages, the most serious being the
long delays involved in removing the ore to the hoists. Only
15,000 tons a month per haulage could be withdrawn under this
system.

The essential improvement took place in 1943 (see page 144).
The haulages were now put in lower down at about fifty feet
below the footwall and the inclined distances between them were
increased to about 180 feet. Approximately equidistant between
the haulages and the footwall—that it, about twenty-five feet
above the haulages—were inserted 'grizzly'[114] drives which linked
up the lower ends of the scraper drifts. Each grizzly led to the
haulage *via* a transfer raise (a short passage down which the ore
passing through the grizzly fell) and at the bottom end of each
transfer raise was a manually operated wooden loading box from
which the Granby cars were filled. The production for each level
now rose to 40,000 tons per month, which was adequate to
supply the 150,000 tons required by the crushers, when four
levels were in operation.

The haulages were now constructed rather larger in cross-
section, 12 ft × 10 ft at first and then 13 ft × 12 ft. Nevertheless, even though production increased, disadvantages remained.
Too many loading boxes were needed—one for each scraper raise
—which meant that cheap and less efficient wooden ones had to
be used instead of much more efficient, but expensive, steel ones.
Extra labour was also required to operate the loading boxes.
Finally, and most serious, the fumes from the necessary blasting
—for example, on the grizzlies—passed into working areas on
higher levels, causing more trouble for the ventilation engineers
and necessitating a strict timetable for blasting.

The delays in removing ore led to experiments which are now
the standard procedure. The ore is scraped laterally from several
scraper drifts into one large pass, which leads to the haulage and
culminates in a steel loading box with a door operated by com-

[114]'Grizzlies' are large gratings through which rock and ore may fall. The
grating holds back oversize pieces of rock, which are then reduced by
blasting.

pressed air. From the grizzly at every scraper drift there is a small sub-transfer chute raise leading to the transfer raise. The ore is scraped from the finger raises along the scraper drift and allowed to fall through the grizzly into the transfer raise, along which it is scraped through another grizzly and into a pass which leads to the haulage below. Auxiliary haulages are driven to increase the production still further. The removal of the ore (tramming) is done by 25-ton side-tipping cars which are pulled by twelve-ton electric locomotives.

The system is highly efficient, the 1963 output being about 150,000 tons per month from each level. Not only that, there is no longer any fear of fumes circulating in other workings. The steel loading boxes are placed every 400 ft along the haulages, thus making loading easy, but this is a danger in that a breakdown would cause considerable disorganisation. Constant checks are made and a system of planned maintenance operates throughout.

Underground workings at Nchanga West ore-body[115]

Shafts   The Nchanga West ore-body is serviced by a total of fifteen shafts, the main hoisting shafts being 'C' and 'D', both situated in the footwall rocks and equipped with steel headframes.

Hoisting shafts   'C' shaft is a square, vertical shaft having six compartments and reaching a vertical depth of 2,521 ft. The main levels are at approximately 500 ft intervals down to the 2,120 ft level. The compartments contain two ten-ton skips, a double-deck cage (capacity 120 men), a counterweight, a ladderway and numerous pipes and cables. All the waste rock is brought up by this shaft.

'D' shaft is a four-compartment, rectangular, vertical shaft which is sited 139 ft west of 'C' shaft and reaches a depth of 1,743 ft. It contains two pairs of ten-ton skips, one pair of which

[115]In the *Transactions* of the Institution of Mining and Metallurgy, vol. 70, part 3, 1960–61, there is a survey of the Nchanga mine at that date by M. W. Rushton and K. E. Mackay, then general manager and manager respectively. I wish to acknowledge my debt to their work and also to Mr Neil Wilkie for his unlimited patience in translating the technicalities of their article into lay terms.

can be replaced by a triple-deck cage to handle men and materials on the day shift. The skips are for hoisting ore only.

Both these shafts are interconnected on all main levels and have a combined hoisting capacity of 500,000 tons of ore and waste a month. They are concreted throughout, and the hoisting is semi-automatic in its operation.

Service shafts A system of service inclines approximately parallel to the footwall but in sound rock well below it have been extended from the surface to the 1,500 ft level. These shafts handle most of the material required underground and provide access to the caving areas. Some of the air supply is also introduced down these shafts. At vertical intervals of 130 ft sub-haulage levels have been driven from which the actual extraction workings are opened up.

Below the 1,500 ft level it was found that sub-vertical shafts with automatic lifts were quicker and more economical. The first of these, known as 'F' shaft, reached the 2,120 ft level in 1960.[116]

Pumping shafts There are independent of, and sealed off from, the other workings and would provide independent entrance to all the pump stations down to the 2,200 ft level in the event of flooding.

Main haulages, or cross-cuts to the ore-body, are sited on the 480 ft, 970 ft, 1,500 ft and 2,120 ft levels. Those on the lower levels below the 970 ft level are now the ones mainly used, as most of the production of the mine now comes from these deeper areas. The 970 ft and 1,500 ft levels have twin cross-cuts to the sub-haulage, extra space being required for ventilation purposes. One-way high-speed traffic operates along them. The purpose of these main haulages is to remove ore and waste from the mine. The material to be removed comes along the sub-haulages above the main haulages (at right angles to them), is transferred into them *via* ore passes and then taken by train to the hoisting shafts.

Sub-haulages, which have been developed from the service in-

[116]Throughout this section reference should be made to Fig. 8.

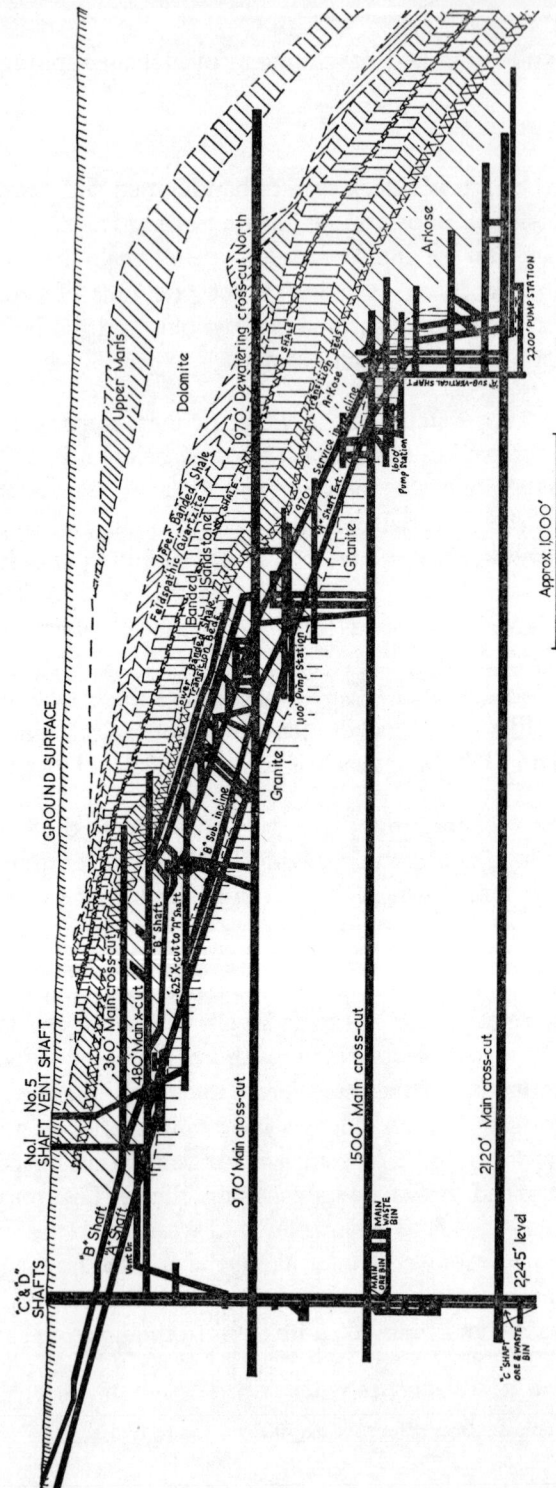

Fig. 8 Cross-section of Nchanga West workings on B incline shaft, 1961. The many sub-haulages, dewatering drives, ventilation and other passages intersecting the cross-section are not shown. (From original in Nchanga files)

clines and from the main levels, provide access to the caved areas above them. All the mined material passes through them *en route* to the surface.

In 1963 two areas were being caved: a length of about 2,400 ft between the 970 ft level and the 1,220 ft level in the centre; and, in the western section, a length of about 1,100 ft between the 970 ft and 1,085 ft levels. Between these two is an area of about 700 ft of barren rock.

As had been anticipated, the outbreak of the war in 1939 and the consequent unavailability of essential materials seriously curtailed the programme as originally envisaged and led to the postponement of capital development. Nevertheless, the output from the mine during the war years was considerable. In the six years from March 1939 to March 1945 the concentrates sent from the pilot plant at Nchanga to the concentrator at Nkana (Kitwe) yielded 76,584 long tons of copper.[117] The capital of the mine was also increased to £7½ million in July 1946.

During the immediate post-war years there was an increasing demand for coal which could not be met by the collieries at Wankie in Southern Rhodesia. Imports from South Africa and the United States *via* Lobito Bay still failed to meet the deficit, and in consequence it proved necessary to convert the power plants at the Copperbelt mines partly to wood burning. Each mine employed large numbers of woodcutters and seriously denuded the surrounding countryside of trees. At the present time it is possible to observe large amounts of new growth springing from the stumps left behind by the cutters. Already the new growth is almost as high as the old, although not as thick, and in a few more years the damage should be altogether made good. The cutting of trees is now forbidden in the peri-urban areas; African contractors cut fire wood under licence and 'charcoal burners' still operate, but that is all.[118]

In spite of the efforts of the mines to maintain their fuel supplies, none was entirely successful. Each mine in turn had to

[117]Figures in the Nchanga files. Naturally, no information was published during the war years
[118]See article by C. E. Duff O.B.E. in the *Northern Rhodesia Journal*, vol. II, No. 1, 1953.

close down temporarily to enable stocks of fuel to accumulate. This explains why for the year ended March 1948 the production of blister copper from Nchanga was only 23,468 long tons, roughly 3,500 tons below the rated capacity of the mine.

During 1948 the two mining groups agreed to link the thermal power plants at Nchanga, Rhokana, Mufulira and the Roan Antelope, and to this end the Northern Rhodesia Power Corporation was created as a subsidiary of the mining companies. The great advantage of this scheme was that to raise the capacity of all the plants it was now necessary to incorporate extra equipment only at one (Nchanga).

Nevertheless, it was realised that expansion of the existing thermal plants was unsatisfactory, and it was in this knowledge that the Belgians in the Congo were contacted about the possibilities of using hydro-electricity. This ultimately led to the setting up of the Rhodesia Congo Border Power Corporation in 1953 to co-ordinate the existing thermal plants and to integrate them with the Congo hydro-electric system and, later, with Kariba.

The Copperbelt system had been integrated with Union Minière by 1956 when power first began to flow from the installation at Le Marinel on the Lualaba river to the Copperbelt central switching station at Kitwe. Early in 1960 Kariba power was linked in and by 1963 provided over two-thirds of the Copperbelt's requirements, which for that year totalled 2,039 million kiloWatt hours.[119]

By 1950 the corner had been turned at Nchanga, and years of progress and profit brightened the horizon ahead. A dividend of 4s a share was declared for the year on the basis of accumulated unappropriated profits of well over £2 million. The price of copper had by now risen to £153 a long ton and the ore reserves developed underground were 8,710,900 tons at an average of 7·51 per cent copper.[120] This was indeed good news for the shareholders. As a means of increasing efficiency, the entire management and control of the company was now removed from the United Kingdom. This change in procedure came into operation on 1 January 1951.

[119]Figures compiled from the various annual reports.
[120]In April 1960, the ore reserves of the Nchanga West ore-body alone totalled 74 million tons averaging 5·96 per cent copper.

6 Developments since 1939

1939 marked a turning point in the development of the Copper-belt, for the outbreak of war at once removed all fears centred around the market. Immediately the demand for copper by the British government became greater than the mines' capacity to fulfil it. But even though markets and employment were secure, this in no way implied an economic boom such as had occurred during the first world war. Labour shortages, difficulties in obtaining raw materials and supplies for maintenance and expansion, transport problems, especially to Europe, heavy taxation, labour unrest, rises in the cost of living and price freezing all combined to reduce dividends and restrict production, even though a maximum effort was made by the companies. The Nkana smelter, already in need of major overhaul, was so affected by the high silica content of the concentrates supplied by Nchanga that by the end of 1940 it was found necessary to reduce production from 9,500 short tons per month, as agreed in December 1939, to a monthly average of 8,100 short tons in 1941. Fortunately this proved to be only a temporary measure, production climbing back to 9,500 tons per month by April 1942. Again, the high silica content of the Nchanga ore played havoc with the waste heat boilers at Nkana, with the result that yet another production cut was forced on the Rhokana Corporation, the output being eventually stabilised in May 1944 at 8,660 short tons per annum. By this time the copper supplies available to the Allied governments were approximately equal to war requirements, and the Rhokana difficulties did not therefore command top priority from the British government. Previously, of course, every effort had been made to maintain Rhodesian copper output at a maximum level. It was on this account that in 1943 the British Ministry of Supply advanced £750,000 to Nchanga to cover half the cost of the immediate Nchanga West improvement and development requirements (see above, page 137), which resulted in the Nchanga output rising from 6,000 tons in 1940 to 20,000 tons in 1944. Similarly, Mufulira and the Roan Antelope increased their annual production to wartime peaks of approximately 86,000 and 75,000 tons respectively. A good example of the prevailing trends may be seen from the production figures for blister copper at Roan Antelope during the war years. This information is extracted from a report by R. M. Peterson (general manager) dated 30 June 1945 and preserved in the Rhodesian Selection Trust archives. For obvious reasons, no production data were published during this period:

PRODUCTION OF BLISTER COPPER AT ROAN ANTELOPE

Year ended 30th June	Blister copper (long tons)	Cost of Production (f.o.b. Beira)
1940	75,195	£21 3s 9d
1941	67,745	£25 15s 10d
1942	65,665	£29 12s 11d
1943	69,188	£33 16s 8d
1944	64,189	£38 13s 11d
1945	54,895	£40 17s 10d
Total	396,877	Average £31 2s 8d
Average	66,146	

All the above production was contracted for by the British government. Although the falls in production in 1941 and 1942 were caused by intrinsic mining difficulties, the impact of British actions is plainly mirrored in the decline in 1944 and 1945. Similarly, the rising costs of production are clearly seen. It might be argued that the fixed price of £62·0 offered a substantial profit, and indeed, this was so;[1] but the intention of the British government (faithfully honoured by the companies) was that

[1]Net profits averaged £7 10s per ton during the war years: *Horizon*, January 1965, pages 21–25.

considerable sums should be ploughed back into further developments. It is, nevertheless, noteworthy that the cost of production per ton (delivered in Europe) of £28·851 in 1931–32 had fallen to £19·586 by 1934–35, a figure which did not change substantially until the outbreak of war in 1939, with the rising costs which followed.[2]

Table 3

Year	Northern Rhodesian copper production (long tons)	Average price (£)
1939	211,668	50·6
1940	262,394	63·6
1941	228,254	62·0
1942	246,597	62·0
1943	250,955	62·0
1944	220,827	62·0
1945	194,014	62·0
1946	182,289	77·2
1947	192,500	130·6
1948	213,633	134·0
1949	259,081	133·0
1950	276,433	179·0
1951	309,141	220.7
1952	312,363	259·5
1953	362,581	256·3
1954	378,611	249.3
1955	342,191	352·3
1956	383,484	329·1
1957	416,211	219·7
1958	374,435	197·6
1959	530,083	237.8
1960	557,676	246·2

1941–52: official control prices.
1953 (January–September): average of control prices.
1953 (October–December): London Metal Exchange cash prices.
1954–60: London Metal Exchange cash prices.

[2]The above figures are quoted in the Peterson report, dated 30 June 1945, in the Rhodesian Selection Trust archives.

Although the relief felt throughout the world at the cessation of hostilities in 1945 was shared in Northern Rhodesia, there was a real fear that a slump, such as had occurred after the first world war and again in 1930, would create unemployment and hardship for many of those involved in the Northern Rhodesian copper industry. Already, in 1944, with the collapse of Germany, the British government had reduced its purchases from the Copperbelt and the Ministry of Supply had ended its bulk purchase programme. It was with this kind of apprehension in mind that the mine workers' union had pressed for wage increases and a 'closed shop' in 1940 and 1941. Certainly there seemed some basis for these fears. Over-production seemed probable if maintained at wartime rates in a post-war age, aluminium was a potential rival metal, and in any case the costs of copper production were not likely to decrease. On the contrary, wages were rising and the technical problems—and therefore expense—of development work were becoming far more serious than ever before.[3] Fuel and power were also serious problems, as was the shortage of railway capacity both for raw materials and supplies and for the export of the finished product.

Nevertheless, the sceptics were soon to be proved wrong, and the Copperbelt entered on an era of unparalleled prosperity during which the price of copper rose from an average of £77 3s 5d per ton in 1946 to an average maximum of £402 10s in 1955 before slumping to £176 5s in 1957. There were many reasons for this extraordinary phenomenon—post-war reconstruction, expanding industry (particularly in the field of electrical goods) and the devaluation of sterling in 1949, which overnight increased the sterling price of copper by 44 per cent.[4] But perhaps most important of all was the rapid realisation by the

[3]Appendix III details production costs for the Rhodesian Selection Trust group. The Anglo-American Corporation refused to supply its own figures. The Rhodesian Selection Trust information was obtained from a memorandum, letter No. 2089/62/K, dated 16 October 1962, from A. C. Annfield, secretary, Northern Rhodesia Chamber of Mines, to I. D. Gregory, then senior lecturer in Geography, the Teachers' College, Bulawayo.
[4]The new valuation of the £ was $2·80 instead of $4·02.

statesmen of the world that although the war was officially over it had merely reverted to another form. The 'cold war' which ensued made further re-armament by the major powers essential, and this, along with stock-piling as a corollary, provided a major incentive to increases in production. Thus new prospecting companies were organised and steps taken to develop further mines. This policy was further encouraged by the amended taxation legislation introduced in Northern Rhodesia in 1951 by which new taxation allowances came into effect, making it possible under certain conditions for capital expenditure on new mines to be 'written off' out of profits before taxes became payable. Briefly, the mines already in existence continued to obtain an allowance of capital divided by x where x was the life of the mine in years (with a minimum of twenty); new mines were permitted an allowance of one-fifth of capital in the first year, one-quarter of the balance in the second year, and so on. From the fifth year onwards any outstanding capital could be set against tax. This was highly advantageous, although very profitable new mines could still pay tax in the first year.

Kansanshi

In 1951 the Anglo-American Corporation was granted an option to purchase Kansanshi. The option was exercised, the Kansanshi Copper Mining Company was registered in March 1953 and the venture was placed under the immediate direction of Rhokana Corporation. Work on the site was renewed in 1952 after the original agreement had been ratified. Again, though, the investigations were inconclusive. Numbers of diamond drill holes were put down, some of which encountered veins of sulphide copper, but it was still impossible to relate them to what was already known or to base firm calculations on the core values recovered. To make matters worse, a large inflow of water began at the bottom of the reconditioned north shaft—now at 300 ft—causing work there to be temporarily suspended. The south shaft seemed more promising, as three of the veins intersected by a cross-cut at 300 ft appeared to be connected to others in the 150 ft level.

From July 1954 until March 1955 shortage of money caused a

temporary hold-up in the work. Subsequently it was decided to begin production so that further exploration could be financed from profits. When exploration recommenced, the main drive on the 300 ft level was extended to the bottom of the north shaft, thus linking the two. The water situation was now greatly alleviated, as the pumps at the south shaft could also cope with the inflow from the north. Working conditions also considerably improved. The south shaft was extended to a depth of 810 ft, disclosing substantial veins of sulphide ore, particularly at the 500 ft level. A power plant was set up and a concentrator to handle sulphide ore constructed. It came into operation towards the end of 1956.

A sound future for Kansanshi seemed assured when tragedy struck. On 31 October 1957 a rush of water on the 500 ft level overwhelmed the pumping station and began to rise in the south shaft, where the pumps on the 300 ft level could not deal with the flood in addition to the normal discharge from the north shaft. These pumps were also drowned, the water level becoming finally established at about 250 ft below the level of the shaft collar. The mine was then closed and left on a 'care and maintenance' basis, in which position it still remains (1969), although a re-opening in the near future is very probable.

One of the major difficulties has been the problem of treating the low-grade oxide ores. Experiments have been conducted in which the oxides have been roasted together with sulphide concentrate to produce copper sulphate for leaching. This was satisfactorily accomplished, but the further complications involved in purifying and filtering the solution proved to be insuperable. Alternatives are still under consideration.

Bancroft

In addition to its supervision of the Kansanshi operations, Rhokana Corporation had a direct interest in the Kirila Bomwe and Konkola deposits in that it held the Special Grants covering the area. As early as February 1949, the Anglo-American Corporation had formed a new company to acquire and exploit these

Special Grants and drilling operations had begun. The new company, which was envisaged on a grand scale with a nominal capital of £5 million, was incorporated in Northern Rhodesia on 21 May 1953 as Bancroft Mines Ltd, with Rhokana Corporation acting as local managers until K. E. Mackay[5] was appointed as manager in February 1954. The intensive drilling programme was greatly reduced from that year, attention being then directed towards exploitation of the enormous ore reserves revealed.[6]

The original development plans provided for the sinking of two main shafts, one at Konkola and the other at the Kirila Bomwe South ore-body. A concentrator capable of handling 150,000 tons of ore a month was also to be constructed. To facilitate the new traffic a twenty-mile extension of the main Chingola–Kitwe railway line was laid to Bancroft from Luano. The main road was also widened to cater for the greatly increased traffic brought about as a result of the new European and African townships which sprang up. These townships, amongst the most modern on the Copperbelt, profited from the experiences of earlier towns and are models of their kind, being situated on the most naturally advantageous sites and enjoying practically every amenity. The mine was officially opened by Sir Ernest Oppenheimer on 29 March 1957, the event being also the last public appearance before his death of the hero of the occasion, Dr Bancroft himself.

Nineteen-fifty-six was a stormy year in the history of the Copperbelt, with numerous strikes and political-industrial disputes disrupting the economic progress of the area. Of greatest

[5]Subsequently general manager, Rhokana Corporation metallurgical division, a personal friend of the writer, who has been of considerable assistance.
[6]At 30 June 1960 these stood as follows:
Kirila Bomwe South
      ore-body: 50,373,700 short tons averaging 4·35 per cent copper
Kirila Bomwe North
      ore-body: 22,476,200 short tons averaging 4·10 per cent copper
Konkola ore-body: 32,073,400 short tons averaging 2·48 per cent copper

     Total: 104,923,300   *Average:*   3·73 per cent

Chamber of Mines *Yearbook*, 1960.

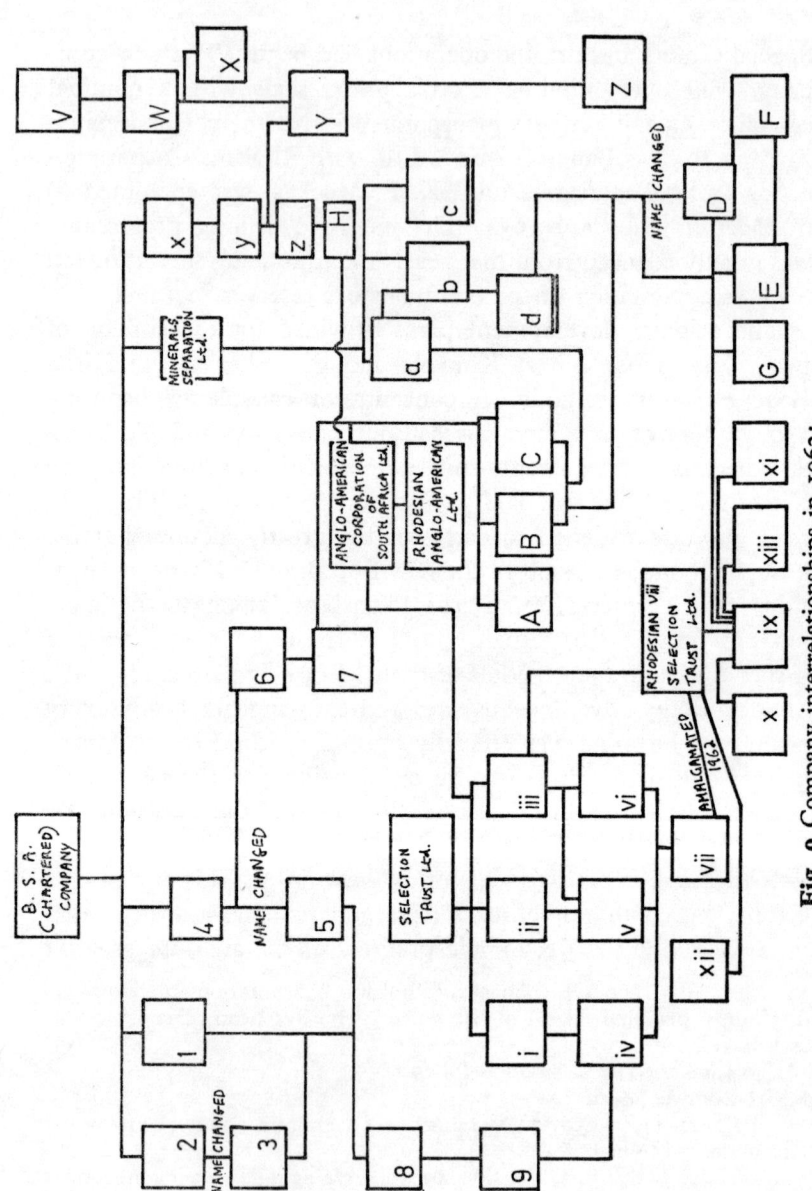

Fig. 9 Company interrelationships in 1962:

1 Bechuanaland Exploring Co. Ltd, 1888: E. Davis
2 Northern Territories (BSA) Exploring Co. Ltd, 1895
3 Northern Copper (BSA) Co. Ltd, 1899
4 Rhodesia Copper Co. Ltd, 1902: E. Davis
5 Rhodesia Copper and General Exploration and Finance Co. Ltd, 1911: E. Davis
6 Bwana Mkubwa mine
7 Bwana Mkubwa Copper Mining Co. Ltd, 1910: E. Davis
8 Roan–Rietbok claims
9 Northern Rhodesia Co. Ltd, 1925: E. Davis

Group 2. Selection Trust Ltd, 1914: A. Chester Beatty

i Northern Rhodesia Venture, 1925: A Chester Beatty
ii Muliashi Venture, 1926: A. Chester Beatty
iii Mineralized Venture, 1927: A. Chester Beatty
iv Roan–Rietbok claims
v Muliashi claims
vi Roan extension claims
vii Roan Antelope Copper Mines Ltd, 1927: A. Chester Beatty
viii Rhodesian Selection Trust Ltd, 1928: A. Chester Beatty
ix Mufulira Copper Mines Ltd, 1930: A Chester Beatty
x Chibuluma Mines Ltd, 1951: Rhodesian Selection Trust
xi Baluba Mines Ltd, 1952: Rhodesian Selection Trust
xii Ndola Copper Refineries Ltd, 1954: Rhodesian Selection Trust
xiii Chambishi Mines Ltd, 1962: Rhodesian Selection Trust

1917: Rhodesian Anglo-American Ltd, 1928: E. Oppenheimer

A Bwana Mkubwa mine
B Nkana concession
C Nkana mine
D Rhokana Corporation Ltd, 1931: Anglo-American Corporation
E Nchanga Consolidated Copper Mines Ltd, 1937: Anglo-American Corporation
F Rhodesia Copper Refineries Ltd, 1947: Anglo-American Corporation
G Bancroft Mines Ltd, 1953: Anglo-American Corporation
H Kansanshi mine (Kansanshi Copper Mining Co. Ltd)

Group 4. Minerals Separation Ltd, 1903

a Copper Ventures, 1921
b Rhodesia–Congo Border Concessions Ltd, 1923: E. Davis
c Rhodesia Minerals Concession Ltd, 1924
d Nchanga Copper Mines Ltd, 1926

Group 5

x Zambesia Exploring Company, 1891: R. Williams
y Tanganyika Concessions Ltd, 1899: R. Williams
z Rhodesia–Katanga Junction Railway & Mining Co. Ltd, 1909: R. Williams

Group 6

v King Leopold II of Belgium
w Comité Spécial du Katanga
x Forminière, 1906
y Union Minière du Haut-Katanga, 1911
z Union Minière, 1936

moment to the situation at Bancroft was the strike of European artisans which began there on 7 December over a triviality and was prolonged and exaggerated out of all proportion to the original incident by the matters of principle involved and by the injuries to their pride suffered by the various organisations during the course of the negotiations. Although by then the Kirila Bomwe South shaft had reached a depth of 1,510 ft and the Konkola shaft was down to 1,400 ft, with a third shaft being sunk to serve the Kirila Bomwe North ore-body, there were grave fears that production would be unable to start on schedule in January 1957. In the event the fears proved unfounded, with production commencing on time at the planned initial capacity of 42,800 long tons of copper per year.

With the decision early in 1958 that a general reduction in production of 10 per cent should be made in copper output to prevent over-trading, the price of copper having then fallen from £437 a ton in March 1956 to £181, the directors found themselves in a dilemma. Bancroft mine has great potential; yet it has a serious problem to face in that the volume of underground water encountered in the workings is enormous. In 1961 a daily average of 33 million gallons was pumped from the mine—representing 27·5 tons of water for every ton of ore. Many minor floodings had occurred and new problems were being encountered daily. It was found to be more economical, under the circumstances, to cease production temporarily for a period of one year, transferring the production quota to Nchanga, which mine was easily able to handle the increase. Apart from those men engaged on further development of the Kirila Bomwe South ore-body, the Bancroft miners were assimilated into the other Copperbelt mines.[7]

[7]This recession affected the economy of the entire federal area, creating a major slump through the fall in income from taxes to all four governments The following table vividly illustrates this:

Taxes received by	1957	1959
Federal government	£16,819,000	£5,418,000
Northern Rhodesia government	11,027,000	5,651,000
Southern Rhodesia government	3,304,000	1,126,000
Nyasaland government	1,518,000	476,000
Total :	£32,668,000	£12,671,000

This closure of Bancroft mine was intended only as a temporary economic measure, and indeed the mine re-opened for limited production on 1 April 1959. Although not operating at full capacity, the mine still produced over 51,000 tons of copper during its first operational year, making from this a profit of almost £3,700,000.[8] In view of the technical difficulties and the need to curtail production, the Konkola shaft was not re-opened, all work being concentrated on the Kirila Bomwe South ore-body through No. 1 shaft. Underground development continued to proceed apace, with twin inclined shafts being constructed to exploit the ore-body below the immediate workings. It was also proposed to exploit the Kirila Bomwe North ore-body by linking it underground to the Kirila Bomwe South ore-body, the ore from the former ore-body being transported underground to No. 1 shaft, near which the surface plant is situated. To handle the additional water involved, the pumping capacity at No. 1 shaft was increased to 57 million gallons a day.[9]

Chibuluma
One of the last discoveries to be made before intensive prospecting was halted on the outbreak of war in 1939 was in the Nkana South Limb area, some seven miles south of Nkana, where a systematic drilling and pitting programme was being carried out in sediments believed to contain copper deposits. The result of this activity—the Chibuluma ore-body, 25 ft thick, 1,800 ft in length and containing approximately eight million short tons of ore averaging 5·04 per cent copper and 0·22 per cent cobalt—is a classic example of the value of modern scientific prospecting techniques in an area where the ore does not outcrop and no obvious

In consequence there were drastic cuts in government and private development. (The above figures were originally published by the Information Department of the former Federal Government and reprinted in e.g. *Horizon*, January 1965).
[8] Bancroft Mines Ltd, annual report, 1960.
[9] It is interesting—and disappointing—to note that Bancroft still fails to stand on its own feet. As recently as August 1964 plans were afoot to amalgamate the mine with Nchanga, and offers of Nchanga shares were successfully made to the Bancroft shareholders. A more balanced economy and production should now ensue.

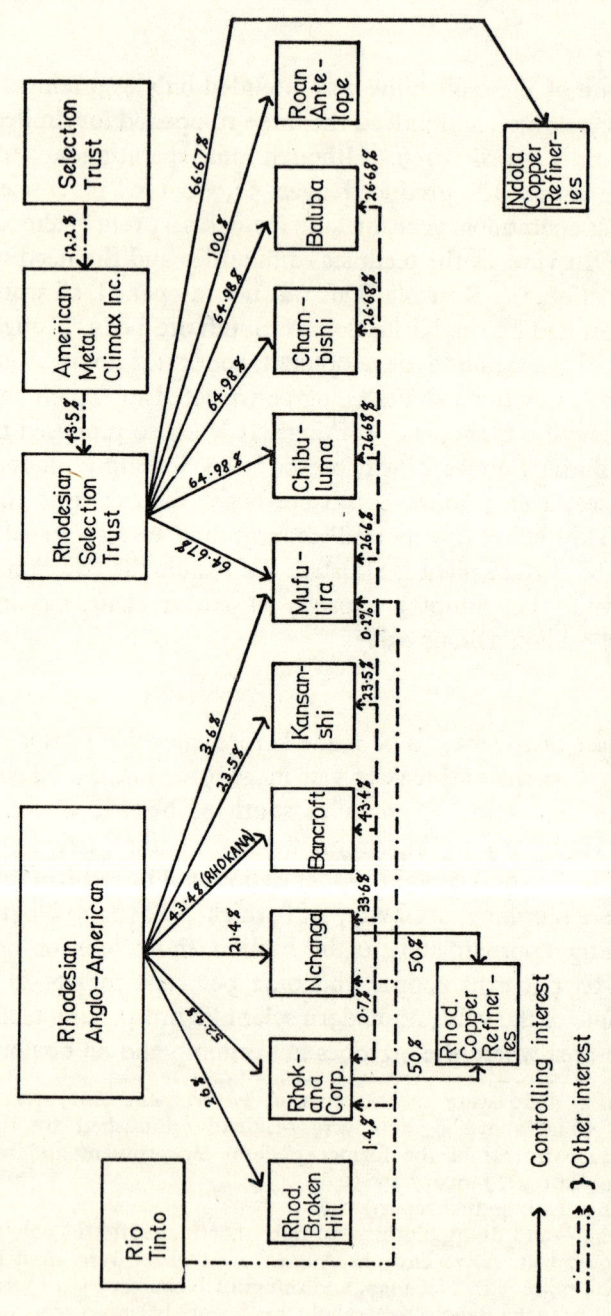

Fig. 10 Financial interrelationships in 1962. Approximate holdings are shown. *Note*: before the incorporation of Roan Antelope Copper Mines Ltd into Rhodesian Selection Trust Ltd in 1962 American Metal–Climax held a controlling 50·6 per cent interest in Rhodesian Selection Trust. The American interest in the combined company was 43·5 per cent

surface indications are visible. The main prospecting drilling had
been completed by 1949 and development began under the local
direction of Mufulira in 1951. The Chibuluma mine and township of Kalulushi then began to appear out of the 'bush'. The
original cost of equipping and developing the mine was approximately £6 million, of which the General Services Administration of the United States government provided £5 million in
terms of an agreement providing for repayment from the copper
and cobalt produced. This loan has since been repaid in full.

By December 1951 the main inclined shaft—Norrie shaft—
had been completed, the erection of the concentrator began in
1954, the first stopes were opened in October 1955. The concentrator began operations in March 1956 and full production began
two months later, with the Mufulira smelter and the Ndola cobalt
plant handling the concentrates resulting from the production of
45,000 short tons of ore per month. Recently, in March 1963,
after four years of development, a second ore-body, Chibuluma
West, some two miles to the west of the main body, was opened
up. These two ore-bodies are now connected by an underground
haulage at the 820 ft level. The 1962 ore reserves were
10,196,000 tons averaging 4·67 per cent copper and 0·15 cobalt.[10]

Mufulira
The exploitation and development of Mufulira, as also the Roan
Antelope, had been steady but unspectacular during the post-war
years. However, in 1948 an electrical survey over the area gave
some indications of mineralisation to the west, and, after drilling
from the surface, a drillhole, MW 62, some 2,000 ft west of the
Mufulira stream intersected what is now known as 'C' ore-body
at a depth of 1,500 ft. The ore-body averaged 72 ft in thickness
and contained 2·8 per cent copper. In the same year, 1952, the
electrolytic refinery which had been begun in 1950 came into
operation.

The improved prospects for copper in the mid-1950's led to a
decision to develop Mufulira West in 1957, the preparations
being finally completed early in 1962. The scheme, which cost

[10]Chibuluma Mines Ltd annual report, 30 June 1962.

£16 million, brought production at Mufulira up to 162,000 long tons of copper a year by 1964, a rise of some 50 per cent, and thus made Mufulira the second largest purely underground producer of copper in the world after El Teniente in Chile. (The largest overall producer in the Commonwealth is Nchanga, some of whose production, of course, is derived from open pits.) Inevitably, the decision to increase production meant also a massive extension of subsidiary workings. The concentrator and smelter were enlarged and five new shafts sunk. A new crushing plant, a tailings dam to extend over more than 3,000 acres, and a surface conveyor system were installed; to cater for the increased labour force, numerous houses, including the new African township of Butondo, were constructed.

The Roan Antelope

The original Beatty shaft sunk at the eastern, shallow end of the Roan Antelope ore-body between 1929 and 1931 was supplemented by Storke shaft as early as 1935. This latter was sited some 7,000 ft west of the first shaft, which gradually became relegated to the function of hoisting waste rock. Eventually, with the practical exhaustion of the ore at the eastern end of the ore-body, Beatty shaft was closed altogether, the headgear being used to equip a new shaft, Irwin shaft, which was started some three miles to the west of Storke shaft in June 1948. Another shaft, MacLaren shaft, a mile further to the west, bottomed in September 1962 at 4,054 ft—the deepest shaft yet sunk from surface in the Copperbelt. All three are linked underground at the 1,900 ft level.

A major engineering work during the immediate post-war period was the diversion of the Luanshya stream, which flowed across the ore-body. The stream was diverted through a tunnel which skirts the east side of the ore-body, and a dam was built to the north. There was almost a mishap in March 1948, when exceptionally heavy rains caused floodings and the consequent suspension of underground work—except for pumping—for five days. Drastic precautions have since been taken to prevent any recurrence of the event.

The underground workings at the Roan Antelope are noted for their great extent, the actual main level development workings in the ore-body being over four miles in length. Smelter and concentrator extensions have also taken place commensurate with increased production, which stood at some 92,000 long tons a year in 1960. Before marketing the anodes produced are further refined by Ndola Copper Refineries Ltd, which company had been formed by Rhodesian Selection Trust and British Insulated Callender's Cables Ltd in 1954 to deal with the increasing demand for highly refined electrolytic copper. By 1961 this refinery was handling the total Roan output.

The copper values at the Roan Antelope, which average under 2·0 per cent for ore hoisted, are clearly the poorest on the Copperbelt.[11] It follows, therefore, that any rapid deterioration in the copper market would have more disastrous effects on this mine than on the others, especially as the mine suffers, like Bancroft and Nchanga, from a severe water problem. It was to mitigate this economic problem and streamline the operations of the whole that Rhodesian Selection Trust and Roan Antelope amalgamated in 1962. The main interest, though, in this otherwise routine business manoeuvre lies in the fact that although the American Metal–Climax company previously held $33\frac{1}{3}$ per cent of Roan Antelope shares and 51 per cent of Rhodesian Selection Trust, in the new combine its holding was 43·5 per cent—no longer an overall controlling interest. It is a reasonable specula-

[11]Although the Roan reserves are given as averaging 3·04 per cent copper (still the poorest on the Copperbelt) in the Chamber of Mines *Yearbook*, 1960, a figure of 'rather under 2 per cent total copper' was quoted to the seventh Commonwealth Mining and Metallurgical Congress in May 1961 and printed in the privately circulated programme of the Northern Rhodesia section of that congress. This discrepancy may be explained partly by inevitable inaccuracies in sampling procedures, by mining techniques, which do not always lead to the removal of a consistent average of the ore values and by dilution of the ore caused by sub-level stoping techniques, especially when pressure increases at depth so that more waste is inevitably mixed with the ore after blasting. Management normally allows for these situations in its mill grade forecasts. Later figures show little change. For 1967 the reserves are quoted as averaging 2·86 per cent copper, and the average grade of ore milled 1·88 per cent (Copperbelt of Zambia Mining Industry *Yearbook*, 1967).

tion that when the Roan Antelope itself ceases to be an economic proposition, attention will be diverted to the Baluba ore-body (see pages 33 and 45). A new company, Baluba Mines Ltd, was floated in 1954 under the chairmanship of Lewin Tucker, but so far only prospecting work has been carried out. It is, however, already clear that the known reserves of 112 million short tons of ore averaging 2·41 per cent copper and 0·16 per cent cobalt[12] provide the potential for a very large future mine.

Rhokana

Within the Rhokana Corporation itself there have been three major post-war developments. The first of these was the decision in 1946 to sell the Rhokana electrolytic refinery at Nkana to a new company, Rhodesia Copper Refineries Ltd, in which control is shared jointly by Rhokana and Nchanga. Then, in 1952, there was set up the Rhoanglo Mine Services Ltd, in which Rhodesian Anglo-American technical services were centralised. This preceded the Rhodesian Selection Trust equivalent by six years. But most important of all was the decision that, as from 1 January 1951, the head offices of Nchanga, Rhodesia Copper Refineries and Rhokana should be transferred from London to Northern Rhodesia. This was not a political decision, although Ernest Oppenheimer himself later pointed out that his company felt a 'moral obligation'[13] to help develop the Rhodesias. The motives were basically economic in that administrative efficiency would be increased by having a locally based headquarters and in addition the heavy taxation liabilities of companies registered in the United Kingdom would no longer apply. Technical control also followed the administration in due course, first to Rhodesia and then to the new State of Zambia, with the removal of the consulting engineer from Salisbury to Lusaka in 1964. The Rhodesian Selection Trust group also adopted similar measures, its headquarters (and archives) being located first of all in Salisbury and subsequently in Ndola.

The two most spectacular post-war developments on the

[12]Baluba Mines Ltd annual report, 30 June 1962.
[13]Statement to shareholders, 1956.

Copperbelt, certainly to the layman and possibly to the tech-
nologist also, involve Chambishi and Nchanga.

Chambishi

It will be recalled that after the initial prospecting by Parker and
Grey from 1927 (see page 51), Chambishi had lain neglected.
The original activity was halted by the depression of the early
1930's. Then, when the devaluation of sterling in 1949 stimulated further development, attention was devoted to opening up
the Chibuluma mine instead because of its rich copper ore and
cobalt (see pages 153–5). Similarly, the increased buoyancy
felt in 1956 led to the decision to exploit the Mufulira West area.
Thus in 1960 Chambishi had reverted to bush, the ruins of the
original buildings overgrown by tropical vegetation. Only in
1962, on 21 May, was it announced by Rhodesian Selection
Trust that a new company, Chambishi Mines Ltd, was to begin a
£7½ million programme to develop Chambishi as an open-cast
mine. This was one of the first fruits of the merger of Rhodesian Selection Trust and the Roan Antelope which had taken
place shortly before. A new mining town therefore rapidly began
to spring up in what is virtually the geographical heart of the
Copperbelt—a remarkable expression of confidence in the future
of the world copper market and of Northern Rhodesia in
particular.

The Nchanga and Chingola open pits

To appreciate the function of the Nchanga and Chingola open pits
it is necessary to consider the ore reserves available for exploitation on the Nchanga property. Comparative figures, as published
by the company, were as follows:

	JANUARY 1955		MARCH 1960[14]	
	Tons	% Cu	Tons	% Cu
The River Lode	2,000,000	4·2	1,731,240	4·29
Chingola ore-body	2,000,000	7·0	14,183,196	4·89
Nchanga ore-body	93,000,000	3·51	88,996,680	3·53
Nchanga West ore-body	46,500,000	6·9	74,558,860	5·96

[14]The total ore reserve at 30 June 1961 amounted to 184,166,000 short
tons averaging 4·63 per cent copper: Chamber of Mines *Yearbook*, 1961.

It is immediately apparent that although the Nchanga West deposit is considerably richer in copper than any of the others, it contains a much smaller tonnage than the neglected Nchanga ore-body. During the early years of development, when one of the main incentives was to produce paying ore in the shortest possible time, all the attention had naturally been devoted to the rich Nchanga West ore-body. Although this meant that the mine came to a profitable stage relatively quickly, it also meant that the exploitation of the property was being conducted in an unbalanced way. The consulting engineer, Nichols, had noted this as early as 1950,[15] without any immediate response. However, the development which took place during the early 1950's, and which has already been discussed in detail, brought the output of the mine to its theoretical potential in 1954, without handling any other than Nchanga West ore. It was then decided, in the long-term interests of the company, that the value of the ore mined in the future should conform as far as possible to the average values of the reserves as a whole. As the full potential of the Chingola ore-body was not known at this stage, and as the River Lode was comparatively small, this decision actually meant that the production from the Nchanga West deposit was to be deliberately diluted with poorer quality ore which could come only from the Nchanga ore-body. A balanced production at this stage would involve reducing the output at Nchanga West and adding each month 150,000 tons of the Nchanga ore.

There were also sound technological reasons why an open pit should be developed to exploit the Nchanga ore-body at this time. It was desirable that the rate of advance of the Nchanga West workings down dip should be slowed up so that the dewatering procedure in all three of the water-bearing horizons could be facilitated. In addition, the advance of the underground workings on Nchanga West was going to cause caving which would ultimately prevent further work on the Nchanga lode itself. If the maximum possible extraction of ore from the open-cast workings on the Nchanga lode was to be accomplished, this exploitation would have to be undertaken before the Nchanga West

[51]Letter dated 2 August 1950. See above page 128.

underground workings had advanced so far as to make the open pit operation unsafe.

The difficulty, of course, is obvious. Whereas the extraction workings beneath the Nchanga West ore-body are in solid arkose or granite, the feldspathic quartzite which contains the Nchanga ore lies immediately above the very soft and loose upper banded sandstones in which extraction workings would have been most expensive to support and maintain. Inevitably, of course, the problem of de-watering the beds had to be overcome before any kind of mining could be attempted. It was eventually proved, after extensive diamond drilling, prospect pitting and cross-cutting from these into the ore-body, that mining by open pit methods would be the most feasible. There were, of course, many difficulties. The angle of dip on the south side of the syncline was between 25° and 30° and the ultimate vertical depth was about 800 ft. Further, the heavy, concentrated rainfall between November and April brought possibilities of floods and landslides within the pit itself.[16]

On the credit side, although the overburden is extremely deep —up to 600 ft when the Nchanga pit reaches its maximum depth of 800 ft—it is composed of earth and soft, decomposed rock which is comparatively easy to remove. Little drilling or blasting is required and large-capacity earth-moving equipment could be economically employed. The ore-body itself is a substantial one —up to eighty feet thick—and at its upper end is only 120 feet from the surface, under a layer of decomposed rock.[17]

The original layout of the pit is along the strike of the

[16]In 1961 Professor J. E. B. Jennings of the Witwatersrand University began an investigation into soil stability in the open pit. The management intended to build a laboratory to investigate what the maximum angle of the pit slopes may safely be. This must determine how deep the pits can be sunk. If the angle is to be very low the economic potential of the pits will be greatly restricted. Nevertheless, under present circumstances (1962) about 33 million tons of the 89 million in the Nchanga ore-body will be recovered from the Nchanga pit (personal information from the former Open Pit Manager, N. A. Wilkie).

[17]Apparently not much. Nevertheless, to expose it required the removal of eight million tons of earth (Anglo-American Corporation annual report, 1956).

Nchanga ore-body for 3,500 ft, which will allow a maximum depth of over 700 ft. The pit is being excavated in a series of steps ('benches') each about 35 ft high and 110 ft wide. Work commenced on 21 April 1955, the development being carried out by three large, electrically operated shovels, each excavating eight tons of earth at a bite. To remove the earth from the pit there were trains consisting of eight trucks, each holding forty-five tons, hauled by diesel locomotives. In addition there were six rubber-tyred trucks each carrying thirty tons and another six with a capacity of twenty-two tons.

In November 1958 a remarkable bucket-wheel excavator was imported from Germany at a cost of £210,000. This enormous machine, with its eight buckets, each holding a ton of earth, can remove the overburden at speeds of up to about half a ton per second. The earth is then transported on a conveyor belt almost three miles long to another gigantic machine[18] which stacks it on a waste dump. The conveyor system and stacker involved a further outlay of £180,000. The actual operating of the excavator is carried out by only one European and four Africans.[19, 20]

The ore itself, in the feldspathic quartzite, has to be blasted into pieces of a convenient size before it can be removed. The monthly output of 80,000 tons for the concentrator is loaded by mechanical shovel into 25-ton trucks which convey it to two 8 ft diametre ore passes, lined with concrete, which are located in the floor of the pit. This ore, which is largely oxide, passes through grizzlies at the top of these passes and falls to a loading point on the 625 ft level sub-haulage which leads to the Nchanga West workings. Here it is hauled to the surface up the main 'C' or 'D' shafts along with the Nchanga West ore. This is a much simpler and more economical process than any scheme of direct removal

[18]66 ft high, 250 ft long and weighing 388 tons.
[19]The total personnel of the pits in 1962 numbered 303 (Nchanga) and 87 (Chingola). Figures supplied by N. A. Wilkie.
[20]The bucket-wheel excavator plus the mechanical shovels still remaining remove almost one million tons of overburden and ore per month between them. By 2 December 1961 over 50 million tons of earth had been removed, giving a yield of 3½ million tons of ore. The planned ore production is 80,000 tons per month, and at all times sufficient ore for eighteen months mining is fully developed. Information by N. A. Wilkie.

from the pit. Low-grade ore is stockpiled for future use as required.

The Chingola ore-body is really only an extension of the Nchanga West deposit after an intervening barren area. But whereas in 1955 it was thought to be a comparatively small deposit of some 2 million tons of high-grade ore, diamond drilling in 1956 and subsequently has increased the reserve to 14 million tons, with the prospect of more yet to be found. The ore-body lies in a shallow syncline which has a very complicated structure due to folding of the strata. The ore-body is 1,500 ft long and 90 ft wide, and is mainly in the form of high-grade oxides.

The decision to mine it by open pit methods was taken in 1957, for similar motives to those which had brought about the Nchanga open pit. The purpose[21] was not to increase output but to permit of the maximum flexibility of output as dictated by prevailing circumstances. A balanced production would be even easier to maintain with three separate sources of supply than before.

As the company did not have the equipment available for developing the pit in 1954, the initial task of removing the overburden was undertaken by contractors until the necessary machinery arrived. The techniques used were much the same as in the Nchanga pit. The excavation of overburden is made by a ten-ton electric shovel which serves ten 22-ton trucks. Another electric shovel removes the ore, which is brought to surface in the same trucks.[22] The benches in the pit are 38 ft high in the overburden and 30 ft high in the ore.

In 1963 the ore was being mined at the rate of 40,000 tons per month, with a developed reserve of 732,000 tons. The overburden and low-grade ore are dumped in separate piles on the surface, while the better ore is taken to the plant by a private two-and-a-half mile railway.[23] The grade varies enormously from

[21]Nchanga annual report, 1957; H. F. Oppenheimer's review.
[22]Equipment is interchanged between the Nchanga and Chingola pits as required. The Nchanga pit workshops are also responsible for repairing the Chingola equipment.
[23]This railway crosses the main road to Bancroft and the Congo by a high-level bridge. During the disturbances inspired by the United

level to level and poses considerable problems to the concentrator staff.

Prospecting

Although Dr Bancroft reduced surface prospecting to a virtual routine and was able, in consequence, to produce the first comprehensive geological map of the Copperbelt, he largely ignored one of the most intriguing surface manifestations of mineralisation—vegetative guides.

It was well known to early prospectors that vegetation was frequently sparse and stunted in areas where copper deposits lay but a short distance below the surface. This manifestation was, for example, most marked at the Roan Antelope. In addition a small blue flower, rather like a forget-me-not, was frequently seen in areas where outcrops of copper ore occurred. However, as the flower is almost always associated with visible outcrops, it was of no real value as a prospecting guide. Still less so was the species of cryptosepalum, known to the Africans as *mpandala* or *sambashi*, whose small pink flowers were believed to be a certain indication of copper. It has been conclusively proved by recent tests that this flower grows equally well anywhere in the district and its presence near copper deposits is purely coincidental.

In October 1949, however, the Kennecot Copper Corporation, of America, sent a cable to the general manager of Roan Antelope requesting that further information regarding the above-mentioned blue flower be provided. This request was passed on to the Roan geological department, with astonishing results. Samples of all the flowers growing on and near the ore-body were collected and it became immediately evident that the unclassified blue flower, which had been the initial cause of the investigation, grew equally profusely on or off the ore-body. So did all but one of the other flowers—a member of the sage family which grew only over the ore-body and could not be found more than a few yards from it. Just in case there might be some significance in this fact, the plant was then extensively plotted throughout the area—with the

National Independence Party in 1961 an attempt was made to blow up the bridge, without success.

disappointing result that it appeared everywhere regardless of the proximity of copper.

Only at this stage was the plant subjected to close scrutiny. On close examination there proved to be two almost identical varieties of the same plant. The mauve-white petals differed very slightly, as also did the calyx and the texture of the leaves—and one type grew only over the ore-bodies.

As information became more abundant, so did the confidence of the investigators increase. The new flower charts followed the contours of known ore-bodies with uncanny accuracy. The plant was sent to the Curator of Tropical Botany at Kew Gardens and there formally identified as *Ocimum homblei de wild*, the 'pseudo' copper flower being also identified as *Becium obovatum E. May* —a different genus altogether.

The plant was now subjected to chemical analysis and proved to be a copper accumulator. Copper in quantities of up to 4,500 parts per million was found, as opposed to the normal copper content in plants of less than twenty parts per million. It was also proved that the seeds of the plant would germinate only if there was a copper content of at least fifty parts per million and not more than 600 parts per million in the water used for their culture. Plants immediately died if planted in copper-free soils.

Tests have been made from areas as far apart as Lusaka and the Congo border, all but two with success. Even in these two cases, rational explanations for failure were available. Further, the testing of areas not previously known to contain copper, on the basis of the discovery of the flower, has given successful results in the form of large new reserves. A new and valuable copper indicator has therefore been found.[24]

Ironically, as more and more deposits have been found, so the actual difficulties of finding them have increased. It is now fairly certain that all the surface outcrops have been discovered and in-

[24]For a most interesting illustrated article on the copper flower, see *Horizon*, January 1959, from which some of the above information was taken. *Note :* although the 'copper flower' is always found growing above ore-bodies the converse is not true. Some ore-bodies have no 'copper flowers' growing on them. Therefore the plant can never replace the more orthodox geophysical investigations.

vestigated, and the geologist is faced with the problem of searching for copper of which no visible signs exist. The Chibuluma and Chibuluma West ore-bodies are cases in point. Further senses other than sight must be brought into operation, the use of super-sensitive chemical assay, and electrical, electronic and magnetic apparatus replacing the relatively insensitive human nose and ear. In this way the development of techniques of tracing mineralisation in streams back to its source has taken place. Very delicate chemical tests are also available to test the amounts of copper in the soils above ore-bodies, and, coupled with the possible visible evidence of the copper flower and the 'clearings' formed by the slight 'poisoning' of other vegetation, these provide a reliable guide on which to base the decision whether or not to drill. Clearings in the bush caused by mineralisation show up particularly well in aerial photographs—a technique in use on the Copperbelt since 1926.[25]

Geophysical methods were first introduced on the Copperbelt in 1926, when an electrical survey over the Nchanga ore-bodies was made.[26] Amongst the numerous geophysical methods now in use are electrical, electro-magnetic, magnetic, gravity and seismic. Unfortunately, as the sulphide ore-bodies are found only at depths of more than 200 ft below the surface, the above methods are not very successful in tracing them, the effects of the laterite layer above them tending to 'blot out' the reactions of the ore-body itself on the measuring instruments. Fortunately the electrical method known as 'self-potential' has proved fairly effective, as has testing for radio-activity, which is often associated with copper. This may be done from low-flying aircraft—helicopters, for example.

Nevertheless, these various scientific methods have rarely proved the existence of a mine, Chibuluma being a notable exception on the Copperbelt; and the geologist is once more forced back to the time-honoured methods of pitting and drilling. The

[25]For details, see Owen Letcher, *South Central Africa*, pages 86–7; also G. L. Walker, 'Surveying from the air in Central Africa', *Engineering and Mining Journal*, January 1929, pages 49–52.
[26]See *Horizon*, September 1959; also Appendix II.

drilling is usually done at the richest point indicated by the prospect pits, and may have to go down to well over 300 ft before
unweathered formations are reached which core well and provide
concrete evidence of mineralisation. Many years of investigation
are usually necessary before sufficient knowledge can be gained
to justify exploitation.

At the present time, transport and supply are carried on mainly
by air, often by helicopter, with the result that the expense of
building and maintaining roads is greatly diminished, porterage
becomes unnecessary and the prospector can be deposited on the
site of his work without the need for prolonged and time-wasting
treks from the nearest centre of civilisation.

A further complication, not envisaged in the early days, has
now arisen to add still further to the difficulties encountered by
the prospector and those who employ him. The Copperbelt contains considerable acreages which are known as 'exclusive prospecting areas' and further large areas known as 'mining special
grants'. The actual position of the prospector and of the mining
companies in these areas deserves careful study.

In *The Laws of Northern Rhodesia*[27] the rights and obligations
of the prospector are clearly defined. His work 'shall not confer
any right, title or interest whatsoever in any land'. Further, he
must obtain the permission of the property owner before he may
work near such items as buildings, ploughed land, growing crops,
roads, dams and various other places. Work in such areas also
embodies further difficulties not encountered elsewhere, for, with
the removal of the natural vegetation, disturbances of the soil,
introduction of metal in the form of fences and so on, the basic
clues by which the prospector is guided tend to disappear. Not
only is his own work rendered more arduous and complicated,
but the disturbance to the property owner is correspondingly
greater.

No individual prospecting is now permitted on the Copperbelt.[28] Four large blocks of Crown land in the middle of the area

[27]Cap. 91, sections 19 and 20.
[28]Except for the residue of land not taken up, which was opened to
individual prospectors in 1941: government notice 37/1941.

are reserved by the Government Mining Engineer. Of the remainder, nine areas were held as exclusive prospecting areas by
the Anglo-American Group under licences valid until 1963 (1960
in the case of Kafue) of which four had already been prospected
and the licences surrendered by 1960. Seventeen further exclusive
prospecting areas came under the control of the Rhodesian
Selection Trust with licences valid until 1961, by which time
most of them had been investigated. Smaller areas may be set
aside for further intensive investigation and possibly later registered as mining special grants.[29]

The problem, then, in exclusive prospecting areas is to decide
how far to permit capital expenditure and development of the
surface of the land in view of what the prospectors might discover underneath it. In general the basic principle would seem to
be that the natural vegetation should not be cleared until the
initial prospecting has been completed, whilst at the same time
ensuring that land be not alienated from normal use merely
because it happens to lie within an exclusive prospecting area.
The Duff report[30] recommends that in doubtful cases the Government Mining Engineer should always be consulted.

The mining special grants provide an altogether different set
of circumstances from the exclusive prospecting areas. Their
holders have not only the right to work minerals over extensive
areas but may also make almost unlimited use of the surface whilst
actually mining.[31] Any surface developments on them would have
to give way to any future development the mining companies
might wish to make. In some cases, farming operations have already begun, but it is obvious that in the event of a grant holder
exercising his right to work his property the farms would have to

[29]For speculation and further details see the *First Report on a Regional
Survey of the Copperbelt, 1959*, chapter 7, sections A and B (the Duff
report), Government Printer, Lusaka, 1960. *Note :* the position regarding
prospecting areas and special grants is in a constant state of flux. The
information given above was correct for early 1961.
[30]Para. 209.
[31]For details, see *The Mining Laws of Northern Rhodesia*, cap. 91, sections
54–57.

be sold to the holder of the grant, even if this meant settling the price by arbitration.[32]

Some of the latest grants to be registered have had farms established in the areas prior to the grant being made. It would appear that in these cases permission to work in the areas near houses, crops and so on would have to be obtained, and in the event of large-scale working the property would have to be bought outright. It is unfortunate for all concerned that very often the land reserved for mining in this way is often also the best and most fertile farming soil.

It may be argued that the payment of full compensation to a farmer who is dispossessed from his property on a mining special grant occasions no special loss to him. This may be true, but it takes no account of the loss to the nation as a whole of capital, time and the fruits of labour over the years. The productivity of farms is built up gradually and cannot be replaced overnight. In view of all this it is desirable that land intended for permanent agricultural or other development should be separated as far as possible from the mining special grants.[33] This has led in some cases, such as Ndola and Mufulira, to the cramping of town planning and development to avoid encroachment on mining grant areas. This problem of the conflicting uses of land is far from being settled and will pose problems for planners for many years to come even after all mining development has ceased, since the effect of caving on the hanging wall side of the outcrops is a perennial limitation on surface development.

[32]Increased land values due to mineral deposits would be discounted in the valuation.

[33]It should be noted that much land is held by the mining companies as freehold, in which case no complications arise. The companies are well aware of the problems involved and now offer considerably longer leases than previously. They also take every precaution to ensure that the minimum disturbance takes place. The number of farms actually taken over for mining development is small.

Appendix I

Some notes on the native development of copper ore deposits in Central Africa

The discovery and working of copper deposits in south central Africa must not be regarded solely as a European phenomenon. It is true that there was never a Bronze Age in Africa south of the Sahara, as there was elsewhere—the earliest metal users in south and central Africa used iron from the beginning and worked it in a manner similar to that evolved by other Iron Age people in Europe and Asia. Nevertheless, where surface deposits of other metals such as copper, tin, gold or silver were found there is no doubt that they too were extensively worked, and the resulting ingots, ornaments and weapons not only retained for local use but also traded, often to considerable distances.

The first reference to copper being worked in south central Africa is to be found in a unique book, *Relatione del Reame di Congo et delle circonvicine Contrade*, by the Portuguese Filippo Pigafetta, published in Rome in 1591. In this volume, written almost three centuries before David Livingstone's journeys, there is reference to the copper mines of the Bembe. If, as is possible, the name relates to the Bemba tribe or to Lake Bembe—the former name of Lake Bangweulu—the mines may well be identified either with those of Katanga or the present Zambian Copperbelt. About the same time also, an Englishman, Andrew Battell, a prisoner of the Portuguese in Angola, spoke of natives in the far interior bringing copper to trade in the central and coastal areas of Southern Angola. 'Again,' writes J. Desmond Clark,[1] 'it is not improbable that this copper may have come from our own Copperbelt.'[2] Occasional copper ornaments have been found on 'stamped ware'[3] sites in both Zambia and Rhodesia, whilst Rhodesia is particularly rich in finds from centres of stone building, of which the

[1] Former curator of the Rhodes-Livingstone Museum. Subsequently Professor of Archaeology, Los Angeles.
[2] 'Pre-European copper working', *Roan Antelope Magazine*, May 1957, pages 12–16.
[3] So called from the impressed designs on their pottery. The sites date back to the fourteenth century in some areas. One example was found in 1956 between Chingola and Bancroft (Kirila Bomwe).

ruins at Khami, Zimbabwe and elsewhere are a silent memorial.[4] Numerous tools, ornaments and weapons in various metals have been found, testifying to an ever increasing development of mining and smelting, particularly of copper, in Katanga and adjacent parts of Zambia. Katanga copper also reached as far as the Portuguese settlements in Mozambique, north-east to the coast of Tanganyika and possibly to the Angola coast also.[5]

The Portuguese, Lacerda, on his journey through central Africa in 1798 noted the use of copper for necklaces, bracelets and anklets.[6] Even he made no direct reference to Katanga, the first European mention of the area being in the companion account to Lacerda's journey by the traders P. J. Baptista and Amaro José, who crossed Africa from Angola to Tete in 1802, after Lacerda's death.[7]

When we started from this farm of Chamuginga Mussenda [wrote Baptista] we travelled across others with valleys and saw on the summit of the hills stones which appear true [green?][8] and where they dig the copper; in the midst of this country is where they make the bars . . . and pay such bars to the Quiburi or his successor for that Lord of the Salina to send them to the Muatayanvo or to whoever the Muatayanvo sends for them. These two proprietors were also at one time sovereigns of the lands as well as owners of the mines left them by their predecessors.

Later, however, the Cazembe acquired them by force and at the time of Baptista's visit they were in subjection to both him and Muatayanvo. The estimated position of these copperfields was between 25–26° E and 11° S.

In the 1850's the famous missionary explorer Dr David Livingstone reported observing the use of copper rings as ornaments[9] and a few years later, in 1873, the explorer Cameron noted what is probably the first written reference to Katanga as a place name:

[4]The most important pre-European stone building in Southern Rhodesia, that at Zimbabwe, may date in part back to the eleventh century. This does not necessarily place the metallic remains at the same early date. For details on Zimbabwe, see R. Summers, *Zimbabwe: a Rhodesian mystery*, Nelson, London 1963.
[5]I am indebted for much of this information to J. Desmond Clark.
[6]*The Lands of the Cazembe—Lacerda's Journey to Cazembe in 1798*, Sir R. F. Burton, Royal Geographical Society of London, 1873, page 18.
[7]*Journey of the Pombeiros or Native Travelling Traders P. J. Baptista and Amaro José*, Sir R. F. Burton, Royal Geographical Society, London, 1873.
[8]Malachite.
[9]*Missionary Travels in Southern Africa*, Murray, London, 1857, pages 276 and 291.

Copper is found in large quantities in Katanga and for a considerable distance to the westward . . . The natives, too, know of the gold, but it is soft and they did not value it, preferring the red copper to the white.[10]

The missionary Arnot was also well aware of the widespread fame of the Katanga mines and noted in 1886 that the copper was traded, through the Arabs, as far north as Uganda.[11] He and Livingstone were the first to bring back any details of the Katanga workings, although the first European actually to see them was probably the German explorer P. Reichard in 1884.[12]

Arnot also visited the sites in 1886. The malachite was found on certain bare hilltops and was removed by the natives, who dug round shafts some fifteen to twenty feet deep for the purpose.[13] The actual mining was restricted to certain families, who formed a kind of trade 'caste' jealously guarding their secrets and handing them down from generation to generation.[14] The mining operations were conducted during the dry season, from May until the onset of the rains in November. Entire families participated, the rocks being dug out with iron picks or, if too hard, being cracked by lighting a fire against them and then suddenly cooling them with water before levering them away. Bark buckets and ropes were used to bring the earth and ore to the surface.[15]

All the accounts mention malachite only, and it appears that this was the only form of copper ore mined and smelted by primitive methods in Central Africa. Smelting was a highly specialised process, carried out under the direction of master smelters. The furnaces were constructed of clay and ant-hill[16] and fired by charcoal from the very hard wood *Afrormosia angolensis*. Although little information was

[10]*Across Africa*, vol. II, chapter 17, Daldy Isbister & Co., London, 1877.
[11]*Missionary Travels in Central Africa*, Holness, London, 1914, page 76.
[12]Owen Letcher, *South Central Africa*, African Publications, Johannesburg, 1932, page 44.
[13]Professor Clark says they were sometimes as much as 100 ft deep. This could only have been in particularly firm ground, for shafts were normally abandoned when any risk became apparent. Probably for the same reason no lateral workings ever extended from the bottom of the shafts. Trench-like cuts were also sometimes made in Northern Rhodesia e.g. at Kansanshi and Bwana Mkubwa.
[14]Arnot, op. cit., page 90.
[15]Progress was often rapid. Livingstone mentions that eleven men dug 3,500 lbs of copper in three months: *Last Journals*, Murray, London, 1874. Entry dated 28 April 1871.
[16]There are tales of the early European miners and prospectors in the Ndola and Solwezi areas finding old furnaces hollowed out from the sides of ant-hills. Personal information W. Pickering, a surveyor in the Nchanga area in 1926.

available until recently, it was known that these furnaces were small, producing about fifteen pounds of copper at one smelting. After a second smelting to refine the metal, the molten copper was collected in a bowl-shaped clay pot and poured directly into the previously prepared moulds, generally made of clay.[17] The resulting ingots were sometimes turned into ornaments or weapons, but more usually traded as bulk metal.

The shape of the ingots varied considerably. Currency bars were manufactured in the form of a capital 'I' about four feet long and weighing sixty to seventy pounds.[18, 19] Others were in the form of a capital 'H' or a Maltese cross. These types were seen by both Livingstone and Arnot. Smaller ingots were also made in various shapes, and in some cases the copper was traded as wire made by drawing the hot metal through a hole of the appropriate diameter in a special plate designed for the purpose. According to Livingstone, much of the copper was traded for beads,[20] but apart from its obvious use as currency it served many useful purposes amongst the African peoples—weapons, ornaments, ceremonial objects and even occasionally for inlay work on iron.

As Professor Clark pointed out in 1957,[21] most of the available facts known up to then regarding early copper mining and smelting in south central Africa referred to Katanga, and not to the Northern Rhodesian Copperbelt at all. Although evidence of ancient workings is widespread on the Copperbelt, the actual methods used could only be assumed to be the same as those in the neighbouring Katanga—and undoubtedly they must have been very similar, if not identical. However, more definite information has since become available. Although the last official native smelting of copper in the Copperbelt area was as long ago as 1912, in November 1960, Mr Chaplin of the Rhodes-Livingstone museum discovered survivors of the smelters living in a village to the west of Solwezi. They were persuaded to recondition their implements and demonstrate their techniques to a number of interested persons, incuding the Central African Film Unit. Iron was successfully smelted on this occasion, but attempts to obtain a workable quantity of copper were a failure, this unfortunate result being blamed by the smelters on the poor quality of the ore provided for the experiment by the Nchanga mine.[22]

[17]Or in sand by the fingers of the workers: Arnot, op. cit., page 90.
[18]One measuring 4 ft 6 in and weighing 30 lbs was discovered nine inches below ground on a farm near Lusaka in 1952: *Rhokana Review*, April 1952.
[19]Livingstone, *Last Journals*, page 179.
[20]Ibid, page 123.
[21]*Roan Antelope Magazine*, op. cit.
[22]Personal information: Mr J. H. Chaplin.

Appendix II

The equipotential line method of electrical prospecting

In 1925, A. Broughton Edge, A.R.S.M., B.SC., M.I.M.M., was engaged by Minerals Separation Ltd to carry out geophysical prospecting by electrical methods in Northern Rhodesia. In that year he obtained excellent results in the Lunsemfwa area, north of Broken Hill, as a result of which he was offered a much bigger contract for 1926–27. This necessitated his engaging four assistants, D. Williams, now Professor of Mining Geology at the Royal School of Mines, S. H. Shaw, now Director of Colonial Geological Surveys, J. H. Taylor, lately retired as a senior geologist for the Central Mining–Rand Mines group, and J. C. Ferguson, who was until recently the Director of Geological Surveys in Southern Rhodesia. The rest of the staff—surveyors, draughtmen and two mechanics to run the generators—were recruited in Rhodesia. They were A. J. Liebenberg, C. W. Scrymgeour, W. A. L. Gordon, C. W. Kerr, W. D. Penny, I. F. Maritz, R. W. Hill, A. M. McKenzie, C. F. A. Dennison, N. M. Airey and P. G. Lendrum. The party was later joined by T. V. Wilson (now Baines) and W. M. Pickering.

The principal method used by Broughton Edge was the equipotential line, with alternating current at 540 cycles 4·5 amps at 80 volts). The generators could also deliver direct current with a 1,080 cycle ripple (16 amps at 50 volts). These generators were small, flat twin petrol engines which were built by Bosch of Germany during the 1914–18 war, possibly for military signalling purposes. The weight of the complete unit was about 200 lbs.

The basic principle of the method was simple. A line measuring one mile was cleared through the bush and along it a power line was suspended on poles, the ends of the line being buried in the ground. When current from the generator at the mid-point of the line was passed along the wire, it continued below ground by passing through any conductive materials, e.g. copper, which might exist. It was then possible to track this and plot the position of these conductive materials. The method worked well at Lunsemfwa, where sulphides lay close to the surface, but proved unreliable in detecting the deeper Copperbelt deposits.

Appendix III

Costs of production (£)

(a) Roan Antelope

Year to 30 June	Coal	Electricity	Transport, etc.	Labour	Royalties	Stores consumed	Total
1947-8	57,581	165,250	36,349	1,168,747	473,572	685,213	2,586,712
1948-9	55,167	164,204	42,778	1,356,563	548,359	962,839	3,129,910
1949-50	54,916	165,609	49,459	1,522,475	679,428	1,169,418	3,641,305
1950-1	91,864	163,248	58,671	1,703,674	1,335,687	1,257,035	4,610,179
1951-2	113,329	187,686	75,781	1,881,745	1,849,516	1,410,450	5,518,507
1952-3	106,116	318,257	102,004	2,150,354	2,517,302	1,882,593	7,076,626
1953-4	182,400	528,099	142,933	2,428,654	2,129,893	2,152,940	7,564,919
1954-5	205,952	547,360	108,376	2,408,032	2,548,762	1,949,961	7,768,443
1955-6	226,481	743,428	118,858	2,777,706	3,650,593	2,302,440	9,819,506
1956-7	233,258	768,636	119,861	2,978,004	2,449,624	2,489,028	9,038,411
1957-8	178,882	661,348	80,489	3,146,487	1,307,566	2,086,569	7,461,341
1958-9	193,852	601,062	87,415	3,257,976	1,732,096	2,057,108	7,929,509
1959-60	243,888	716,971	118,945	3,329,309	2,290,122	2,440,611	9,139,846
1960-1	239,949	727,654	136,001	3,330,974	1,810,529	2,205,196	8,450,303

Appendix III—*continued*

(b) *Mufulira*

Year	Electric power imported	Railage to African port (including handling charges freight and insurance)	Labour	Royalty	Stores consumed (including coal)	Total
1948	12,105	237,683	1,073,552	502,648	1,135,448	2,961,436
1949	12,587	312,964	1,267,276	723,745	1,338,885	3,655,457
1950	5,560	321,570	1,435,013	759,422	1,565,793	4,087,358
1951	6,032	469,452	1,989,333	1,494,867	1,986,151	5,945,835
1952	3,455	428,589	2,393,641	1,744,413	2,043,028	6,613,126
1953	62,137	418,612	3,022,813	2,116,632	2,467,311	8,087,505
1954	61,732	1,103,693	3,223,346	2,017,395	3,071,369	9,477,535
1955	167,621	1,171,504	3,581,518	2,576,531	3,060,049	10,557,223
1956	337,070	1,407,913	4,611,663	3,888,632	3,713,902	13,959,180
1957	659,978	2,202,099	4,406,919	2,746,260	3,648,285	13,663,541
1958	936,156	2,103,830	4,306,869	1,589,633	3,188,343	12,124,831
1959	839,232	1,807,549	4,761,355	2,005,085	2,981,464	12,394,685
1960	1,029,965	2,288,851	6,144,969	2,590,180	3,733,618	15,787,583
1961	1,111,499	2 139,613	6,144,190	2,445,653	3,651,062	15,492,017

Appendix III—*concluded*

(c) *Chibuluma*
Began production May 1956

Year to 30 June	Electricity	Transport and insurance	Labour	Royalties	Stores consumed	Other	Total
1956	62,890	55,712	119,482	152,277	92,791	99,354	582,506
1957	125,201	312,496	434,372	395,349	331,229	33,576	1,632,223
1958	151,037	588,857	524,641	465,171	403,359	605,407	2,738,472
1959	122,840	424,578	528,672	438,398	388,502	663,603	2,566,593
1960	119,779	84,144	584,600	546,006	429,566	908,479	2,672,574
1961	123,797	87,757	637,792	449,476	438,774	755,499	2,493,095
1962	132,116	81,973	691,181	388,387	471,084	673,895	2,438,636

Production capacity (short tons)

Year ending	Bancroft	Chibuluma	Mufulira	Nchanga	Rhokana	Roan
1951			90,000	61,096	94,554	83,462
1952			90,000	77,074	86,850	90,749
1953			95,000	104,515	80,457	97,784
1954			95,000	128,953	93,900	99,319
1955			95,000	115,205	80,237	92,620
1956			112,000	128,490	94,328	99,360
1957		22,000	112,000	126,093	94,992	96,649
1958		22,000	112,000	135,744	98,252	89,523
1959	13,595	22,000	112,000	156,175	89,820	90,643
1960	57,627	22,000	112,000	199,410	112,689	103,028
1961	57,988	22,000	143,000	206,080	123,406	91,621

Specimen rates of pay: Roan Antelope, 1929

(from Rhodesian Selection Trust files)

EUROPEAN	Maximum			Minimum		
Monthly paid (per month)	£	s	d	£	s	d
Assayers	50	0	0	35	0	0
Caretaker	45	0	0			
Clerical staff	55	0	0	27	10	0
Draughtsmen	60	0	0	30	0	0
Foreman carpenter mechanic	65	0	0	45	0	0
Gardener	40	0	0	30	0	0
Geologist and junior mining engineers	45	0	0	30	0	0
Hospital nurses	25	0	0	15	0	0
Mine captain	60	0	0			
Stenographer	35	0	0	15	0	0
Shift bosses	62	10	0	47	10	0
Surveyors	55	0	0	35	0	0

Daily paid (per hour)						
Bricklayer			3	6		
Crane driver			3	0		
Electrician			3	6		
Fitter			3	6		
Handyman			2	10½	2	6
Locomotive and lorry drivers			3	4½	2	6
Motor mechanic			3	6	2	9
Miner (per shift)	1	10	0	1	7	6
Underground timberman (per shift)	1	10	0			
Night watchman			2	9		

AFRICAN						
Daily rates (not including bonuses)	Range					
Recruiting	5d–1s 1d					
Watchman	6d–1s 5d					
Caretaker	1½d–1s 3d					
Garden	1½d–9½d					
Compound police	6d–2s 1d					
Head police	6d–2s 10d					
Garage	1d–1s					
Office boy	2d–2s 10½d					

Appendix V—*concluded*.

Bricklayer	7*d*–2*s* 9*d*
Bricklayer's labourer	2*d*–8½*d*
Time office clerk	9½*d*–2*s* 10½*d*
Compound clerk	11*d*–2*s* 11½*d*
Engine driver	8*d*–1*s* 3½*d*
Boss boy	8*d*–1*s* 4*d*
Timbering	8*d*–1*s*

Basic rates of wages of African mine workers before and after the Guillebaud award, 1953

Pay per ticket (30 shifts) before the award	Pay per ticket (30 shifts) after the award	Pay per ticket (30 shifts) before the award	Pay per ticket (30 shifts) after the award
Surface		*Surface*	
Group 1		Group 5	
45s 0d	80s 0d	172s 6d	217s 6d
47s 6d	82s 6d	175s 0d	220s 0d
50s 0d	85s 0d	177s 6d	222s 6d
52s 6d	87s 6d	180s 0d	225s 0d
55s 0d	90s 0d	182s 6d	227s 6d
57s 6d	92s 6d	187s 6d	232s 6d
60s 0d	95s 0d	192s 6d	237s 6d
62s 6d	97s 6d		
65d 0d	100s 0d		
67s 6d	102s 6d		
Group 2		Group 6	
52s 6d	87s 6d	190s 0d	235s 0d
55s 0d	90s 0d	195s 0d	240s 0d
57s 6d	92s 6d	200s 0d	245s 0d
60s 0d	95s 0d	205s 0d	250s 0d
62s 6d	97s 6d	210s 0d	255s 0d
65s 0d	100s 0d	215s 0d	260s 0d
67s 6d	102s 6d	217s 6d	262s 6d
70s 0d	105s 0d		
Group 3		Group 7	
62s 6d	97s 6d	222s 6d	272s 6d
65s 0d	100s 0d	227s 6d	277s 6d
67s 6d	102s 6d	232s 6d	282s 6d
70s 0d	105s 0d	237s 6d	287s 6d
72s 6d	107s 6d	247s 6d	297s 6d
75s 0d	110s 0d	257s 6d	307s 6d
77s 6d	112s 6d	267s 6d	317s 6d
		270s 0d	320s 0d

Appendix VI—*continued*

Pay per ticket (30 shifts) before the award	Pay per ticket (30 shifts) after the award	Pay per ticket (30 shifts) before the award	Pay per ticket (30 shifts) after the award
Group 4		*Special group*	
75s 0d	115s 0d	290s 0d	340s 0d
77s 6d	117s 0d	300s 0d	350s 0d
80s 0d	120s 0d	310s 0d	360s 0d
82s 6d	122s 6d	320s 0d	370s 0d
85s 0d	125s 0d		
87s 6d	127s 6d		
90s 0d	130s 0d		
Underground		*Underground*	
Group 1		*Group 5*	
55s 0d	90s 0d	187s 6d	232s 6d
57s 6d	92s 6d	190s 0d	235s 0d
60s 0d	95s 0d	192s 6d	237s 6d
62s 6d	97s 6d	195s 0d	240s 0d
65s 0d	100s 0d	197s 6d	242s 6d
67s 6d	102s 6d	200s 0d	245s 0d
70s 0d	105s 0d		
72s 6d	107s 6d		
75s 0d	110s 0d		
77s 6d	112s 6d		
Group 2		*Group 6*	
65s 0d	100s 0d	197s 6d	242s 6d
67s 6d	102s 6d	202s 6d	247s 6d
70s 0d	105s 0d	207s 6d	252s 6d
72s 6d	107s 6d	212s 6d	257s 6d
75s 0d	110s 0d	217s 6d	262s 6d
77s 6d	112s 6d	222s 6d	267s 6d
80s 0d	115s 0d	225s 0d	270s 0d
82s 6d	117s 6d		
Group 3		*Group 7*	
77s 6d	112s 6d	232s 6d	282s 6d
80s 0d	115s 0d	237s 6d	287s 6d
82s 6d	117s 6d	242s 6d	292s 6d
85s 0d	120s 0d	247s 6d	297s 6d
87s 6d	122s 6d	252s 6d	302s 6d
90s 0d	125s 0d	257s 6d	307s 6d
92s 6d	127s 6d	260s 0d	310s 0d

Appendix VI—*concluded.*

Group 4		Group 8	
90s od	130s od	257s 6d	307s 6d
92s 6d	132s 6d	262s 6d	312s 6d
95s od	135s od	267s 6d	317s 6d
97s 6d	137s 6d	272s 6d	322s 6d
100s od	140s od	282s 6d	332s 6d
102s 6d	142s 6d	292s 6d	342s 6d
105s od	145s od	302s 6d	352s 6d
		305s od	355s od
		Special group	
		325s od	375s od
		335s od	385s od
		345s od	395s od
		355s od	405s od

Bibliography

Personal information or assistance
Note: the current activities of the persons listed may vary from those stated, which are correct for the time at which assistance was rendered to the author.

Airey, N. M.: Lonrho Ltd; former manager, Ethel asbestos mine; Rhodesian Congo Border Concession Ltd, 1926–27, field work with geophysical prospecting team; underground at Nchanga, 1929–31.

Beaton, J. J.: recently Director of Federal Public Works, Salisbury; discoverer of Nchanga, 1923.

Beatty, Sir A. Chester: pioneer and director of many early copper companies.

Bradley, Sir Kenneth: Director, Commonwealth Institute, London.

Chaplin, W.: Rhodes-Livingstone Museum, Livingstone.

Clark, J. Desmond: former curator, Rhodes-Livingstone Museum.

Cullen, H.: field geologist, Rhodesian Congo Border Concession Ltd, Nchanga, 1929.

Douw, A. H.: consulting geologist, Bulawayo; rediscovered Bancroft, 1928.

Fallon, M.: editor, *Luntandanya* (Nkana African magazine).

Ferguson, J. C.: recently Director of Geological Surveys, Southern Rhodesia; Nchanga geophysical prospecting, 1926.

Gann, L.: former editor, national archives, Salisbury.

Hall, B.: editor, *Rhokana Review*.

Harrison, A. Royden: consulting engineer, Anglo-American Corporation of South Africa Ltd, Johannesburg; early Nchanga.

Hill, G.: former editor, *Nchanga News* and *Nchanga Drum*.

Horner, Mrs P. K.: wife of former general manager of Union Minière du Haut-Katanga, director of Rhodesian Congo Border Concession Ltd, etc.

Lambertsen, J.: diamond driller, Nchanga and Bancroft, 1920's and 1930's.

Liebenberg, J.: diamond driller, Nchanga and Bancroft, 1920's and 1930's.

Mackay, K.: former manager of Bancroft and Nchanga; subsequently general manager, Rhokana Corporation metallurgical division.

Matthews, W. A.: chief surveyor, Nchanga.
McGrath, E.: late Federal MP; at Nchanga in 1930's.
McKinnon, D.: consulting geologist, Anglo-American Corporation of South Africa Ltd.
Mitchell, J. C.: Professor of Sociology, University College, Salisbury.
Morris, Rev. C.: missionary and economist; formerly vice-president of the Northern Rhodesia Liberal Party.
Mullen, W.: early surveying, Nchanga.
Oxford, D. de Villiers: research manager, Nchanga.
Pickering, W.: geophysical survey, Nchanga, 1926; Roan Antelope from 1929.
Scrymgeour, W.: electrical prospecting, Nchanga, 1926.
Smit, N. J.: chief geologist, Nchanga.
Spires, G.: Nchanga, 1929; later general secretary, Northern Rhodesian Mineworkers' Union.
Stokes, E.: former Professor of History, University College, Salisbury.
Tucker, L.: director, Rhodesian Selection Trust Ltd, etc.; secretary, Rhodesian Congo Border Concession Ltd, 1923.
Wilkie, N. A.: manager, Open Pit, Nchanga; Copperbelt and Nchanga in 1930's.
Williams, J. E. G.: discoverer of Bancroft mine, 1924; early Bwana Mkubwa and Nkana.
Winward, H. E.: secretary, Rhodesian Congo Border Concession Ltd, 1920's.

I am also indebted to the managers of the various mines who gave me access to company files; also the staff, the former Rhodes- Livingstone Institute, Lusaka, the former Rhodes-Livingstone Museum, Livingstone, the National Archives, Salisbury, the public relations officers of Rhodesian Selection Trust and Anglo-American Corporation of South Africa, and the archives staff, A. A. Cole and Mrs M. Thysse of the Rhodesian Selection Trust archives, Salisbury

Unpublished material
Reports, letters and memoranda on the files of the Copperbelt companies and in the archives of the Anglo-American Corporation of South Africa, Salisbury and Johannesburg, and the archives of Rhodesian Selection Trust, Salisbury, now Ndola (detailed separately). Some company reports, etc., may be found in the Central African Archives, Salisbury, but the bulk of the material consulted may be seen only on the premises of the relevant companies.

Andrews, T. F. (1927), 'Final report on the reconnaissance of the Nkana Concession western and southern areas.' Rhodesian Selection Trust.

— (1927), 'Geologic report on the Roan Antelope extension. Report to manager, Roan Antelope mine.' Roan Antelope/Rhodesian Selection Trust.

Bancroft, J. A. (1930), 'Memorandum on water in Nchanga mine.' Nchanga.

— (1931), 'Memorandum on the flooding of No. 1 shaft, Nchanga.' Nchanga.

Bateman, A. M. (1929), 'Preliminary report on Selection Trust properties, Nkana concession.' Rhodesian Selection Trust.

Brummer, J. J. (1952), 'The discovery of Mufulira copper mine.' Mufulira.

Ellis, D. H. (1930), 'Note on Mimbula.' Nchanga.

Ellis, M. W. (1957), 'Notes on the geological history of the Copperbelt and its relation to modern prospecting techniques.' Rhodesian Selection Trust.

Emery, A. D. (1920), 'Report on the property of the Bwana Mkubwa Copper Mining Company Ltd.' Rhokana/Anglo-American.

Gilchrist, W. (1933), 'Report on Nchanga West mine.' Nchanga.

Gray, A. (1927), 'Report on a reconnaissance of the Nkana concession east of the Kafue river.' Rhodesian Selection Trust.

— (1929), 'Outline of the geology and ore deposits of the Nkana concession.' Rhodesian Selection Trust.

Horscroft, F. D. M. (1954), 'A contribution to the geology of the Katanga system in the Nchanga district, Northern Rhodesia.' MSc thesis, University of the Witwatersrand.

Howard, A. W. (1939), 'Report on the geology of Roan Antelope.' Roan Antelope/Rhodesian Selection Trust.

Romig, W. E. (1939), 'Report on Nchanga West mine.' Nchanga.

Rosenthal & Co., A. J. (1929), 'Report on the copper district of Northern Rhodesia, Africa. Rhodesian Selection Trust; prepared by Rogers Meyer & Ball, New York, USA.

Sharpstone, D. C. (1929) 'Outline of geology and development of the Roan Antelope mine.' Rhodesian Selection Trust.

Rhodesian Selection Trust archives

In addition to the material referred to above, the Rhodesian Selection Trust archives contain a collection of memoranda, including notes, articles, etc., under various heading and catalogued as memoranda Nos. 1–14. Nos. 6 and 7 were not made available for this study. The others include:

(a) 'Opening up of the Rhodesia–Congo divide copper mining field' by G. Macpherson.

(b) Data on the formation of the British South Africa Company, the occupation of Northern Rhodesia and the granting of the early concessions, 1899–1922.

(c) Details of Copper Ventures Ltd, 1921–25, including original material from C. Gordon James.

(d) 'History of the prospecting for copper in Northern Rhodesia, 1921–25' by P. K. Horner.

(e) Data on the Roan and Rietbok claims and the formation of Roan Antelope Copper Mines, 1902–27, including original material from W. C. Collier and R. J. Parker, and extracts from the British South Africa Company archives on the registration of claims.

(f) Details of the Nkana concession, the formation of Rhodesian Selection Trust Ltd, Mufulira and Nkana mines.

(g) Details on Rhodesian Congo Border Concession Ltd, Rhokana Corporation Ltd and Nchanga, including original material from W. C. Collier, R. Brooks, W. Selkirk, R. J. Parker and L. Tucker.

(h) 'Notes on the copper history of Central Africa' by G. L. Walker (not made available for this study but known to be very inaccurate).

(i) Voluminous correspondence between D. C. D'Eath (Rhodesian Selection Trust) and others on all the above topics.

(j) Data on the business interests of Alfred Chester Beatty, dated November 1938.

In addition an amount of printed material not generally available elsewhere is held in the Rhodesian Selection Trust archives. It includes:

(a) A translation of Hemptinne's 'L'industrie du cuivre de Katanga avant l'arrivée des Européens', Brussels, Goemaere, 1926.

(b) Address by A. Chester Beatty, A.I.M.E., New York, 1931, on the discovery of Roan Antelope.

(c) 'Outline of the geology and ore deposits of the Roan mine' by D. C. Sharpstone (undated).

(d) Speeches by Sir Ronald Prain, notably:

    (i) 'The position of copper in the federal economy', to the National Affairs Association, Bulawayo, 22 May 1956.

    (ii) 'The position of the copper mining industry in the economy of Northern Rhodesia', to study conference No. 2, sponsored by the United Northern Rhodesia Association, Lusaka, 26 October 1948.

(iii) 'The problem of African advancement on the Copperbelt of Northern Rhodesia', to a joint meeting of the Royal African Society and the Royal Empire Society, London, 26 November 1953.

Books

Arnot, F. S., *Missionary travels in Central Africa*. London, Holness, 1914.

Bancroft, J. A., *Mining in Northern Rhodesia*. Private publication, British South Africa Company, 1962.

Bradley, K., *Copper venture*. Private publication, Mufulira and Roan Antelope mines, 1952.

Bulpin, T. V., *Trail of the copper king*. Cape Town, H. Timmins, 1959.

Burton, Sir R. F., *The lands of Cazembe: Lacerda's journey to 1798*. London, Royal Geographical Society, 1873.

— *Journey of the pombeiros P. J. Baptista and Amaro Jose*. London, Royal Geographical Society, 1873.

Cameron, V. L., *Across Africa*. Two volumes. London, Daldy Isbister & Co., 1877.

Davis, J. Merle, *et al.*, *Modern industry and the African*. London, Macmillan, 1933.

Gann, L. H., *The birth of a plural society: the development of Northern Rhodesia under the British South Africa Company, 1894–1914*. Manchester, University Press for the Rhodes-Livingstone Institute (now the Institute for African Studies, University of Zambia), 1958.

— *A history of Northern Rhodesia: early days to 1953*. London, Chatto & Windus, 1964.

Gregory, Sir T., *Ernest Oppenheimer and the economic development of Southern Africa*. London, Oxford University Press, 1962.

Guernsey, T. D. (ed.), *A prospector's guide to mineral occurrences in Northern Rhodesia*. Salisbury, British South Africa Company, 1952.

Hamilton and Cooke, *Geology for South African students*, Johannesburg, African Publications, 1939.

Hanna, A. J., *The beginnings of Nyasaland and North Eastern Rhodesia, 1859–95*, Oxford, Clarendon Press, 1956.

Hemptinne, Monseigneur de, *L'Industrie du cuivre de Katanga avant l'arrivée des Européens*. Brussels, Goemaere, 1926 (contains details of African smelting techniques).

Letcher, O., *South Central Africa*. Johannesburg, African Publications, 1932.

Livingstone, D., *Last journals*. London, Murray, 1874.

— *Missionary travels and researches in southern Africa*. London, Murray, 1857.
— *Narrative of an expedition to the Zambesi and its tributaries and of the discovery of lakes Shirwa and Nyasa*. London, Murray, 1865.
Malcolm, Sir D. O., *The British South Africa Company, 1889–1939*. London, British South Africa Company, 1939.
Mendelsohn, F. (ed.), *The geology of the Northern Rhodesian Copperbelt*. London, Macdonald, 1961.
McKinstry, H. E., *Mining geology*. New York, Prentice-Hall, 1948.
Prain, Sir. R., *Selected papers: vol. I, 1953–57; vol. II, 1958–60*. London library committee, Rhodesian Selection Trust, 1958 and 1961 respectively.
Schweinfurth, G., *The heart of Africa: three years' travels and adventures in the unexplored regions of Central Africa from 1868 to 1871*. London, Sampson Low, 1873.
Stephenson, J. E., *Chirupula's tale*. London, Bles, 1937.
Wienthal, L. (ed.), *The story of the Cape to Cairo railway and river route*. Four volumes. Pioneer Publishing Company, 1923.
Williams, H. M., *The mining laws of Northern Rhodesia*. London, British South Africa Company, 1964.

Also the Copper Development Association publications *Copper through the ages* (fourteenth edition, 1957), *Introduction to copper* (second edition, 1958), the Northern Rhodesia Chamber of Mines *Yearbooks*, and Copperbelt of Zambia Mining Industry *Yearbooks*; *The laws of Northern Rhodesia*.

Other works of more general interest to students of the Copperbelt include:

Ansell, W. F. H., *Mammals of Northern Rhodesia*. Lusaka, Government Printer, 1960.
Bloomhill, G., *Witchcraft in Africa*. Cape Town, Timmins, 1962.
Clark, P. M., *The autobiography of an old drifter*. London, Harrap, 1936.
Clegg, E. M., *Race and politics: partnership in the Federation of Rhodesia and Nyasaland*. London, Oxford University Press, 1960.
Cullen, L. P., *Beyond the smoke that thunders*. New York, Oxford University Press, 1941.
Davidson, J., *The Northern Rhodesian Legislative Council*. London, Faber & Faber, 1948.
Doke, C. M., *The Lambas of Northern Rhodesia: a study of their beliefs and customs*. London, Harrap, 1931.

* 14

Epstein, A. L., *Politics in an urban African community*. Manchester, University Press, for the Rhodes-Livingstone Institute (now the Institute for African Studies, University of Zambia), 1958.

Gelfand, M., *Northern Rhodesia in the days of the charter: a medical and social study, 1878–1924*. Oxford, Blackwell, 1961.

Gibbs, P. B., *Avalanche in Central Africa*. London, Barker, 1961.

Gray, R., *The two nations: aspects of the development of race relations in the Rhodesias and Nyasaland*. London, Oxford University Press, 1960.

Hole, H. M., *The making of Rhodesia*. London, Macmillan, 1926.

Jones, T. J. (ed.), *Education in East Africa*. New York, Phelps–Stokes report, 1924.

Lewin, J., *The colour bar in the Copperbelt*. The Institute of Race Relations, for the Southern African Committee on Industrial Relations, 1941.

Masters, H., and Masters, W. E., *In wild Rhodesia: a story of missionary enterprise and adventure in the land where Livingstone lived, laboured and died*. London, Griffiths, 1920.

Mathers, E. P., *Zambezia, England's Eldorado in Central Africa*. London, King Sell & Railton, 1891.

Moubray, J. M., *In south central Africa*. London, Constable, 1912.

Moore, R. J. B., *These African copper miners*. London, Livingstone Press, 1948.

Phillips, C. E., Lucas, *The vision splendid: the future of the Central African Federation*. London, Heinemann, 1960.

Powdermaker, H., *Copper Town: changing Africa. The human situation on the Rhodesian Copperbelt*. New York, Harper & Row, 1962.

Richards, A. I., *Land, labour and diet in Northern Rhodesia: an economic study of the Bemba tribe*. London, Oxford University Press, 1939.

Sampson, R., *So this was Lusaakas: the story of the capital of Northern Rhodesia to 1936*. Lusaka Publicity Association, 1959.

Selous, F. C., *A hunter's wanderings in Africa*. London, Bentley, 1881.

Smith, E. W., *The blessed missionaries*. Cape Town, Oxford University Press, 1950.

— *The way of the white fields in Rhodesia: a survey of Christian enterprise in Northern and Southern Rhodesia*. London, World Dominion Press, 1928.

Taylor, J. V., and Lehmann, D., *Christians of the Copperbelt: the growth of the Church in Northern Rhodesia*. London, SCM Press, 1961.

Watson, Sir M., *African highway: the battle for health in Central Africa*. London, Murray, 1953.

Worthington, F. V., *The witch doctor, and other Rhodesian studies.*
London, Field Press, 1922.

Reports
1 Annual reports of the mining companies, of Rhodesian Selection
Trust, Anglo-American and Rhodesian Anglo-American.
2 Miscellaneous occasional reports:
'Memorandum by the Anti-Slavery and Aborigines Protection
Society on the report of the commission appointed to enquire into
the 1940 disturbances in the Copperbelt of Northern Rhodesia.'
London, The Society, 1941.
'Report on Northern Rhodesia African demographic surveys, May
to August, 1960.'
'First report on urban African budget surveys held in Northern
Rhodesia, May to August, 1960.'
'Second report on urban African budget surveys held in Northern
Rhodesia, May to August, 1960.' Salisbury, Central Statistical
Office, January 1961, December 1960, January 1961.
Duff: 'First report on a regional survey of the Copperbelt, 1959.'
Lusaka, Government Printer, 1960.
Wilson: 'Report of a soil and land use survey, Copperbelt, Northern
Rhodesia.' Lusaka, Government Printer, 1956.
Morison: 'Mining development in Northern Rhodesia.' Rhodesian
Anglo-American Corporation, 1933.
'Report on the discoveries made by Mr George Grey's expedition.'
London, Tanganyika Concessions Ltd, 1902.
Short accounts of present technology published by each mining
group (public relations offices, Rhodesian Selection Trust and
Anglo-American).

Other reports on social and economic affairs on the Copperbelt
include:

1 Miscellaneous annual reports:

Department of Labour.
Department of Native Affairs.
Department of Native Education.
London Missionary Society.
Medical officers of health (Copperbelt towns).
Provincial Commissioner, Western Province.
Bledisloe: 'Report of the Rhodesia–Nyasaland Royal Commission.'
London, HMSO, 1939 (Cmd. 5949).
Keir: 'Committee report on technical and commercial education.'
Lusaka, Government Printer, 1960.

14

Orde-Browne: 'Labour conditions in Northern Rhodesia.' London, HMSO, 1938 (Colonial No. 150).

Pim: 'Report of the commission to enquire into the financial and economic position of Northern Rhodesia.' London, HMSO, 1938 (Colonial No. 145).

'Report on the Ndola anti-malarial scheme by the Ross Institute representative' [A. Harrison]. Livingstone, Government Printer, 1931.

Pim: 'Report of Northern Rhodesia Government Unemployment Committee.' Livingstone, Government Printer, 1932.

'Report of a commission appointed to enquire into the administration and finances of native locations in urban areas.' Lusaka, Government Printer, 1944.

Saffery: 'A report on some aspects of African living conditions on the Copperbelt of Northern Rhodesia.' Lusaka, Government Printer, 1943.

'An account of the disturbances in Northern Rhodesia, July to October, 1961.' Lusaka, Government Printer, 1961.

2 Official reports, etc., on Copperbelt mining affairs:

Alison Russell: 'Evidence taken by the commission appointed to enquire into the disturbances in the Copperbelt, Northern Rhodesia, July to September, 1935.'

Report of above, Lusaka, Government Printer, 1935.

Branigan: 'Report of the Commission appointed to inquire into the unrest in the mining industry in Northern Rhodesia in recent months.' Lusaka, Government Printer, November 1956.

Dalgleish: 'Northern Rhodesia—commission appointed to enquire into the advancement of Africans in industry. Report.' Lusaka, Government Printer, 1948.

Forster: 'Report of the commission appointed to enquire into the disturbances in the Copperbelt, Northern Rhodesia, July 1940.' Lusaka, Government Printer, 1941.

'Statement by the government of Northern Rhodesia on the recommendation of the report of the Copperbelt Commission.' Lusaka, Government Printer, 1941.

Forster: 'Report of the board of inquiry appointed to inquire into the advancement of Africans in the copper mining industry in Northern Rhodesia.' Lusaka, Government Printer, 1954.

Honeyman: 'Report of the commission appointed to inquire into the stoppage in the mining industry in Northern Rhodesia in July, 1957, and to make recommendations for the avoidance and quick settlement of disputes in the industry.' Lusaka, Government Printer, 1957.

Morison: 'Report of the commission appointed to inquire into the mining industry in Northern Rhodesia.' Lusaka, Government Printer, 1962.

Published papers
Anonymous, 'Notes on the Bwana Mkubwa and Nkana mines, Northern Rhodesia.' Presented by the Bwana Mkubwa Copper Mining Company to the third (triennial) Empire Mining and Metallurgical Congress, South Africa, 1930.
'Brief description of Roan mine and development plans, 1930.' (Presented as above.)
Bancroft, J. A., 'Notes on the geology of the Bwana Mkubwa mine.' 'Notes on the geology of the Nkana mine,' 'Notes on the geology of the Nchanga mine,' in the International Geological Congress *Yearbook*, 1929.
Guernsey, T. D., 'Report on the four mines of the Anglo-American Corporation in Northern Rhodesia.' (Presented to the symposium on the geology of copper in Africa by the Association of African Geological Surveys, 1959.)
Wilkie, N. A., and Holt, W., 'A description of open pit mining at Nchanga Consolidated Copper Mines Ltd. Northern Rhodesia.'
Presented to the Northern Rhodesian section of the seventh Commonwealth Mining and Metallurgical Congress, May 1961.

Other more general papers include:

Conference Proceedings: Rhodes-Livingstone Institute (especially vols. 11, 12, 13, 1958–59).
Mackintosh, C. W., 'Some pioneer missions of Northern Rhodesia and Nyasaland.' Livingstone, Rhodes-Livingstone Museum, 1950.
Mitchell, J. Clyde, 'African urbanisation in Ndola and Luanshya.' Lusaka, Rhodes-Livingstone Institute, 1954.
— The Kalela dance. Rhodes-Livingstone Paper No. 27. Manchester University Press, for the Rhodes-Livingstone Institute (now the Institute for African Studies, University of Zambia), 1956.
Wilson, G., *An essay on the economics of detribalisation in Northern Rhodesia*. Livingstone, Rhodes-Livingstone Papers Nos. 5–6, 1941–42. Reprinted by Manchester University Press for the Institute for Social Research (now the Institute for African Studies), University of Zambia, 1968.

Newspapers
Bancroft Bulletin and Kasanbankanya (Bancroft African employees, from 13 January 1961), *Bulawayo Chronicle, Central African Daily*

News, Central African Mail, Chibuluma News (Newsletters), from June, 1961, *Economist, Financial Times, Livingstone Mail, Mufulira Star* (formerly *Mufulira African Star*), *Nchanga Drum* and *Nchanga News* (replaced on 5 October 1962 by *Nchanga Weekly*), *News Comments, Reviews* (Ndola Copper Refineries Ltd, November 1959 to August 1960. Out of print), *Northern News, Roan Antelope* (formerly *African Roan Antelope*), *Johannesburg Star, Sunday Mail, Times* (London), *Union News, Graywacke News, Mufulira Kasobela* (Wall sheets; replaced from 18 January 1963 by weekly *Mufulira Mirror*).

There are at present (1963) no newspapers on the Copperbelt produced entirely for Africans by Africans, although some employ Africans on the reporting and editorial staff and are designed for the African market.

Magazines and Journals
(Only articles of major interest and importance are noted.)
African World Annual
African Administration, Journal of
   Vol. 3, pages 113–17, 1951: Conyngham, L.D., 'African towns in Northern Rhodesia.'
Central Africa Examiner
Engineering and Mining Journal, New York
   1922, April: Ball, S., 'Copper smelting by Central African natives.'
   1929, January: Walker, G. L., 'Surveying from the air in Central Africa.'
   1944 (series): Brooks, R., 'How the Rhodesian coppers were found.'
Geological Society, London, Journal of
   Vol. 88, 1932: Jackson, G. C. A., 'The geology of the Nchanga district, Northern Rhodesia.'
Horizon (monthly magazine of the Rhodesian Selection Trust group, successor to *Roan Antelope* and *Mufulira Magazines*)
   1959, January: Anonymous article on the copper flower.
   1959, March, May, June: Prain Sir R., 'How the copper industry developed.'
   1959, May: Brooks, R., photographs of pre-European smelting.
   1959, August: pages 10–19: Garlick, W.G., 'How the Copperbelt ore-bodies were formed.'
   1959, December, pages 28–32: 'Underground operations at Roan.'*
   1960, January, pages 20–25: 'Underground operations at Mufulira.'*
   1960, February, pages 12–17: 'Underground operations at Chibuluma.'*
   1960, March, pages 30–32: 'Ventilation.'*

1960, May, pages 18–24: 'Concentrator operations.'*
1960, July, pages 14–18: 'Smelting operations.'*
1960, August pages 16–20: 'Refinery operations.'*
[*General series by *Horizon* entitled 'A guide to copper mining.']
1960, August, pages 24–25: early photographs of Roan Antelope.
1960, December, pages 26–28: White, C. M. N., 'The role of witchcraft in Central Africa.'
1960, December, pages 4–11: Mackersey, I., and Moir, J., article on discovery and career of James Moir.
1961, January, pages 22–24: articles on Mufulira West.
1961, March, pages 18–19: 'The ghost mines of Mumbwa.'
1961, April, pages 4–10: Scannell, T., 'A dynamic union with a turbulent career.'
1961, May, pages 28–35: Juretic, F., 'Shafts—their role in mining operations.'
1962, July, pages 12–15: 'Headframes.'
1962, October: Scannell, T., article on J. E. G. Williams.
Il Missionario Francescano
1956, November: Mazzieri, Very Rev. F., article on Copperbelt missionary work (in Italian).
Institution of Mining and Metallurgy, transactions of
1934–35: Pickard, T. A., 'Primitive smelting of copper and bronze' (extract in Rhodesion Selection Trust archives).
1935–36, pages 317–64: Parker, R. J., and Gray, A., with comments by Horner, P. K., 'Prospecting and geological survey (1927–1929) of the "Nkana Concession".'
1949: Pettijohn, W. T., and Norrie, J. P., 'An outline of underground operations at Mufulira Copper Mines Ltd' (extract in Rhodesian Selection Trust archives).
1953–54, vol. 63, pt. 1, pages 1–8: Guernsey, T. D., 'Summary of early prospecting in Northern Rhodesia.'
1960–61, vol. 70, pt. 3, pages 77–131: Rushton, M., and Mackay, K., 'The Nchanga mine.'
Luntandanya (Nkana African magazine)
Mining Magazine
Mufulira Magazine
MOSSA (Mine Officials and Salaried Staff Association Magazine)
1952, December, page 13–19: Brummer, J. J., 'Discovery of the Mufulira mine.'
Nkhwazi (Northern Rhodesia Police magazine)
1957, June: 'Report on the Mongu witchcraft trials.'
Northern Rhodesia Gazette
1950, vol. I, No. 2: Brooks, R., 'How the Rhodesian coppers were found.'

1953, vol. II, No. 2: Beech, A. E. 'Early days around the copper-belt.'
1954, vol. II, No. 3: Munday, Rev. J. T., 'The fear of witchcraft.'
1957, vol. III, No. 3: Jordan, E. Knowles, 'Old Ndola.'
1958, vol. III, Nos. 5–6: Butler, L. G., 'Lusaka African community Chilenje.'

Northern Rhodesia Mining Journal
Nshila (Northern Rhodesia government magazine)
Optima (quarterly, Anglo-American Corporation of South Africa.)
1955, March: Nelems, T. E., 'Open pit mining at Nchanga.'
1956, September: Nichols, C. P., 'The Bancroft mine—a tale of tribulation and triumph.'

Rhodesian Mining Journal
1959, vol. 24, No. 13: Armstrong, D., 'The geology of Bancroft mine.'

Rhodes-Livingstone Journal
1950, No. X: King, E. R. G., 'On educating African girls in Northern Rhodesia.'
1951, No. XII: Mitchell, J. Clyde, 'A note on the urbanisation of Africans on the Copperbelt.'
1954, No. XIV: Cunnison, I., 'A note on the Lunda concept of custom.'
1954, No. XIV: Mitchell, J. Clyde, 'The distribution of African labour by area of origin on the copper mines of Northern Rhodesia.'
1954, No. XVI: Gann, L. H., 'The end of the slave trade in British Central Africa, 1889–1912.'
1955, No. XVIII: Gann, L. H., 'The Northern Rhodesian copper industry and the world of copper, 1923–52.'
1961, No. XXIX: Rotberg, R., 'The Lenshina movement of Northern Rhodesia.'

Rhokana Review
1951, November: article on malaria control.
1952, January: McDermott, E. K., 'Shaft sinking.'
1953, January: Guernsey, T. D., 'Bancroft mine.'
1956, January: Guernsey, T. D., 'Bwana's baby—the Nkana claims.'

Roan Antelope Magazine
1957, May: Clark, J. Desmond, article on pre-European copper working in Central Africa.

Royal African Society, Journal of
1937, vol. XXXVI (supplement): Spearpoint, F., 'The African native and the Rhodesian copper mines.'

South African Engineering and Mining Journal
1957, June: Clark, J. Desmond, 'Pre-European copper working in South Central Africa.'
Hansard, Northern Rhodesian Legislative Council and Federal Assembly.

Minor private publications
The African mineworker in the Copperbelt of Northern Rhodesia, Rhodesian Selection Trust, 1960.
O'Brien, P. L. A. (1958), *Copper deposits and their environment in Northern Rhodesia.* Publication No. 44 of the Commission for Scientific and Technical Co-operation in Africa, South of the Sahara. Réunion Conjointe, Leopoldville.
The history and progress of the Anglo-American Corporation of South Africa Ltd, Anglo-American Corporation of South Africa Ltd, 1961.
Minor private publications

Index